UGC (NET) Manual for Library and Information Science

Paper-II (Objective Questions) &
Paper-III (Descriptive Questions)
(In Accordance With New Syllabus For UGC (NET), SET, SLET, JRF & Other Tests)

Anil K. Dhiman
Yashoda Rani

Ess Ess Publications
4837/24, Ansari Road
Darya Ganj
New Delhi-110 002
Phone: 51563444
Fax: 51563334
E-mail: info@essessreference.com
url: http://www.essessreference.com

First Published 2005

ISBN: 81-7000-424-1

Rs.750/-

Published by:
Ess Ess Publications
4837/24, Ansari Road, Darya Ganj,
New Delhi-110 002.
Phone: 51563444
Fax: 51563334
E-mail: info@essessreference.com
url: http://www.essessreference.com

Printed in India at:
Printline, New Delhi

Contents

SECTION TWO : OBJECTIVE QUESTIONS (SOLVED)

Preface

Clearing competitions has become a necessity in today's world where all national and state level agencies conduct examinations for various posts in degree colleges at state level and universities at national level.

University Grants Commission (UGC) conducts National Eligibility Test popularly known as NET Examination for according eligibility for appointment as Lecturer in all subjects including Library and Information Science and Assistant Librarians for university and college libraries. NET is also the basis for the award of Junior Research Fellowship (JRF) for pursuing the award of M.Phil. and Ph.D. degrees. In our country, it is mendatory to clear NET to apply for the posts of Lecturer/Assistant Librarian in the universities and now many states have adopted the same model of NET an conduct their State Level Eligibility Tests (SLET) for recruitment as Lecturer/Librarians in Government Degree Colleges and other educational institutions run by the state governments. Seeing the success of NET and SLET examinations, now even some State Public Service Commissions and College Service Commissions have started conducting examinations on the pattern of NET.

The UGC-NET consists of three papers: Paper-I (General Awareness, Reasoning and Mathematical Ability) which is compulsory for all the candidates from all subjects and consists of 50 objective type questions of 2 marks each thus making the total to 100 marks. Then there are two more papers, Paper-II (Objective type questions) and Paper-III (Descriptive or Essay type questions) from the subject the candidate has chosen.

Paper-II consists of 50 objective type questions with 100 marks; Paper-III consists of two parts, Part-A and Part-B; Part-A consists of 10 short essay type questions (300 words) with 16 marks allocated to each; Part-B has questions from all 1-10 units one of which has to be answered by the candidate. This is long essay type question (800 words) and carries 40 marks thus making the total marks of Paper-III to 200 (Part-A-160+Part-B-40=200). The syllabus for both the units is common which consists of ten units covering all the major aspects of Library and Information Science.

The present work covers both Paper-II and Paper-III of the Library and Information Science discipline. Care has been taken to design this book on the pattern of revised syllabus of UGC. Past question papers of these examinations have been kept in mind while designing this manual.

This book has been divided into parts and chapters on topi cal basis and in a very logical manner. Special attention has been allotted to prepare an exhaustive question bank for the objective part and enriched material and write-ups for the descriptive part of the examination papers. The unnecessary heap of questions and answers has intentionally been avoided to deliver the chosen and the very best to the readers.

All efforts have been made to provide the aspirants with an authentic and comprehensive book to serve their purpose. All that is required to clear the NET, SLET and JRF examinations is given in a nutshell, to say the least.

Anil K. Dhiman
Yashoda Rani

SECTION ONE

STUDY MATERIAL

One

Introduction

Fundamental Perception

The word 'social' is derived from the Latin "sccius" which means companion, ally, friend, follower, etc. It has acquired numerous meanings in modern usage, all of which pertain to playing a role in groups.

It acquired its dominant position in our thought patterns in the late nineteenth and twentieth century when social policy, social economics, socialism, social work, social legislation, social psychology, social medicine, etc., became household words. This shift from individualism towards collectivism occurred due to increased interaction between individuals and groups. The term 'social' also shows a great affinity to terms like 'function' or 'functional' to determine more specific relationships of the different parts to one another.

Role in Society

If we speak about 'social function' it is essential that we should specify the group in relation to which we are trying to determine the function.

Social Function and Library : Library as a social institution brings into relation the writer, publisher, librarian and reader. This relationship can also be viewed in terms of producer, intermediary and consumer. In case of the library authors and publishers are producers-who produce books; Librarians serve more like distributors or middle men; and readers are the consumers.

Dr. Ranganathan described books, readers and staff as the basic trinity of the library and the social function of the library is to bring the best interaction among these three basic constituents.

S.R. Ranganathan mentioned the following social functions of the library:

1. To increase the economic resources of humanity to the extent necessary to maintain the ever increasing population, in comfort and free from want of any kind, and also

2. To help in the elevating, self-dependent use of leisure with the aid of freely served books, pictures, sound records, and other graphic materials; and

3. To help in increasing the opportunity for the spiritual awakening of one and all of the members of humanity.

Main Objectives

Robert D. Leigh mentioned the following as the Social Objectives of a library:

1. "To assemble, preserve and administer books and related educational materials in order to promote, through guidance and stimulation, an enlightened citizenship and enriched personal lives."

2. "To serve the community as a general centre of reliable information."

3. To provide opportunity and encouragement for children, young people, men and women to educate themselves continuously.

These objectives clearly indicate the functions of public library in the community. It is important to note that the social role of library has never been a single one or uniform. It has been changing with the course of time and the emphasis has been shifting from one aspect of the function to another.

Historical Significance

Barnes has mentioned that social heritage is a manifestation of the people's ideas, views, thoughts, customs and beliefs, built up as a result of their needs, objectives and activities in the society (Barnes : 1942). This heritage is transmitted from one group to another and from one generation to the next. Hertzler says : 'Institutions are the great culture carriers, the depositors of the social heritage; the media of its operation and perpetuation.... In them are the most constructive culture elements that the centuries allowed to endure and develop. A group's culture is largely a summation of its institutions and its institutions are largely the embodiment of its culture."

The recorded knowledge and descriptions of human social history, art, literature, science and technology are stored on the long shelves of the library, which go down from generation to generation. These shelves depict the life and character of the human race. As an instrument of social control in the community, the library conserves the social heritage and then transmits it.

The function of the library can be seen under the aspects of the various social institutions which make-up our society. The library can be seen as an agency of communication, agency for preservation of culture, agency of change and an economic institution.

We shall first ask ourselves why people communicate with one another, secondly why writing and reading have emerged as specific forms of communication and thirdly why it has proved necessary to build-up collections of written materials.

With the increase in interaction among the individuals and starting of social life, there arose the need for communication. Even some of the primitive animals do communicate by emotions, feelings, gestures, etc. The increased interaction of man with nature resulted in accumulation of more and more of information which he wished to share with his fellow beings. Thus the spoken language was developed. Spoken language led to written language. Written documents gave rise to the need for collection, storage, care and preservation. These activities took the shape of the institution which we call the "library." The social function of a library is to communicate or to facilitate communication.

Cultural Aspects

The written word is revealing, not always by what it states but by what it implies. It shows, although it operates under the limitations of the value-system of the culture under which it appears, the entire fabric of this society. In writing, the values of a society are not only developed and expressed but also doubted and denied. The whole range of human emotions expresses itself in writing, not only in literature but even in the staid language of government reports and scientific works.

The Effects

The library may have the function of a sieve but it is a sieve with very uneven meshes, which themselves reflect the structure of its society. This structure is far from being a neat logical unity- it is a product of social growth, with all the disproportion and unevenness that this growth displays to the minds of those who prefer to think in the earlier terms of logic and rationality. We collect the records from the past to find security for the future although the future always presents new problems for which past experience offers but slim support. The function of the library not only expresses a higher rate of social communication, but it is one of the main contributory factors for social change.

Economic Aspects

Out of the numerous functional aspects under which the library can be considered, a choice will have to be made. As modern society devotes the greatest part of its energy to economic activities, it is obvious that the library must be dealt with as an economic institution. This involves not only its own economic processes but also the general influence which it exercises on the economy through its cultural and intellectual function.

Role in Education

The library is the most effective and economic medium for spread of education and dissemination of information. Education is a process and from childhood to old age every one continuously passes through this process. In the whole life the human passes through or receives education in two forms: formal education and informal education. The library plays vital role by helping the citizen pursue both forms of education.

Education implies cultivation of the intellect. The formal education is achieved through educational institutions like schools, colleges, universities and other institutions. Here, there will be a continuous interaction between the teacher and the taught. Various apparatus like libraries, laboratories, educational technology, etc., are used for effectiveness of formal education.

But education has to be a life long process. Formal education ends after a certain stage in one's life. It is through informal education, man keeps himself abreast with the new knowledge, new skills and new means and methods of development. Here libraries play a major role. There is no limit to knowledge and there will be no limit to learning through libraries. This is the reason why public libraries are described as "people's university."

As a social agency, the library has to stimulate reading habit. Attract the readers to the library and make them beneficiaries of the knowledge available in various documents. Public libraries since long has been playing a vital role in disseminating information to literates as well as illiterates and neo-literates through adult education classes, reading programmes, book-talks, displays and exhibitions, special lectures, organising fairs and festivals, etc.

Special libraries started appearing in a big way with the acceleration of research.

Research is the life-blood of modern society; as our economic standard of living, our culture, and our age of progress depend upon it. Research is an endeavour, to discover, develop, and verify knowledge. It is an intellectual act that begins with the asking of question and progresses through the critical examination of evidence that is both relevant and reliable, to the revelation of truth that is generalization and universal. Its goal is the pursuit of truth, a goal that can never be attained, but which must always to be attainable.

Research, whether it endeavours to formulate new principles or theories and generalizations or concepts without concern for their application, requires an awareness of the state of existing knowledge and a free flow of information. It is at this point that library enters into the research process and helps in its advancement.

By and large, the library offers many types of specialized services to help in the advancement of research in society. The basic services elaborated by Mr. J.K. Gates are:

(a) Identifying, accumulating, processing for use needed and pertinent materials speedily;

(b) Preparing and circulating lists of latest additions,

(c) Evaluating and interpreting new documents and providing to the right users requisite information contained in them in the form of reviews, abstracts, tables of contents, and photocopies of excerpts;

(d) Maintaining highly specialized reference files and indexes;

(e) Conducting literature searches;

(f) Providing accurate, factual and relevant information to inquirers;

(g) Preparing bibliographies;

(h) Translating publications wholly or in part;

(i) Providing cheap and rapid means of photo-copying;

(j) Providing quick reference and referral services;

(k) Extending the limitations of its own resources by inter library loans, cooperative acquisitions and through such methods of bibliographical cooperation as union lists, and catalogues and the exchanging of catalogues and bibliographies.

Two

Origin and Growth

Historical Background

The discovery of innumerable seals from Mohenjodaro, Harappa, Lothal and other places confirm the fact that writing was well known in the so-called pre-historic India and Indians had the conception of reduplication on the basis of a printing technique.

Universities : By 700 B.C. universities or centres of learning were started in Panchala, Kuru, Videha, Matsya, Usinara, Taxila, Naimisharanya, Kasi and other places.

Scribes : Vinaya Pitika and Nikayas mention a list of games of which one is called 'Akharika' (= lettering). It was guessing of letters in the air or in a play fellows back. The great grammarian Panini used the term 'Lipikara' for scribes in the eighth chapter of his work.

Libraries : Acharya Nagarjuna, the founder of Mahayana Buddhism is known to have maintained a library on the top-floor of the university building. Taxila was one of the most important seats of learning in Ancient India. It was in existence from 700 B.C. The teaching was mostly in Vedic literature, philosophy and eighteen shilpas. It was said that there was a rich library. The great grammarian Panini and great economist Kautilya were students of this university. Another important library of great significance was that of the Nalanda University established in the fourth century A.D. The area of the library was called as "Dharma Ganja" (= Mast of religion). The library was said to be in three grandest buildings named as 'Ratna-Sagar', Ratna Dadhi' and 'Ratna Ranjaka'. Of these, the last one is said to be of nine storied building.

The other important academic libraries of ancient India were Odantapuri, Vikramasila, Somapuri, Jagadala etc.

The Beginning

Muslim Contribution : Muslim rulers were patrons of education, literature and libraries. Babur brought with him to India all the specimen he could collect from the library of his ancestors. He authored many works on jurisprudence and prosody. He encouraged calligraphy and himself invented a new type of writing called Baburi Hand. Humayun was also a lover of books and it is said that he converted a pleasure house in purana-qi1a in Delhi into a library. Akbar maintained an "Imperial Library" and Mulla Pir Muhammad was his Librarian. The books in his library were classified and catalogued according to a scheme developed by them. He encouraged translations and illustration of manuscripts. Jahangir is said to have maintained a personal library which moved with him wherever he went. Aurangazeb also encouraged, libraries and Islamic learning.

Printing Press in India : Christian missionaries were responsible for the introduction of printing press in India. The first press arrived in Goa on September 6, 1556 from Portugal. It was accidental. The press which was landed in India was bound for Abyssinia. By the time the press reached Goa, the relations between the Abyssinian ruler and the Portuguese missionaries were strained and the press was retained in Goa.

David Library : The East India Company established the fort St. David Library at Cuddalore in 1707. In the year 1709, The Society for Promotion Christian Knowledge sent out a circulating library to Calcutta, the first of its kind in India.

The Asiatic Society, Calcutta was established in 1784. It started Asiatic Researches, a scientific journal in 1787 which continued till 1939.

Early Libraries : The concept of 'public libraries is an exotic one. It was the British who introduced this concept by starting a few public libraries in the chief metropolitan cities of this country in the late 18th Century. Prior to these, there were libraries, rich in many ways but were purely private, owned by the native rulers, their officials and a few feudal lords. The access was to a chosen few.

Middle Age : When the British established their rule and started settling in big colonies in this country, felt the need of libraries. The residents of Kolkata made an appeal to the Society for the Promotion of Christian Knowledge to dispatch a 'circulating library" to meet their reading demands. The Society had conceded to their request and sent on in the year 1709. The concept of libraries for all had dawned on this soil. Subsequently a number of such libraries were established in this country. Notable among them are fort St. George Library (1714), East India Company's Library, Bombay (1715); John Andrews Circulating Library at Fort Williams, Calcutta (1770), The Calcutta Circulating Library started by Messrs Cock, Marxwell & Co. (1787); and The Calcutta Literary Society's Library (1818).

Academic Libraries : The East India Company had faced administrative difficulties on account of language barrier. As a solution they started establishing schools to train local people in English who can serve as the middle men between the Government and the public. The first school to be started thus was the one at fort St. George in 1715. This was followed by the Fort William School in Calcutta founded in 1729. Thereafter a number of schools, colleges and universities were started in the course of time by the rulers as well as by the public. The first college to be started in this country is the fort William College in 1800. The first three modern universities were started in 1857 in Calcutta, Bombay and Madras successively.

Research Libraries : The Asiatic Society was established in Calcutta in the year 1784. Mr. Warren Hastings was its first Patron and Sir William Jones, Judge of the Calcutta's Supreme Court was its first President, which post he retained till his death. This society has started building-up a good research library since its inception. The Asiatic Society, Bombay founded in 1804 also developed a good library. The first technical library to be founded in this country is the Victoria Technical Library in Nagpur in 1806. The Madras Literary Society had founded its library in 1812.

Registration of Libraries : The Government of Bombay Province started a scheme for registering libraries in 1808 with the intention of supplying copies of books to be published from the "fund for the Encouragement of Literature" This has been the first attempt to register the libraries and assist them with literature by the Government.

Public Libraries : The subscription Library started at the Fort Williams in 1770 was later on converted into a public library in the early 19th century. A few public libraries started appearing sporadically here and there during the same period in this country. Notable among them are : The Asha Granthalaya, Waltair (1800); United Services Library, Poona (1818); Raghunandan Library, Puri (1821); Bombay General Library (1830). These were followed by those started in Cochin, Ernakulam, Serampore, Trichur and Nasik.

Calcutta Public Library : Mr. J.H. Stocquel, the editor of the local daily Englishman drafted a scheme for the establishment of a public library in Calcutta and convened a general meeting at Town Hall on 31 October. Indians and Europeans all supported the scheme. As a result a public library was established and was first house in the lower appartment of Dr. E.P. Strang's house at Esplanade, Calcutta. The Government of India put the final seal to the Imperial Library Act in 1902 under which it became the owners of the Calcutta Public Library and its building. The new library was renamed as the 'Imperial Library'.

Evolution and Growth

The library consciousness has started developing from the beginning of this century. There are various reasons for this. Important among them are :

The division of Bengal in the early part of this century brought in the people a smouldering political consciousness, which culminated into a struggle for freedom. The leaders of the nation, spear-heading the movement realised that the literacy of the masses is an essential prerequisite to arouse public consciousness in this direction and the libraries will play a vital role in educating the masses and creating political consciousness among the people.

People's Interest

'Mitra-Mandal' Libraries : As a result, a number of public libraries started appearing in various parts of the country. Notable among them are the 'Mitra Mandal Libraries' opened in Gujarat. About 150 libraries were opened under this banner in different parts of Gujarat. This scheme was engineered by Mr. Motibhai Amin and his associates. Under this scheme, a village has to contribute Rs. 10 or Rs. 15 a year and get in return newspapers, periodicals and books worth double the amount. The loss was met from concessions secured from the editors of the papers, authors of books and from funds privately raised for the purpose. A similar movement under the name of "Gokhale Libraries" were started under the guidance of Mr. I.K. Yagnik by the Kalavani Mandal.

Royal Patronage : The Sayaji Rao Gaikwad of Baroda is regarded as an "Apostle of Indian Library Movement". He introduced the free primary compulsory education in his princely state in the year 1907. In 1908, while touring in America wired to his Prime-Minister to open circulating libraries in villages of the Baroda State for diffusion of knowledge among the masses forthwith sanctioning Rs. 30,000 for this very project. The Education Department of the State thereupon worked out the scheme of establishing libraries in the State and offered Rs. 24 a year for periodicals, provided the villagers contributed a similar sum and also a set of new books worth Rs. 100 each on payment of

Rs. 25 made by the people. He brought with him Mr. W.A. Borden from America for organising the 'library system' of the State. Mr. Borden had established the State Central Library, and a number of branch libraries. He organised library training classes and a journal by name 'Library Miscellany'. He also designed a classification scheme suitable to the local needs and an alphabetical list of author's surnames. Children and Womens' libraries were also organised. In about 20 years almost all the towns and about 1,100 villages in the State had a library of their own.

Mysore State : At the recommendation of the Education Committee of the Economic Conference the State of Mysore had sanctioned grants for a period of three years, to all the then existing public libraries in the State with, the aim of providing 'free book service for all'.

Peoples Movement in Andhra : The public library movement in Andhra is regarded as a "People's Movement" as the Library consciousness in Andhra arose as a mass movement. It was carried to the nook and corner of the State by enthusiastic library. The Andhra Desa Library Association founded in 1914 is the first of its kind in India. Soon after its formation the Association had compiled a Directory of Andhra Libraries and started the publication of its monthly organ Granthalaya Sarvaswamu in 1915. They had also organised library training classes and the All India Public Library Association (in 1919). Of the various activities which the Association had carried out in the early days, the 'library pilgrimages' can be regarded as unique and superb. This consisted of six sections and their activities were in short as follows:

The advance party first used to enter into a village, paste down the posters etc. and meet the local libraries, elders and officers of the village and discuss about the library matters in general and about the programme of the pilgrimage. The second party consisted of Exhibition Section, which used to arrange an exhibition in order to arouse public interest in libraries. The third party used to play gramophone records to attract people for the meeting. The fourth one which is called as 'Bhajan Section' used to go round the village with songs and bhajans and reach the place of meeting by time. The 'Lecturing Section' consisted of eminent personalities who used to deliver lectures for the establishment of libraries, inspect the various local libraries if there were any and give suggestions for their improvement. After the meeting the 'Magic Lantern Section' used to exhibit informative pictures on library propaganda, health, cooperation etc. 'Ibis is a unique ingenious method of library extension technique devised by the Andhra Desa Library Association.

Other State-Level Associations : The Andhra Desa Library Association also took lead in convening the first All India Library Conference in Madras which converged into the formation of the All India Public Library Association. It has also started the first full fledged professional periodical in English in 1925 under the title Indian Library Journal. This Association had also encouraged the formation of the Bengal Library Association, Madras Library Assoiciation and the revival of Punjab Library Association.

Bengal Library Association : The Bengal Library Association founded in 1925 took an active part in spreading the library movement in that part of the country. It has organised regular conferences and periodical training classes for library workers. Kumara Munindra Deb Roy Mahasay took keen interest in library matters and gave a lead in the early days of its activities.

Madras Library Association : The Madras Library Association, formed in the year 1928 had done yeoman service in 1940s under the able leadership of its Secretary Dr. S.R. Ranganathan. This Association apart from running the library training classes introduced the first mobile library service at Mannergudi in 1931 and prison and hospital library services in 1931-32.

Punjab Library Association : The Punjab Library Association after its reorganisation in 1929 had done a commendable work. It had hosted in the 7th All India Public Libraries Conference in December, 1929 and published its organ the Modern Librarian successfully for about a decade. It was the only journal in English when it was started in 1930.

Indian Library Association : The Indian Library Association was founded in the year 1933 with its head-quarters in Calcutta. In the earlier years it had compiled a directory of libraries and encouraged training of Library personnel in the country. It had organised conferences in alternative years. In 1943, it had started its quarterly organ the Library Bulletin. After the partition of the Country in 1947, the then Secretary, Mr. K.M. Asadullah had resigned and left for Pakistan. The office of the Association was shifted to Delhi. Under the Presidentship of Dr. Ranganathan, the Association had done a lot of work. The organ of the Association was started under the title Abgila (this included a Hindi section also) in 1949. Conferences were held regularly. Symposia were organised alongwith the Conferences. The association had started its publication, series and a few publications were brought out in English and Hindi. It also took up the project of the compilation of the Union Catalogue of Scientific Periodicals in S.E. Asia in collaboration with the UNESCO. Using the good offices of ILA Dr. Ranganathan initiated the Delhi Public Library project and the INSDOC. The Association became inactive after 1954. In the recent part Mr. D.R. Kalia had rejuvenated the organization by creating various Sectional Committees and also provided a house to the Organisation.

Working Group on Libraries : While preparing the Fourth Five Year Plan, the Planning Commission had appointed a Working Group on Libraries in 1964 with Dr. V.K.R.V. Rao as its Chairman. After conducting an intensive survey, this Group had put forth the following objectives before the Planning Commission for preparing a Library Plan:

1. Sharing of the responsibility among the Centre and the States of providing adequate public library service to the citizens;

2. Setting up an All India Library Advisory Council at the Centre; and State Library Advisory Councils in the States;

3. Financing Library Legislation for providing adequate library service; and

4. Promotion of book production.

The working Group envisaged that within a period of ten years all the villages over two thousand population will have their own libraries, with an estimated expenditure of 310 Million Rupees.

National Advisory Board for Libraries : In pursuance of the Recommendations of the Working Group on Libraries, the Union Government had constituted a National Advisory Board for Libraries with the Union Education Minister as its Chairman in 1966 for advising the Union and State Governments on matters relating to the reorganisation and coordinated development of libraries in the country. To promote closer contacts between different libraries, and closer association of Government and the public with the activities of the different libraries in India. The members of the Board included five nominees of the Union Government: two Members of Lok Sabha: one Member of the Rajya Sabha: a nominee each of the UGC: Librarian of the National Library, and one representative each of the ILA, All India Federation of Publishers and Book Sellers' Association, the NCERT, the Indian Adult Education Association, the National Book Trust, and the Children's Book Trust.

Raja Ram Mohan Roy Library Foundation : The Raja Ram Mohan Roy Library Foundation was set up as a part of the bureaucracy celebration of the birth anniversary of Raja Ram Mohan Roy. The main objective of the foundation is to promote and support the public library services in the country particularly in the non-metropolitan areas. The foundation is assisted by the State Library Planning Committees set-up in each State, which consists of a representative of the foundation and of the State Government. The officer-in-charge of the library services in the State is the Convenor of the Committee. It is the responsibility of the Committee to recommend proposals for assistance to the libraries of the State by the foundation.

The foundation has taken up the following programmes during the fifth Five Year Plan period :

1. Assistance towards building up of adequate stock of books and reading and visual material in the District Libraries and the Nehru Yuvak Kendras.

2. Assistance towards development of the Rural Book Deposit Centres and Mobile Library Services;
3. Assistance towards processing, binding, preservation of out-of-print and rare books and of manuscripts, and
4. Assistance to rural libraries run by voluntary organizations.

The organization since its inception in 1972 to the middle of 1977 covered more than 6,000 libraries at various levels all over the country.

National Library, Calcutta : Soon after independence, the Government of India had passed the National Library Act in 1948 with the effect of which the Imperial Library was renamed as the National Library of India. Today this (National) Library is having 1.5 million collection and a staff of over 700 including technical and non-technical. In 1958 the Central Reference Library was established in Calcutta at the National Library which took up the work of the compilation and issue of Indian National Bibliography on the lines of BNB. The first issue of the Bibliography was released on 15th August.

Institutional Libraries

Today there are about 6,00,000 primary schools, 80,000 secondary schools and 223 universities in India. All the universities have good library facilities. Their collection range from few thousands to a million. The growth of the university of the libraries is very rapid on account of the generous grants from the UGC. Statistics with regard to school libraries is unfortunately not available. However, we can say that very few schools have good library facilities and even in those schools where there are libraries, they have been playing a very insignificant role. Most of these are managed by unqualified people. Almost all the colleges numbering 10,000 are having library facilities though their contributions to the development of education and skills is not much.

Special Libraries

Most of the special libraries are those run by the Government Departments or Quasi-Government organisations and research institutions. There are a few run by learned societies and business houses. All the Union and State Governments are having their own libraries. Government is the main agency supporting research in this country as like in any other State. There are number of special libraries attached to these organisations. There are about 34 research establishments under CSIR which include national and regional laboratories, institutions, organisations, and two information centres. The ICAR has 25 research establishments under its control. Two more are in offing. The ICMR has several permanent and semipermanent research institutions that are being organized by the Union Government in different fields like, Food, Family Planning, Housing, Mines, Observations, Oil and Gas Standards etc. These are equipped with good libraries. The Automatic and Space Research organisations are also having big libraries with best facilities.

Three

Development as a Discipline

Evolution in Modern Times

The first ever library school was started by Melvil Dewey in USA in 1887. WA Bordon, a disciple of Dewey initiated training in librarianship in India in 1911 at Baroda to create a cadre of men to man the newly established libraries in the State library system. In 1913, another training class for working librarians of town libraries, was started. These classes continued even after the departure of Bordon. However, the existence of in-service training was initiated by John Macfarlane, the first librarian of the Imperial Library (now National Library) at Calcutta from 1901 to 1906 as mentioned in some reports. In subsequent years, the training programme was opened to the staff of other libraries and even to non-librarians but dealing in books and other documents.

Punjab University : A more systematic training programme was initiated by another American librarian by name Asa Don Dickenson at Punjab University, Lahore (now in Pakistan). This happens to be the first university course in India. Mr. Dickenson also prepared a manual for the use of students namely, The Punjab Library Primer.

Andhra Desa : Library movement in Andhra is described as the 'peoples movement' because, it was the common man who took lead in the establishment of the libraries and the reading rooms. With the coming-up of innumerable libraries, there arose the need for people with some background knowledge and technique of library management. The Andhra Desa Library Association (founded in 1914) started conducting 'training classes' for the library workers in the state in 1920 at Vijayawada. The classes covered a module on running adult education classes in addition to library techniques.

Mysore State : In the same year, i.e. in 1920, a course for the training of librarians was conducted at Bangalore under the 'programme of library development' initiated by the then Dewan of Mysore, M. Visweswarayya.

Madras Library Association (MALA) : A regular certificate course in Library Science was organised by MALA from 1929. A 'Summer School' for college librarians and Lecturers-in-charge of college libraries in Madras was held in 1928 and repeated in 1930. University of Madras took-up the training course of MALA in 1931 and started offering the course on a regular basis.

Andhra University : Andhra University started a certificate course in 1935. But, the course was abandoned shortly, thereafter. In 1970 the university started B. Lib. Sc. Course.

Imperial Library, Calcutta : The Imperial Library, Calcutta started a training class under the supervision of its Librarian Mr. K.M. Asadullah in 1935. It was a full time regular Diploma Course in Librarianship at the Imperial Library (now National Library), Calcutta. It continued till 1946.

Bengal Library Association : The Bengal Library Association under the leadership of Kumara Munindra Deb Rat Mahasay arranged a 'Library Training Camp' at Banasberia in 1935.

University of Madras : With the experience in conducting the certificate course, the University Librarian, S.R. Ranganathan proposed to the University of Madras to introduce a postgraduate degree course in 1936. This was not accepted then on the ground that "the subject is not a discipline of sufficient calibre for which the university can give a degree" However, undaunted

Ranganathan could succeed in convincing the authorities in the next year, i.e., in 1937 and the university introduced a one year postgraduate diploma course in place of the certificate course of three months duration.

Banaras Hindu University and Bombay University : The second university to start a post-graduate diploma course was the Banaras Hindu University in 1942. University of Bombay initiated a similar diploma course in 1943.

Delhi University : Sir Maurice Gwyer, the then Vice-chancellor of University of Delhi invited Dr. S.S. Ranganathan to organise a Department of Library Science. The Department was started in 1947 to conduct Post-Graduate Diploma in Library Science. Dr. S.R. Ranganathan worked as Hon. Professor at the University during 1947-1955.

First Degree Course : The University of Delhi instituted the first post-diploma degree course in 1948. In 1949 the structure was changed. The programme of Master of Library Science was introduced as a two year course with the first year leading to Post Graduate Diploma in Library Science (later changed into Bachelor of Library Science).

GOI's In-service Training Course : The Government of India Libraries Association approached the Union Government to start an in-service training course for the staff working in various government organisations to meet the shortage of qualified librarians. Accordingly, a training course was started in 1953. This course was recognised as equivalent to the university diploma course.

Educational and Training Facilities

An Institute of Library Science was established at the University of Delhi with a grant from the Union Ministry of Education. Its main objectives were to train public librarians and to prepare teaching aids and materials. This Institute was inaugurated in 1959. Unfortunately this Institute was closed down in 1964 and the staff was got merged with the University Department of Library Science.

Diploma to Degree : The full-time one year Diploma Course was converted to degree course (B Lib. Sc.) in 1960 by Madras University. By mid-1960s many other universities had fallen in line with University of Madras and the recommendation of Review Committee Report of UGC.

First B.Lib. Sc. Course : In 1957 Aligarh Muslim University started B Lib Sc. Course for the first time in the country. It had been conducting certificate course since 1951.

Polytechnic Diploma Courses : The Government Polytechnics for women at Ambala, Bangalore, Chandigarh, Delhi, Jallandar and Rourkela started post-matric Diploma courses of two year duration in late 1960s.

DRTC Course : Dr. Ranganathan started Documentation Research and Training Centre (DRTC) at Bangalore in 1962 under the auspices of Indian Statistical Institute (ISI) Calcutta. Its training course was of 14 months duration (Recently it has been made a two year programme).

INSDOC Course : INSDOC conducted a short-term course for Asian documentalists in 1963. Later in 1964, it started a one year postgraduate course in 'Documentation and Reprography' leading to "Associateship in Documentation and Reprography." Now it is called "Course, in Information Science."

Degree Courses

Bachelor of Library and Information Science : Most of the university departments today are offering Bachelor of Library and Information Science (BLI Sc) course, though in some universities still they are calling it as Bachelor of Library Science (B Lib Sc) course (e.g. Punjab University, SNDT Women's University, Bombay University, Delhi University etc.). This course is of one academic year in duration. In addition, there are a few universities which are offering BLISc as a Correspondence Course. Two open universities are also offering this course. Some colleges are also conducting BLISc programme. Presently there are 78 universities in India offering BLISc programme at 86 institutions.

Master of Library and Information Science (Earlier M.Lib. Sc.) : There were only three schools offering M Lib Sc course till the end of 1960s. These were University of Delhi (1948); Banaras Hindu University (1965); and University of Bombay (1967). However a large number of schools initiated MLISc Course in 1970s. Four universities namely Aligarh, Karnataka, Mysore and Vikram started M Lib Sc in 1971. Today there are about 40 universities offering this programme through 44 institutions.

M.Phil Programme : With the recommendation of the Sen Committee (UGC), M.Phil programmes were initiated in various disciplines in different universities. University of Delhi was the first to introduce M.Phil programme in library and information science in 1980. Today 5 more universities are offering this programme.

Ph.D. Programme : University of Delhi instituted doctoral programme leading to Ph.D. in 1951. Dr. D.B. Krishnarao was the first awardee of Ph.D. in library science from University of Delhi in 1958. Then it could be only after 19 years in India that Dr. Pandey, S.K. Sharma became the second person to receive Ph.D. in library science from Punjab University in 1977, however, 1970s marked the beginning of research programmes in library science in several universities. Today there are 30 universities in India offering Ph.D. programme.

Official Steps

UGC Review Committee Report : There was no written document laying down certain norms and prescribed standards or projecting a policy, etc., till 1958. A policy on library science education was partially covered by the UGC Libraries Committee headed by Dr. Ranganathan in 1957. A Review Committee on Library Science was appointed by the UGC in 1961 again under the chairmanship of Dr. Ranganathan. This Committee in its report laid down for the first time in the country a detailed pattern for library and information science education. The report of this committee was published by the UGC under the title Library Science in Indian Universities (1965).

***Salient Features of the Report*:** The Report in its introduction mentioned the importance of proper training for librarians; and the growing need for qualified and competent librarians in the country with the developing network of libraries, democratisation, research institutions and nevertheless the planners and policy makers. It also gave a brief historical account of library science education in India. It identified the following problems with library science education in 1960s:

(a) No assessment of the value of training programmes was made till then. There is no uniformity with regard to admission qualifications, scope of practical training, quality of teachers, etc.

(b) The quality of entrants to the schools was poor.

(c) Teaching in most of the schools was conducted by part-time staff drawn from the university library.

(d) Certificate course was being conducted in certain universities along with high level courses.

(e) Need for more intensified research.

The Committee laid-down the following three-fold functions for a department of library science:

(i) to train professional librarians;

(ii) to prepare the holders of B.Lib.Sc. degree for the additional course leading to the degree of M.Lib.Sc.; and

(iii) to engage in research and to train the professionally qualified staff to do research.

A questionnaire was issued by the committee (the same was given as appendix 1) and the replies received were analysed and presented under the title "Existing Facilities of Teaching and Research." Following are some of the important findings:

1. Five universities were conducting Certificate course; eleven were offering Diploma course; only University

of Delhi was offering Master's degree and Ph.D. programme.

2. The number of papers to be offered at Certificate level ranged from 3-7; whereas, at B.Lib Sc./ Diploma level they ranged from 7-9, and at M.Lib.Sc., there were in all 8 papers including one optional and one literature survey.
3. The duration varied from 3-4 months in case of certificate course; one full academic year in case of Diploma/B.Lib Sc. and M.Lib.Sc.
4. The total number of hours assigned to course work in majority of the schools were found to be inadequate.

Staff Requirement

Staff-student Ratio (full time)

At B.Lib.Sc.	1:10
At M.Lib.Sc.	1:5

Minimum Staff (full-time) :

For B.Lib.Sc.	One reader and two lecturers.
For M.Lib.Sc.	One professor, two readers and four lecturers.

Scheme of Papers : The scheme of papers suggested by the Committee for each course was given. Though research was at its lowest off in 1960s, the Committee detailed and discussed the various areas of research in the field.

University Courses : The Committee laid down the minimum qualification for admission to various courses and recommended that the universities should be concerned only with the Ph.D., M.Lib.Sc. and B.Lib.Sc. courses.

Equivalence of Diploma and Bachelor's Degree: The Post Graduate Diploma courses in the universities should be redesignated as the postgraduate B.Lib.Sc. course and should enjoy the same status for all purposes.

Non-professional Subjects: Non-professional subjects like general knowledge, language, cultural history, etc. should be dropped as in those days only graduates were being admitted and such courses increase the load beyond the proper limit.

Cooperation between the Department and the University Library : There should be a close cooperation between the library and the department of library science in a university. It would be useful for the teachers to work in the library for short periods and similarly, it would be useful for the librarians to maintain an academic interest in the subject by delivering a few lectures in the department.

The Purposes

The Review Committee tried to enumerate the functions of a library science department and objectives of various courses. It has not recommended any major change in the scheme of papers. Interestingly it devoted a full chapter on sectors for research, even though the research work was almost nil in library science departments. Suggestions for discontinuation of Certificate course by university departments; equivalence of diploma and degree; dropping of non-professional subjects, staff-student ratio, grant to books, training of teachers and desired cooperation between the school and the university library are some of the important recommendations.

UGC Panel on Library and Information Science (1979) : The Department of University of Delhi organised two national seminars with the financial support of UGC in 1973 and 1977 on the themes mentioned below:

(i) All India Workshop on Methods of Teaching and Evaluation in Library Science. May 15-30, 1973: and

(ii) All India Seminar on Library and Information Science Education in India. October 3-8, 1977.

The recommendations of these programmes alongwith the proposed syllabi for various courses were discussed by the Panel on Library and Information Science of UGC at its meeting held from 17-18 December 1979. The Panel made a number of recommendations.

The Suggestions

Two Year Integrated Programme : While accepting the usefulness of Bachelor's and Master's courses of one year duration the panel recognised the need for a two year integrated programme leading to M.L.I.Sc. and recommended that the universities having adequate facilities may start such a course on an experimental basis.

Independent Status to the Department : A university department of library and information science should be the constituent department of the university having the same status, privileges as other departments in the university and should have adequate full time teaching staff and also a full-time Head.

Change in the Nomenclature of the Department : Taking into consideration the introduction of the new areas of study of information science, it would be appropriated if the nomenclature of the department is suitably changed to reflect such changes in its curriculum.

Promotion of Research: Research programmes leading to the award of M.Phil and Ph.D. degree should be undertaken by departments having adequate facilities. Research projects also be undertaken by the university departments in order to raise the quality of teaching and to relate the educational programmes to the needs of the society.

Towards the late 1970s, the demand of information science component was increasingly felt. Many library schools giving room for the 'new technology' and even started changing the nomenclature of the departments to 'department of library and information science'. The new component of the curriculum made the syllabi heavy. The panel recommended for a two year integrated programme leading to Master of Library and Information Science. The panel stressed on the independent status of the department. The syllabus do not carry any drastic change, except introduction of new subject areas like information storage and retrieval, computer application, operation research and systems analysis, etc. It was right in recommending to UGC to support a survey to study utilisation of the product from the schools, standards and guidelines for schools to raise the quality of their educational programmes, and financial assistance for continuing education programmes. The suggestion for cooperative programmes among library schools is a welcome one. The Panel made an elaborate and detailed recommendation with regard to space requirement and budget.

Government's View

An All India Seminar on 'National Policy for Library and Information Science Education' was organised by the Department of Library and Information Science, Nagpur University, Nagpur from 23-26 September 1983 in collaboration with Indian Association of Teachers of Library and Information Science (IATLIS) under the sponsorship of UGC. This seminar discussed in detail the need for a national policy; levels of training and agencies that should handle, bibliographic organisation and control in LIS: policy for research and training: and monitoring evaluation and standardisation.

RRRLF and ILA : The Raja Rammohun Roy Library Foundation and Indian Library Association brought out separate drafts on national library and information policy in 1985. Both these drafts touched upon library and information science education.

Conpolis of Ministry of Human Resource Development : Government of India set-up a Committee on National Policy on Library and Information System (CONPOLIS) in October, 1985 under the chairmanship of Prof. D.P. Chattopadhyaya with Dr. B.P. Barua as the Member-Secretary. After a series of seminars, symposia and meetings, the Committee submitted to Government its report entitled "National Policy on Library and Information System-A Presentation" on 30 May 1986. Thereafter, the Government of India set-up an Empowered Committee again under the chairmanship of Professor D.P. Chattopadhyaya to assess the policy document and draw-up an action plan. The Empowered Committee submitted its report in March, 1988.

Recommendations on LIS

- In view of the rapidly expanding library and information services and the fast changing character of library and information science, the development of manpower in a planned manner becomes essential. The Indian librarian and information scientist in particular will face the difficult task of carrying the literacy drive on the one hand and dealing with the technological revolution on the other.
- The literary and information science courses run by the universities and comparable institutions at the post graduate level should continue to maintain the high standards that have been reached and improve their quality, in particular by the incorporation of advancing information technology.
- Para-professional training courses may be undertaken by other appropriate agencies, but care must be taken to ensure uniformity and quality of such training all over the country.
- In view of the challenging and dynamic situation in the profession, the Indian library and information professional must be given every facility to refresh his/her expertise, so as to keep abreast of advancing knowledge by a planned development of continuing education programmes in the field.
- Considering the fact that library and information science courses tend to proliferate, introducing on occasions a dilution of standards, there should be an accreditation agency to ensure the standard and the quality of the training imparted.

- The national need of furthering higher education and research in library and information science may be undertaken by a National Centre to be established for the purpose.
- Library and Information Science professionals should be given the status and pay scales as well as academic facilities commensurate with their responsibilities with due regard to the fact that every library is an academic/research centre and has to function as such.
- The Government of India should recognise the need for the creation of an All India Library Service and implement the plan when feasible. The creation of such a service will strengthen the national network of library and information systems.

Rules and Regulations

ILA : The Central Sectional Committee on Library and Information Science (E&T) of Indian Library Association organised a workshop on "Norms, Guidelines and Standards of Library and Information Science Education" on 31 July 1991 in Nagpur. The CSC prepared a working document covering a brief history of education for library and information science in India, present educational frame work, admission criteria, enrolment, medium of instruction course contents, structure of papers, research, working hours, teaching methods, teaching aids, teaching staff, library, workshop, physical facilities, accreditation, standards for evaluation of library schools, etc. These were further discussed at the All India Library Conference held at Pune in 1989.

IATIS Seminar on Standards in LIS Education : The ninth National Seminar on IATLIS held at Visakhapatnam in August 1991, discussed in detail the problems and procedure for accreditation.

CDC of the UGC : On the recommendation of the Panel on Library and Information Science, UGC constituted a Curriculum Development Committee on L.I.Sc. in Sept., 1990. The committee was to:

(i) review the existing curricula of L.I.Sc. in the university system,

(ii) take the responsibility of modifying or changing the existing curriculum by incorporating the changes in the field of L.I.Sc. and to meet the manpower needs of libraries and information centres in the modern age,

(iii) develop model curricula for course programmes at various levels,

(iv) prepare the report of the Curriculum Development Committee on the following terms of references,

(v) Achieve the objectives that the "Libraries should be transformed into information centres and steps to link the library with various departments through modern communication technology, library service be strengthened to extend its access with a view to making it whole-day institution working with modern facilities including computer search and documentation services."

ILA Guidelines : The guidelines prepared by the ILA Central Sectional Committee on Library and Information Science and discussed at the All India Library Conference at Pune in 1989 set-out certain guidelines for LIS Schools.

Basic Conditions

1. Starting of new courses, and the number of seats in each of the existing course is to be decided by conducting a study of the manpower needs of the region and its employment potential.

   Not the demand from students, but the demand for qualified personnel should decide the intake of library schools.

2. As subject background is going to play an important role in special libraries and in handling specific needs of subject specialists, students with varied backgrounds

be admitted in the courses. A proportion of 2:1:1 be followed for candidates with science, social and arts (including commerce) background. Special consideration be given to candidates from the fields of medicine, engineering, agriculture, technology etc.

The Objects : Each LIS school should spell out the basic objectives of each course being offered by them. Such a set of objectives should indicate:

(i) Aims;

(ii) Level of professionals to be developed;

(iii) Jobs for which they will be suitable;

(iv) Skills to be developed;

(v) Means of achievement; etc.

Note: Objectives stated under norms are illustrative.

Higher Courses

Certificate Course : SSC should be the minimum qualification for admission to CLSc course.

Degree Course

1. Bachelor's degree or its equivalent qualification. However, preference be given to postgraduates. The following order of preference be followed:

   (i) Master's degree holders with first division;

   (ii) Degree holders with first division;

   (iii) Master's degree holders with second division;

   (iv) Degree holders with second division.

2. The following reservation criteria be followed:

(i)	Backward classes	40%
(ii)	Working/deputed	10%

(iii)	Defence personnel/wards	10%
(iv)	Science graduates	20%
(v)	Social sciences	10%
(vi)	Arts/Commerce	10%

3. Selection be based on the academic achievement, admission test and interview.

The following scale be applied for these criteria:

(i)	Academic achievement	50%
(ii)	Admission test	40%
(iii)	Interview	10%

4. Weightage be given to CLISc holders among equals.

Postgraduate Course : Basing on the demand from working librarians, a maximum of 50% seats be reserved for them.

Selection of working librarians be based on (i) experience; (ii) qualification; and (iii) interview.

Freshers be selected on the basis of : (i) qualification; (ii) admission test; and (iii) interview.

About 5% of the seats be spared for candidates seeking admission from outside the university area, both at BLISc and MLISc level.

Enrolment : The staff-student ratio suggested by the UGC Review Committee (1: 10 at the BLISc level and 1:5 at the MLI Sc level) be followed scrupulously.

Taking note of the present day employment market, the following enrolment is suggested for various courses:

BLISc	20-30
MLISc	5-10
M.Phil	5

Medium of Instruction

CLSC	English or regional language
+2, +3, BLISc level	Preferably English
MLISc, M. Phil	English only

Curriculum : It is not desirable to prescribe uniform syllabi for various LIS courses run in our country. However, a set of core and optional papers can be listed here. The individual school will have the freedom to choose.

CLSC : At CLSc level there be five theory and one or two practical papers:

(i) Library Administration and Organisation

(ii) Classification (Theory)

(iii) Cataloguing (Theory)

(iv) Bibliography and Book Selection

(v) Reference Sources and Services

(vi) Practical test in Classification and Cataloguing

BLISC : There is almost uniformity in the content of BLISc courses run by various universities.

Foundation Course

Library and Society

Core Courses

1. Library Organisation and Management
2. Library Classification
3. Library Cataloguing
4. Documentation
5. Reference Sources and Service

Auxiliary Courses

1. Bibliography
2. Book Selection

Applied Courses

1. Classification Practice
2. Cataloguing Practice
3. Bibliography/Bibliographical essay
4. Library records
5. Evaluation of reference sources
6. Fact finding
7. Book Selection

Optionals/Electives

1. Information Science
2. Subject indexing/ Indexing theory
3. Computer applications

Work Experience

1. Educational tour
2. Internship

MLISc

1. Universe of Knowledge
2. Research Methodology
3. Statistical Methods
4. Systems Analysis

5. Comparative Librarianship
6. Management Techniques
7. Operations Research
8. Linguistics
9. Behavioural Science
10. Communication Theory

Core Courses

1. Classification, Advanced/Depth
2. Cataloguing, Advanced
3. Information Science and Technology
4. Information systems and programmes

Applied Courses

1. Classification, Advanced/Depth (Practical)
2. Cataloguing, Advanced (Practical)

Optionals Electives

1. Information and literature sources in:
   - (i) Humanities
   - (ii) Social Science
   - (iii) Science
   - (iv) Medical Science
   - (v) Engineering and Technology
   - (vi) Agricultural Science etc.
2. Computer Applications
3. Library and Information Science Education

4. **Library systems:**

   (i) **Public**

   (ii) **Academic**

   (iii) **Research and technical**

   (iv) **Agricultural**

   (v) **Medical**

   (vi) **Engineering and technology**

   (vii) **Medical etc.**

5. **Bibliographical control**

Work Experience

1. **Seminar**

2. **Project**

M.PHIL

Research methods

Core Courses

Library Planning and Management

Optionals

1. **University and college library system**

2. **Research and technical library system**

3. **Public library system**

4. **Information processing and organisation**

5. **Information transfer and dissemination**

6. **Comparative librarianship**

7. **Education for library and information science**

Work Experience

Dissertation

Projections

1. Internship programme of 1-3 months be introduced at BLISc level.

2. Educational tours and visits to local libraries be carried out on regular basis.

Teaching Methods

1. Last 15 minutes of the lecture hour be spared for discussion.

2. Weekly seminars be organised.

3. Initiate group discussions and cooperative projects.

4. Tutorials be organised on regular basis.

5. New techniques like role-playing, management games, etc. be used.

6. Computer simulations be developed to provide 'hands-on' experience to students.

Teaching Devices

The departments of library science should possess and use the following teaching aids to make teaching-learning process more effective:

(i) Over-head projector

(ii) Slide projector (with synchroniser)

(iii) Video equipment

(iv) Personal Computer, etc.

Necessary software be prepared locally.

Teachers' Responsibilities

1. No new department or course be started without proper infrastructural facilities and availability of qualified full-time staff.

2. The recommendation of the UGC Panel on Library and Information science (1982) be followed with regard to staff requirement.

3. General UGC recommendations issued be time with regard to qualifications shall have, followed.

Each department should be given supportive staff as detailed under the 'Norms'.

Significant Features

Finances : Non-recurring Expenditure. Provision should be made for the following non-recurring expenditure while planning for a new department or for further strengthening the existing department:

(i) Department's Library

(ii) Workshop/ Laboratory

Recurring : In addition to the provision such as salaries, contingencies, office/library equipment etc. the budget of a department of library and information science should include provisions for expenditure for the following purposes:

(i) Establishment and maintenance of :

(a)	Department's Library	Rs. 25,000/
(b)	Workshop/ Laboratory	Rs. 6,000/

(ii) Adhoc grants for acquiring the editions of manuals, reference tools etc., like, classification schedules, catalogue codes, subject heading list etc., should be calculated on the basis of actual need by the department (UGC Panel, 1982).

Building Accomodation : It will be ideal to have a separate, building for the department of library and information science. If not, the minimum accommodation prescribed by the UGC Panel in 1982 should be provided.

Research : Apart from the research for the award of Ph.D., pragmatic, applied, empirical and a priori research should be done by teachers, students of library and information science, as well as, practising librarians. Such studies should have a direct bearing on day-to-day library organisation and management, application of new technology, introducing new services, building-up vital statistical data on library and information services, and the profession in general.

Evaluation and Measurement

UGC, Curriculum Development Committee (India) (1992) : The UGC's Curriculum Development Committee on Library and Information Science in its Report gave separate schemes of papers and Bachelor of Library and Information Science and Master of Library and Information Science.

(a) Bachelor of Library and Information Science:

- (i) Library and Information Society.
- (ii) Library and Information Management.
- (iii) Library Classification-Theory and Practice.
- (iv) Library Cataloguing and Subject Indexing-Theory and Practice.
- (v) Information Sources and Services.
- (vi) Computer Application.

(b) Master of Library and Information Science

- (i) Information and Communication: Evolution and Development.

(ii) Library and Information Management: Sources and Services.

(iii) Computer Technology, Library Automation and Information Systems.

(iv) Information Processing and Retrieval.

(v) Research Methodology and Informatics.

Electives : In addition, the following electives were suggested at the Bachelor of Library and Information Science Level :

(i) School and children libraries.

(ii) University and college libraries

(iii) Public library system.

(iv) Government department libraries.

(v) Research and development libraries.

(vi) Archives Librarianship.

(vii) Engineering and Technology Information System.

(viii) Medical librarianship.

(ix) Agricultural Library and Information System.

(x) Law libraries.

(xi) Music libraries.

(xii) Industrial Library and Information System.

(xiii) Manuscriptology.

(xiv) Library buildings, fittings and furniture.

(xv) Local studies librarianship.

(xvi) Non-book materials.

The following electives were suggested at Master of Library and Information Science Level:

(i) Comparative and International Librarianship.

(ii) Higher Education and Academic Library System.

(iii) Communication, Mass Media and Public Library.

(iv) Bibliographic control.

(v) User Education and User Studies.

(vi) Education for Library and Information Science.

In the above curricula, one can observe a gradual shifting from documentation work to total information oriented syllabus from the one suggested by Prof. Foskett to the 'criteria' suggested by the Institution of Information Scientists (UK). However, in the syllabus suggested by UGC's CDC (India) still a large part is devoted to librarianship, which is justified considering local needs and local situation. It is essential to think loudly whether there is a need for specialised courses for information science parallel to librarianship. If the present practice is to be continued, how to incorporate the new technology and trends in information science in the Library and Information Science courses?

UGC Model Curriculum (2001) : UGC constituted a Curriculum Development Committee as per the recommendations of the Subject Panel in 1998. Dr. C.R. Karisiddappa was the 'nodal person' (Convenor). This committee recommended an integrated 2 year (=4 Semester) programme leading to Master of Library and Information Science.

The scheme of papers is as following :

Module Nomenclature of the Paper

1. Foundations of Library & Information Science
2. Knowledge Organization, Information Processing & Retrieval (T)
3. Knowledge Organization, Information Processing & Retrieval (P)

4. Information Technology : Basics
5. Management of Library & Information Centres
6. Information Sources & Services (T)
7. Information Sources & Services (P)
8. Library & Users
9. Fundamentals of Information Science
10. Information Analysis, Repackaging, Consolidation
11. Information Retrieval
12. Research Methods & Statistical Techniques
13. Information Technology Applications (T)
14. Information Technology Applications (P)
15. Elective
16. Dissertation/Project Work.

Four

Institutional Libraries

University Libraries

The importance of libraries in academic institutions and the like was recognised in India even in remote past and the teacher was held in high esteem who was considered as the living library. In the Vedic age the system of education was Sruti and Smriti based. Instructions were imparted "orally, without the medium of book" . And this, perhaps, is the reason that no "libraries have so far been discovered at Taxila" in archaeological excavations, "which was a famous seat of learning for nearly a thousand years (700 BC-300 AD)". With the advent of Buddhism, however, the teaching came to be practised through written word and this in turn gave rise to libraries. The existence of such libraries was noticed at Jetavana monastery by Fahien, a Chinese monk who visited India in 4th century AD. In Pag-sam-jong-ang, Zang, (a Tibetan text) the Nalanda University, which flourished between 300-850 AD in Bihar, is mentioned to have had a huge library complex known as Dharamganj comprising "three grand buildings called Ratnasagar (sea of gems), Ratnodadhi (ocean of gems) and Ratnaranjak (collection of gems)." The Ratnodadhi was the biggest of the three and was a huge and spacious" nine storeyed" building. Vikramsila, Odantapuri, Somapuri, Jagaddal, Mithila, Vallabh,

Kanhery and Ujjain were the other seats of learning which had good collections of manuscripts in libraries attached to them. They were all destroyed at one time or the other by fire or Muslim invaders about which mention is found in various and numerous historical records. The medieval period of Indian history is silent about the existence of libraries in academic institutions. But there is no denying the fact that Muslim rulers who finally decided to settle down in India did patronise libraries in their own palaces. During the whole of this period we find a lone example of a library attached to a college at Bidar which was built by Mehmud Gawan, who was a Minister in the Court of Mohammad Shah Bahmani III (1463-1482). It is mentioned to have 3,000 books on different subjects. During the reign of Aurangzeb this library was also transferred to Delhi and amalgamated with the library of the palace.

The Beginning : College libraries, which are the fore-runners of modern university libraries, were the first to develop. A brief historical description of their origin and development will be relevant here to give us necessary background information. A maiden move was made by Warren Hastings in 1781 who founded a Madarsa at Calcutta for the "study of Arabic and Persian languages and of Muhammadan law with a view to supplying officers for the courts of justice." Eleven years after its establishment in 1792, Jonathan Duncan emphasised the need to collect books "of the most ancient valuable general learning and tradition." Lord Minto in his Minutes dated 6th March, 1811 wrote: "Library be attached to each of the College under the charge of a learned native with a small establishment of servants for the care of manuscripts. This is, perhaps, the first explicit statement on record pertaining to the desirability of library in an academic set-up. Lord Auckland went a little further and outlined the library policy in his Minutes dated 24th November, 1839 in the following words: "In order to make the greatest use of the advantages of the colleges, I would attentively watch the degree to which the students profit by their access to the considerable libraries which are now attached to many of our institutions. Important deficiencies in these libraries should be promptly supplied." Gradually the colleges started collecting books.

While assessing the situation of college libraries, the Hunter Commission observed: "As regards the extent to which libraries are used, the information obtained seems to show that among the students of some colleges a perceptible taste for general reading has sprang up. Yet, the Bombay, the Bengal and the North Western Provinces reports agree in saying that the general reading of students is confined to a very narrow range, being almost entirely limited to the books which have some bearing on the subjects of examinations, though an exception to a limited extent is made in Bombay in the case of the Elphinstone College."

Special mention may be made here of the Forman Christian College Lahore, whose library was inaugurated in 1889. Within five years 13,000 books were purchased and a librarian named H.M. Grawold appointed. The prominent place given to library and reading room facilities in the College marked a new era. It "became an integral part of students' education. Besides financial resources, donations of books, magazines and periodicals from the United States made it far easier for the college to build up and maintain a library than was possible for other private or aided institutions. The reading room was opened twenty-four hours and the students were encouraged to go in at all hours. Being a residential campus this facility proved a great asset to the students. It helped promote the habit of self-study and stimulated general reading outside the prescribed text books."

Attempts were made to start universities at Madras and Calcutta in 1834 and 1845 respectively, but they were of no avail. The proposals did not meet the approval of the Court of Directors of the East India Company, who had taken up the control of educational affairs after 1823. But the rapid spread of liberal education among Indians on one hand and requirements of an increasing European and Anglo-Indian population on the other made them revise their opinion which was reflected in Despatch No. 49 of 19th July 1854 addressed to the Governor-General in Council by Charles Wood. Lord Dalhousie in his Minutes described it as "a scheme of education for all-India, far wider and more comprehensive than the local or Supreme Government could ever have ventured to suggest." An immediate outcome of the Despatch was the establishment of three affiliating universities at Calcutta, Bombay and Madras on the model of the London University which was itself an examining body at that time and could "give little guidance over quality of teaching and even as an examining body, it offered no safeguards of achievement." Thus it brought an end to "the arrangements which had for many years been in operation for testing the powers and attainments of the young men educated in colleges and more advanced schools." As per their preamble these universities were established "for the purpose of ascertaining, by means of examinations, the persons who have acquired proficiency in different branches of literature, science and arts, and of rewarding them by academical degrees as evidence of their respective attainments and marks of honour." Since there was no mention of teaching or research in the preamble, no need, therefore, was felt immediately after their inauguration to create a library as an organ of the university. They came to be established at a much later date.

The first reference to the library in the chronicles of Indian university libraries occurs in the form of a letter addressed to the authorities of Bombay University "in August 1864 by Seth Prem Chand Roy Chand offering a munificent sum of Rs. 2,00,000 specially for meeting the cost of a building for the university library." The building however, took 14 years to be completed and was released for library use only in 1880.

The library activity of the University of Calcutta began a little later. In February 1869 Babu Joy Kissan Mookerjee offered to donate a sum of Rs. 5,000 for purchasing books for the University Library. As a result of this on 1st March, 1873, the Syndicate of the University appointed a Committee to prepare a list of books to be purchased for the University Library.

The library of the University of Madras owes much to William Griffith, who in his will dated 9th September, 1897 bequeathed to the University a legacy of Rs. 25,619. The University with the approval of the Government decided to utilise this amount for the establishment of Library. The Provincial Government not only approved the suggestion but also sanctioned a sum of Rs. 13,600 for making additional book-cases to accommodate the University library books in Connemara Public Library.

Official Steps : Two more universities, namely the University of Punjab at Lahore in 1882 (now in Pakistan) and the University of Allahabad in 1887 had been established before the close of 19th Century. The story of all these five University libraries has one thing in common, that is, the absence of 'library head' in the priority list of university development. The Report of the Indian Universities Commission (1902) was very critical of this. It remarked: "Of the present university libraries there is not much to be said. The Library at Madras appears to be entirely neglected. Bombay has a good collection of oriental and other books; but the Library is little used by graduates and hardly at A by students. Calcutta has a library and moneys have been granted for the purpose of making it supplementary to other libraries in Calcutta. It is open to fellows and to persons permitted by the Syndicate to use it for the purpose of literary search. The Allahabad University has no library. Lahore has not a very large University Library," and recommended: "Good reference libraries should be provided in connection both with universities and colleges in order that students may have an opportunity of forming the habit of independent and intelligent reading." An immediate outcome of these observations and recommendations was the enactment of University Act of 1904 which was quite specific as to the place of library in University set-up. The Punjab University, Lahore was the first University to take a note of this and secured the services of Asa Dickinson, an American librarian and student of Melvil Dewey, "to reorganise and catalogue and administer the University Library and to give a course of training in modern library methods." The Calcutta University Commission (191719) too considered "the maintenance of an adequate University library kept up to date as essential to a first class university." It recommended that the University should have the services of a librarian, who "should have the salary and status of a professor and should be ex-officio member of the Academic Council." The University of Madras gave a lead in this direction and appointed S.R. Ranganathan as its librarian. He was sent abroad to undergo the course in librarianship. After his return from London he introduced lending and reference service which was much appreciated by the readers. Thus by the end of the first quarter of the 20th Century necessary climate had been created for the establishment of university libraries almost simultaneously with the incorporation of new universities. The University of Agra established its library after 7 years while Kerala established it after 5 years. The libraries of Indore, Ranchi and Sambalpur came to be established after 3 years while Mysore, Sardar Patel, Rajasthan, Dibrugarh, Saurashtra and SNDT were established after two years. Karnataka, Gujarat, Poona, Punjab, Jabalpur, Jiwaji, Kanpur, Kurukshetra, Meerut and Punjab established their libraries within one year from the date of their inauguration.

Banaras, Aligarh, Annamalai, Bangalore, Gorakhpur, Jadavpur, Lucknow, Madurai, Rabindra Bharti, Sri Venkateswara and Udaipur lost no time in establishing their libraries.

Radhakrishnan Commission, 1948 : When the Government of India appointed a Commission in 1948, under the chairmanship of Dr. Radhakrishnan (President of India) there were expectations and high hopes that this Commission appointed by the Government of a free and independent country, will do something about the shocking conditions prevailing in the existing university libraries and will give due consideration to the importance of the library in the general set-up of the universities. The Commission, it appears did realise to some extent, the role of the libraries in the educational system and noted the very unsatisfactory conditions in them yet it also, like the others did very scanty attention to it, in their otherwise very voluminous and scholarly report. It, however, noted that "while at a few universities the libraries are fairly well stocked, grants for their upkeep are more or less reasonable... it was distressing to find that in most colleges and universities the library facilities were very poor indeed."

The scant attention paid by the Commission to the importance of the libraries is evident from their questionnaire.

Apparently the Commission readily sidestepped the fundamental issues and gave an exercise in the second, the development stage; the problem whereas is not how to extend, improve, develop or correctly administer a library, it is how to initiate. Unfortunately no remedies were suggested, though here and there they recommended for strengthening of the libraries, appointment of qualified staff and opening hours.

The Milestone : The turning point and landmark in the development of the university libraries was the year 1956, when the University Grants Commission-an autonomous body—set up by an Act of Parliament came into existence under the chairmanship of Dr. C.D. Deshmukh—a well-known scholar, a man of immense capability and a great lover of books. Thus the UGC, under Deshmukh's guidance, gave top priority for the improvement of the libraries. It granted building grants even upto Rs. 1,000,000 to all universities which needed a library and submitted the plans. Later, it started giving grants for the purchase of books also sometimes 2 or 3 times more than the actual library budget allocated by its parent body, i.e., the University. Dr. S.R. Ranganathan was appointed as the chairman of the library committee of the UGC to advise it on library matters. This committee after convening a seminar in 1958, put forward concrete recommendations to the UGC for approval, and further implementation by the various universities. The UGC decided to accept the said recommendations as a norm of working.

Wheat Loan Programme : Mention may also be made of the Wheat Loan Programme under Public Law 480, under which the United States Government in 1951 decided that Rs. 25,000,000—the amount which the Government of India had to pay to the US Government towards the Interest of loan of Rs. 950,000,000 be used on behalf of higher education for the purchase of American books and scientific equipment and for the exchange of academic persons between India and the United States. Rs. 8,500,000 was allocated exclusive of administrative cost; out of this Rs. 7,000,000 allocated for the purchase of American scientific, technical and scholarly books and books of American literature for higher educational and research institutions; Rs. 800,000 for study travel grants in the United States for 33 Indian librarians; Rs. 200,000 to bring 5 American librarians to India, and Rs. 375,000 to provide Indian Government documents to American libraries.

The Wheat Loan administration also organised 5 workshops; each workshop was attended by from fifteen to twenty Indian librarians. The workshop centred on problems which librarians talked about before and discussion techniques were varied using working papers, panel discussions, case studies and role playing etc. Discussions were pointed out toward what librarians could do to solve their own problems. Some results of these workshops were immediate, as several librarians immediately held staff meetings to acquaint them with the deliberations and as a result, amusingly, some members paid their dues and subscription to the Indian Library Association as a first step toward a dynamic association programme.

The visit of 12 Indian librarians in 1955, 11 librarians in 1956, 4 librarians in 1959 and 5 librarians in 1960, to the United States, was a right step in orientating the Indian librarians. It at least showed them, what a university library is and what it can achieve in the real sense of the word. Whether this had any effect on the development of the libraries is very difficult to measure and state.

Five Year Plan : A brief reference may also be made of the India's Five Year Development Plans, which contributed a good deal towards the development of the libraries not only in the universities but in all other educational institutions. At the time of the partition of the Indian subcontinent into two political units, India and Pakistan, the population of India alone was 308 million and the literacy figure was only 12 per cent. Naturally, the framers of the plans realised the utmost need for mass education and allocated a substantial sum for the spread of education; Rs. 1,530,000,000 in the First Five Year Plan; (1951-1956); Rs.

2,560,000,000 in the 2nd Plan (19 56-1961) and Rs. 5,600,000,000 for the Third Plan (1961-1966). Many new schools, colleges, research institutions, universities have been set up during these five year plan periods and naturally some new libraries not only in the universities but also in colleges, schools, etc., have come into being. These all have contributed to the development of the country and as a result the literacy figure now stands about 23.9 per cent. But if we take the increase in population which has gone up to 438 million, according to the latest figures of 1961, 23.9% literacy figure is quite an achievement. With the increase in literacy, demand for more and more libraries arose and the Government of India, on the recommendations of a seminar on the "'Role of libraries in Social Education," organised by the Indian Adult Education Association at Delhi, appointed in 1956, an Advisory Committee consisting of 9 members, under the chairmanship of Mr. K.P. Sinha, Director of Public Instruction, Bihar, Patna. The Advisory Committee went into the whole question of libraries thoroughly, gathered evidence and made certain recommendations in its report, published in 1959, governing the structure, the education and training of personnel, legislation, finance and administration of public libraries. Though the recommendations of the Committee are mainly concerned with the whole question of public libraries, but it throws light on the importance of the libraries and stresses the need for more and more libraries. It had its impact on the university libraries too in one way or the other, e.g. hours of opening, inter-library loan, etc.

As is natural, the university libraries now are at various levels of development. So far as the stock of the individual libraries is concerned, there are some libraries (e.g. Aligarh, Annamalai, Banaras, Bombay, Calcutta, Delhi, Jadavpur, Lucknow, M.S. Sayyaji Rao, Madras, Nagpur, Osmania, Punjab, Patna, Visva Bharati universities) which have got books and manuscripts etc., from 100,000 to 410,000, whereas other (e.g. Agra, Andhra, Bihar, Gauhati, Gorakhpur, Gujarat, Jabalpur, Jammu & Kashmir, Karnataka, Kerala, Kurukshetra, Marathawada, Mysore, Poona, Rajasthan, Saugar, Utkal, Venkateswara, Vikram Universities) possess a stock less than 100,000. Figures for some of the university libraries (e.g. Bhagalpur, Burdwan, I.I.T. Kanpur and Madras, Kalyani, Magadha, Punjab, Ranchi, Shivaji etc.) which came into existence in early 1960s are not available and they have not published any statistics, but it is hoped that some kind of libraries would be in operation.

The Personnel **:** The greatest stimulation which the librarians of the university libraries have got, is the acceptance by the UGC the norm that the professional (with recognised qualifications and experience) librarians be treated at par with the university professors, readers and lecturers. But the decision to treat the librarians like other faculty members, has been left to the universities concerned, but it is, anyhow hoped that they would implement it, when some genuine case arises.

The Cooperation **:** There should be a close cooperation between the library and the department of library science in a university. It would be useful for the teachers to work In the library for short periods and similarly, it would be useful for the librarians to maintain an academic Interest in the subject by delivering a few lectures in the department.

There exists in India, an all India Library Association, the activities of which are so insignificant that it loses its stature being representative of all India calibre. The position of its membership was 183 in 1949 and 207 in 1950. But during the last few years there have been variations in the total number of membership. Majority of members do not pay their subscription in time and in most cases, cease to be members. It has no headquarter of its own and no staff. The headquarter changes with the election of the new office bearers.

The Indian Academic Library Association, the constitution of which was adopted at the "5th Wheat Loan Library Workshop" came into being in 1962. As evident from the name, its activities cover the libraries of university, colleges, research institutions and institutions of higher learning. As it has been formed not far long, nothing substantial has been achieved by this organisation also.

The Functioning : The University Library in India should perform its functions keeping in view the objectives of higher education. It should be a significant partner in the conservation of knowledge and ideas, teaching, publication, extension services and interpretation of research.

The basic function of the library is educative. Realising the importance of libraries in the fulfilment of objectives of higher education, the University Grants Commission says, "the library is the heart of all the university's work; directly so as records its research work and indirectly as regards its educational work, which derives its life from research work."

Any discussion of the organisation, administration and functions of the university library should be related to the university. This is because the library tries to translate the objectives of the university. The library has to support the teaching and research of the university. To fulfil these the library requires the following requisites:

(1) resources for Instruction, research and extension,

(2) competent library staff,

(3) organization of materials for use,

(4) adequate space and equipment,

(5) integration of the library with the administrative and educational policies,

(6) integration of the library resources with those of other libraries, and

(7) A clear cut library policy.

Seminar on Libraries in India (Jaipur) (1965)

1. The practice prevailing in certain universities of appointing Professor as Honorary Librarian be abolished.

2. The University Librarian (a) be given statutory recognition (b) be directly responsible to the Vice chancellor of the University (c) be an ex-officio member of all academic bodies (d) be the Member-Secretary of the Library Committee which will function only in an advisory capacity and (e) be accorded the status and privileges of a university teacher and the Head of a university post-graduate Department.

3. The designation of the various cadres of the library staff be rationalised as under:

	Designation	*Equivalent Status*
	Librarian	Professor
	Deputy Librarian	Reader
Group. I	Sr. Asst. Librarian	Lecturer
	Sr. Librarian	Senior Research Assistant
	Jr. Library Assistant	Junior Research Assistant
Group. II	Jr. Library Assistant	U.D.C.
	Assistant	L.D.C.

4. The UGC scales of pay for the library staff be implemented by all universities.

5. The UGC may not make financial grants to libraries of such universities as do not implement the Commission's scales of pay to the library staff.

6. The professional staff of the library be accorded the status and privileges of the corresponding cadres of teaching faculty.

7. Upto ten per cent of the university budget be set apart for the library.

8. All book grants be deemed as non-lapsable grants.
9. The policy of calling for tenders for the supply of reading materials be dispensed with to reconcile service with cost and encourage competition.
10. The University libraries be allotted sufficient foreign exchange for the duty free import of books, periodicals, audio-visual and reprographic materials.
11. UNESCO coupons be made freely available to enable libraries to procure reprographic and audio-visual materials without import restrictions.
12. The restrictions imposed by the Government on the import of research materials like maps, globes, atlases etc., be lifted.
13. The duty free import of films, filmstrips, slides, linguaphones, longplaying records etc. of an educational value be freely allowed.
14. There be separate textbook collections for the benefit of teachers/students who can borrow books at a nominal charge, for the full academic session.
15. The programme of establishing extension libraries be continued and extended to other universities.
16. The University libraries be regarded as depository centres for all Union and State Government publications.
17. In view of the fact the INSDOC has already undertaken the work of compiling Union Lists of Serials in Science and Technology, a similar Union List of Serials in Humanities and Social Sciences be compiled by a suitable institution or organisation.
18. The draft code for inter-library-loan as formulated by the IASLIC be implemented. All academic libraries should (a) compile and issue a catalogue of thesis and

manuscripts with them; and (b) provide reprographical facilities.

19. Postal rates for books on inter-library-loan be reduced in order to promote the maximum use of available book resources in the country.

20. The system of getting security bonds executed for purposes of lending out manuscripts and other rare items to institutions or libraries, be abolished.

21. Sample stock taking be done only on a quinquennial basis and the normal loss of books be written off.

22. A separate library wing be established at the UGC with a highly qualified librarian as its head.

23. A librarian be nominated on quinquennial visiting committees appointed to scrutinise plan proposals submitted by universities.

24. A standing library committee be appointed to advise the Commission on all matters concerning the working and development of university libraries.

25. The earlier practice of allotting 2.0% of the book grants for the appointment of additional temporary staff etc. be revived.

26. The UGC should finance the holding of seminars and refresher courses in library science at regular intervals.

27. The Indian Academic Libraries Association be revived.

28. The forecast of finance involved in a planned development of the University Library system in the country for the decade 1966,-1976 be undertaken.

29. The term 'University Library' in the above recommendations would apply also to those institutions on whom a University has been conferred.

30. The Seminar records and conveys its grateful thanks to: (a) the UGC for its encouragement and support in the holding of this Seminar; and, (b) the University of Rajasthan for the exemplary conduct thereof.

The Details

(i) Nearly one-third of the university libraries in India are functioning without University Librarians;

(ii) Nearly half of the university libraries in the country have their book budgets less than Rs. 10 lakhs (one million);

(iii) About 70% university libraries have book collections of less than 2,00,000 volumes (not a single library has a collection exceeding I million), and subscribe to not more than 1000 current periodicals;

(iv) Majority of the university libraries (70%) provide Open Access to their collections; only a microscopic minority (6%) still practice Closed Access; and

(v) Only 2% of the university libraries have some of their library operations computerized.

These are some of the facts that emerge out of the analysis of information provided by one hundred university libraries in the country to the Indian Library Association for its project Indian Library Directory, Ed. 4 (1985). This publication came out after a long gap of 35 years of its preceding edition. The information included herein pertains to the period mid-1984 to mid-1985, The following analysis of university libraries is based on the information provided in this Directory, and hence is limited to such areas only which are covered in the publication. It may also be mentioned here that though the number of university libraries in the country now exceeds 150, the Directory incorporates information of 100 libraries only.

The Evaluation

Year of Establishment : The decade of 1960-70 saw the emergence of the maximum number of universities in the country. Nearly two-third of the universities were established between 1951-80. the decline in the number thereafter is the outcome of the policy of the Government of India to apply a check on the unwarranted growth of general-type universities in the country.

The Staff : More than half of the number of university libraries in India have library staff numbering less than 40; more than three-fourth have staff less than 60; only 6% libraries have a staff strength of more than 100. More than 56% libraries have professional staff (excluding semi-professionals) numbering 10 or less; about 77% have professional staff numbering 20 or less; only 2% libraries have professional staff strength exceeding 50. The overall ratio between professional, semi-professional and other staff for all the university libraries is 1. 5 : 1.3.

Only 67% of the university libraries are being headed by the University Librarians; 13% by the Deputy Librarians; 8% by the Assistant Librarians, and the rest by Acting/ Officiating Librarians (substantive posts not known). This reflects both on the lackadaisical attitude of university authorities towards their libraries, as well as on the availability of competent librarians to head the university libraries.

The Budget : There does not seem to be much variance in the allotment of funds to university libraries in the country.

Nearly half the number of university libraries have book budget of less than Rs. 10 lakhs; only 7 libraries have budgets ranging between 25 lakhs and 50 lakhs, and just 1 library crossing the figure of Rs. 50 lakhs.

Library Holdings : Nearly 45% of the university libraries in the country possess moderate collection of 1,00,000 volumes or less; about 70% libraries have collections not exceeding 2 lakh volumes; Only 3% libraries can boast of having their collections exceeding 5 lakhs, and not a single one has hit the figure of 1 million.

The Subscriptions : The meridian figure of periodicals subscriptions in Indian university libraries is 3,000 with only 1 library crossing the figure of 5,000; about 72% libraries subscribe to less than 1000 periodicals; 15% libraries subscribe between 1,000 to 1, 500 periodicals; only 12% of them acquire between 1, 501 3,000. Thus 99% university libraries subscribe to less than 3,000 periodicals annually.

The Clientele : There seems to be a wide-ranging variation in the figures of clientele attached to university libraries if the Directory figures are to be taken at their face value. While about 10% libraries have as little as less than 500 members, about 15% of them have as high as between 5,000-30,000 membership. Overall, 500/6 of the libraries have clientele upto 3,000, and about 25% between 3,000-5,000 readers to serve.

The Services : Among the services provided by the university libraries, Reference, Circulation and Inter Library Loan are the most common; these Services are being provided by more than 95% of the libraries.

Reprographic service (excluding microfilming) is provided by 80% of the libraries, and the microfilming facility by 13% only.

While 65% libraries claim to be engaged in Bibliography Compilation work, only 11% libraries do the Indexing/ Abstracting work. Similarly, while 51% libraries provide Current Awareness Services, only 20% make SDI facility available.

Press Clippings service is available in 2% university libraries only. So also is the Translation service.

Though computerization has been the subject of discussion of many a library conference/ seminar/workshop in the country over the past decade, only 2 libraries so far are reported to have introduced automation in some of their operations.

Only one library has claimed to provide User Education to its clientele.

Branch Libraries : Nearly 60% university libraries in the country are unitary in character, while 40% have federal character. The number of branches maintained by the latter category of libraries ranges from I to 110. Five libraries maintain more than 25 branches each.

Special Collections : While 29 university libraries have Microform collections; 23 have Manuscripts collections; 17 possess Audio-visual material; 4 have collections of Maps; 3 possess Standards; 2 are in possession of Braille books, and 1 each has collection of Patents and Coins.

Days Open : Majority of the libraries (53%) keep their gates open for 6 days in a week, while 44% remain open on all the 7 days; only 3% libraries are open on 5 days in a week.

The Timings : A substantial number (38%) of university libraries keep open for 11-12 hours a day; 22% libraries are open for 6-8 hours; 17% for 9-10 hours; 19% for 13-15 hours; 4% libraries keep their shutters down just for 6-8 hours.

The university libraries in India are said to be a pampered lot, considering the pitiable condition of other types of libraries-school, college and public-in the country. They are said to be in a reasonably comfortable situation in the matter of funds, space and staff.

Nevertheless, some unsavoury conclusions that can be drawn from the above analysis of university libraries are given below:

(i) The most obvious conclusion is that there is too much of disparity among the top few and the bottom too many university libraries in the country. There are some libraries-mostly attached to Central Universities or Institutes financed by the Centre which are literally slushed with funds, there are others-too many of them-which are worse off than some of the better college libraries in the country. The solution does not lie in slashing a pound from the former, but in adding a penny to the kitty of the latter.

(ii) That almost 30% university libraries should be operating without University Librarians is a matter of concern both to the University Grants Commission and the library profession. The UGC must call for the explanation from the erring institutions, while the profession-through its bodies-must put pressure on the authorities to rectify the situation without further delay.

(iii) There are still a number of university libraries almost 250/6—with little staff, ranging between 3-20 in number. No university library worth the name can be run with this much staff.

(iv) The same inference is valid with reference to budgetary position as well. A little more than 25% of the libraries are managing with annual budgets of Rs. 5 lakhs or less. Considering the whooping prices of books and periodicals, of the latter in particular, the funds are meagre.

(v) As a consequence of the above factors, most of the libraries are providing conven-tional services Circulation and Reference-only. Services like Indexing and Abstracting, SDI, Press Clippings etc., are outside of their purview. Given sufficient funds and staff, these libraries should be able to serve their clientele more effectively.

Indian Library Directory : The above analysis of university libraries in India suffers from some constraints since it is based on the data available in the Indian Library Directory (Ed. 4) which itself suffers from one big drawback that its coverage of libraries is very limited. There are said to be more than 40,000 public libraries, 5,000 college libraries, 150 university libraries and a substantial number of special and governmental libraries in the country. The Directory, on the other hand, provides information about only 100 university libraries, 435 college libraries, 403 special libraries, 113 government libraries, and 559 public libraries—of 1,610 libraries in all.

Another limitation of the Directory has been in the area of authenticity of information provided by the respective university library in the questionnaire sent to them. While some questions seem to have been understood wrongly by some of the respondents, others have provided information which cannot stand the test of scrutiny.

The conclusions drawn on the basis of the data given in the Directory can, therefore, be only tentative (and subject to verification) and not final.

College Libraries

Lyle distinguished three levels of college use:

1. The type of curricular programme.
2. The method of teaching.
3. The attitude toward the use of the library in teaching.

The first one is called the textbook level; the second, the reserve book level and the third the independent study level. While the first two types of library use are common everywhere, the third one, independent library use is gaining importance gradually. This happens especially in science, where the teacher does the minimum teaching work and guides the student for independent study by way of suggesting proper reading materials. The librarian has to play an important role in the promotion of independent study by the student. His role should be:

1. To keep in constant touch with the teachers to know their research problems, methods of teaching.
2. To attend faculty meetings so that he is kept informed of the changes taking place in curriculum. This helps

the librarian to plan to support the teaching programmes.

3. To bring to the notice of teachers now and then the resources and services that the library can make available.

4. To inform the teachers about new additions of books to the library. This can be done by sending a list of the additions every month.

5. To determine, with the help of teachers, what materials the library lacks and the steps to be taken to acquire them.

The Instruction : College students do not understand how to locate and use the library resources. Library collections are growing and a variety of documents are added to the library. Therefore there is a need to instruct the user how best he can reach the materials independently. Instruction in the use of libraries is planned in three ways. They are :

1. An orientation tour of the library for new students at the beginning of the year;

2. Instruction in how to use the library, card catalogues, periodical indexes and reference books effectively; and

3. Giving lectures or participating at the seminars at the invitation of the class teachers.

Orientation: This is good opportunity for the librarian to meet the students at the beginning of the year. He can explain to the students a number of things during the orientation programme, the students are taken to different sections of the library and given instructions about the use of catalogues. It is desirable at this stage that the students are served a handbook which gives them particulars of the library.

Library Instruction : Library instruction takes any of the three forms:

(a) a library lecture or lectures offered in a subject course;

(b' as an optional subject; and

(c) bibliographical instruction to graduate students by invitation of the professor.

The Status : The Calcutta Education Commission (called the Sadler Commission) appointed in 1917 in its Report has aptly summarized the state of college libraries as follows:

> "From this point of view one of the greatest weaknesses of the existing system is that extraordinary unimportant part in it which is played by the library. Few colleges have good libraries. Even the best, that of the Presidency College, is very defective at many points."

The Radhakrishnan Commission on Higher Education also found the state of develop-ment of college and university libraries in general in the country not quite satisfactory. To quote from its report:

> "While at a few universities the libraries are fairly well stocked, grants for their upkeep are more or less reasonable, arrangements for leading books to teachers and students are efficient and the reading room space is reasonably adequate, it was distressing to find that in most colleges and universities the library facilities are very poor indeed. Not only is the provision of keeping the library upto date very inadequate but at one place no attempt had been made to weed out old and obsolete books or old editions and replace them with newer editions of the same books."

Role of the Librarian : The librarian has a definite role to play in the promotion of higher studies. Some may not properly evaluate the place of the librarian in the educational organisation of a college or university. But there are educationists who are convinced about the indispensability of the services of a trained librarian in the academic set-up for higher education. For example Dr. V.K.R.V. Rao in one of his contributions stated the role of a librarian in the following words:

> "In fact, I am of the opinion that in a post-graduate institution a trained librarian is absolutely essential and he should be given an honoured place on its academic staff. It is only when the post-graduate student develops the habit not only of going to the library but also of taking advantage of the knowledge and experience of the librarian that he gets fully equipped for pursuing an advanced study of his subject."

This he opined in 1954. Since then the situation has further drifted in favour of libraries and librarians. But still there is need to come to certain decisions based on informed thinking. These decisions need be taken regarding the effective role, the library has to play, to augment the class room instructions. This can be possible if the following are agreed upon and implemented.

The Correlationship : Close and intimate relation between the faculty members and library staff is desirable for the use of the library in a college. These relations should be based on the services rendered by the library. The teachers should inform the librarian about their tentative teaching programme on a monthly basis. In return the library staff should prepare comprehensive bibliographies on the topics to be covered by the teachers. Making use of these bibliographies, the teachers will definitely not confine their teaching to a single textbook. This will naturally create a curiosity amongst the students to find out further references on the same topics by making use of the resources of the library. At this stage the library staff will again get the opportunity to explore and accelerate the use of the contents of the library. This will create a sense of self-dependence in students in regard to the pursuit of higher studies. They will, thereby, acquire a command over the possible references helpful in their studies. Such a state of affairs will help place the library properly in the organisational set-up of the institution.

Official Steps

Recommendations of UGC Committee on College Libraries : The UGC Libraries Committee after giving serious consideration to the needs of college education, made the following five recommendations which were accepted by the UGC itself-

(i) Each college library should be aided by UGC to purchase sufficient number of books.

(ii) In each college there should be a Textbook library in addition to a general library.

(iii) Each college library should have a librarian in the lecturer's grade. But he will have to be in reader's grade in a large college library. He should be graduate with degree in library science. Library should have staff depending on the strength of the students. Professional assistants should be appointed with degree in library science and semi-professional assistants with certificate course.

(iv) Each college library should be aided by UGC to have library building, fittings and furniture.

(v) Proposal should be given and efforts be made as much as possible in the Third Plan period and widely in the Fourth Plan period.

The above proposals were also emphasised in the UGC sponsored library seminar on "Work Flow" in 1959 which was directed by Dr. S.R. Ranganathan himself. The findings of the Seminar were as follows:

1. Book selection, book purchase and preparation of books should be spread evenly throughout the year.
2. Open access system should be introduced with all the necessary safeguards.
3. The administrative work should be streamlined so that library staff can give maximum time to reference service.

4. The librarian should be the member of the faculty of the college.

5. The librarian should be in close contact with the progress of work in each class. He should provide assistance to students in pre-class preparatory reading and post-class follow-up reading.

6. College library should be opened all the days of the year for 12 hours with a provision of two shifts of staff each day and of the extra staff necessary for each member of the staff to have normal holiday in the year. This should mean 2.35 staff needed for one shift alone with the library closed on all the weekly and other holidays.

The Suggestions : The following guidelines approved by UGC Standing Committee of the University and College Libraries are worth studying in this context:

1. The library material should be of requisite size, scope and quality and should meet the needs of college teaching and research programmes.

2. Multiple copies of textbooks and copies of collateral reading materials could be acquired.

3. Reference and bibliographical tools, journals and serials and latest works in different disciplines should be procured to assist the teachers in their professional growth.

4. Standard works on cultural heritage and books relating to recreational reading should form the part of college library collection.

5. The medium of instruction and curriculum of the studies should be kept in view in building the library resources.

Notwithstanding the above guidelines, it is noticed that in practice the procedure followed in colleges are not conducive to building a balance of quality and relevant collections. Some of the problems are listed below that arise in selection and acquisition of books:

1. The faculty and even the expert committees do not pay required attention to this work.

2. Most of the books acquired are the ones received on approval basis from the booksellers, resulting in lopsided collection.

3. Quite a few colleges have not constituted library committees, expert committees. The purchases are made at the fag end of the financial year. Obviously at the cost of quality and relevance.

4. Mostly UGC and budgeted grants are released late during the financial year and thus rhythm and regularity in acquisition in not maintained.

5. Standard book selection tools like 'choice,' standard catalogue for college libraries, etc., are not available in our country.

6. Some colleges still follow the practice of quotations/ tenders, etc.

7. The audit rules are not very conducive in the matter of discounts and weeding out materials.

8. In the matter of losses also standard practices of writing-off the lost books are not followed.

9. Inadequate resources inhibit the college to go in-for-materials in all formats and provide minimum standard service.

Financial Side : The different norms laid down for allocation of funds to college libraries by committees and commissions are given below:

a. Radhakrishnan Commission (1948) has suggested 6.5% of the total budget of a university or college.

b. The Kothari Commission has suggested that it should be 6.5% to 10% of the university/ college budget depending on the state of development of the library. XVII All India Library Conference also supported this percentage.

c. Khandala Workshop on College Libraries (organised by UGC 1979) recommended 4% of the college budget for books, journals, binding and other library materials; staff salaries and capital expenditure is not a part of this ratio. The Standing Commission of UGC for university and college libraries has approved this standard.

d. K.N. Raj Committee, Karnataka University (1980-81) suggested 20 to 25% of university/college budget for libraries.

e. AIU Report on National Policy on University Libraries (1986) suggests 10% of total budget of university/ college for libraries.

But in actual practice lot of adhocism exists in providing grants to libraries. The majority of college libraries get 2% or less amount of the total college budget. The grants given by UGC are not properly utilized by colleges.

The following factors could be taken as base for allotting funds to libraries:

1. The scope, nature and level of college curriculum;

2. Instructional methods used;

3. The adequacy of existing collection, publishing rate of materials, relating to curriculum;

4. The size or anticipated size of the student body and teaching faculty;

5. The range of services offered by the library; and

6. Resource sharing arrangements with university network and other libraries in proximity.

The Personnel : Adequate, trained and motivated staff is central to the matter of vitalizing the college libraries. It is heartening that UGC, and the Governments of Karnataka, Andhra Pradesh, Tamil Nadu and Maharashtra have equated the posts of college librarians with that of lecturers. But it is seen that still in a large number of colleges this is not done. Even in colleges where UGC scales are implemented, in practice the status and facilities to librarian are not accorded.

Not standard staffing pattern is followed; the management does not go beyond the appointment of the Librarian. They do not think of other required staff. Particularly the newly established affiliated private colleges never appoint the college librarians with requisite qualifications and salary. As a result the library staff is unable to understand the professional responsibilities. The extreme pathetic situation could be understood from the fact that in quite a few colleges the libraries are kept closed whenever librarians take leave.

The college authorities should follow the existing three norms for staffing pattern:

a. UGC's staff pattern (1965) for college libraries affiliated to Delhi University.

b. INSDOC norms;

c. Pattern recommended by Khandala Workshop; and

d. UGC Standing Committee (1980) pattern.

UGC Workshop at Khandala (1979): The UGC workshop on formulating standards for college libraries was held at Khandala from 5-7 March, 1979. Recommendations made were approved by UGC subcommittee at its meeting held on 30th August, 1979.

The recommendations made regarding library staff were important.

An ideal system of higher education is supposed to play a more innovative, more aggressive and more revolutionary role in the affairs of the lives of individuals, communities and nations. But a close look at the academic pursuits in our universities and colleges will reveal that courses offered are archaic, curricula are irrelevant, syllabi are anaemic. The uninitiating instructional materials, unchallenging methods of teaching, unreliable procedures of evaluation and examination, create freezing and demotivating climate in our institutions of higher learning.

It is high time that teacher centred-teaching/learning system yields place to student centred teaching/learning methods. The New Education Policy therefore recommends for recasting, the teaching/learning system and examination methods. The recommendations imply the following:

(i) The elimination of excessive element of chance and subjectivity;

(ii) The de-emphasis of memorisation;

(iii) Continuous and comprehensive evaluation that incorporates both scholastic and non-scholastic aspects of education, spread over the total span of instructional time;

(iv) Effective use of the evaluation process by teachers, students and parents;

(v) Improvement in the conduct of examination;

(vi) The introduction of concomitant changes in instructional materials and methodology;

(vii) Introduction of the semester system from the secondary stage in a phased manner; and

(viii) The use of grades in place of marks.

These reforms if implemented earnestly will have more demands on college libraries. The teaching/ learning processes will be library centred and college libraries will be obligated to revitalize themselves to play a meaningful role in this new bold experiment.

The Management : In general the college library is considered as an administrative unit. Authoritarian attitude on the part of management hinders the smooth running of the library. The library staff feels demoralized.

In many colleges the age old practice of making a Professor incharge of library in spite of a highly qualified professional Librarian looking after the library is still in vogue. The Librarians are not consulted for taking decisions in library matters. In the matter of losses of books, the administration penalises librarians. The changes in audit rules and recommendations of governments and associations in this regard have proved so far of no consequence to them.

In majority of colleges, there are no library committees, Individual whims and fancies of Principals and faculty members incharge mar all chances of libraries to play an active role in academic programmes of colleges. All this is having dampening effect on staff and vitality of libraries. It is therefore necessary that UGC, professional associations, and universities take immediate steps to remedy the situation.

New Trends : Modernization of college libraries is very essential. But modernization should not be equated just with computerization. I feel any innovation that helps in bringing efficiency to the system should be introduced. Thus college libraries, to revitalize themselves, adopt modem management procedures and techniques, system analysis and design, etc., and of course Information Technology.

Information explosion and publication deluge have tremendously transferred the ecology of book world and reading habits of people. To cope with the changing mood and media of information, libraries should collect all types of recorded sources; audio-visual and microforms in addition to print media. The use of communication technology and computers is equally important for both resource sharing and house keeping operations. Let us hope the UGC succeeds in getting its plan on Networking of Libraries (INFLIBNET) including college libraries implemented. It is necessary that college libraries keep themselves abreast with these modern developments.

Success on computerization can be achieved with proper and comprehensive planning, keeping in view the objective of automation, financial and manpower support available. This requires external and internal management support. Cost factor is also a major component of planning. Planning should be in view of perspective requirement. It should be strategic. Staff and financial support should be on regular basis. The objective of automation has to be worked out on the basis of what is needed by the users and not on the basis of what is an ideal system. Computerization can be planned partially even for one aspect i.e., information storage and retrieval to start with, if resources do not permit full automation. It can be further expanded in course of time. It is not at all essential at college level to have all the facility such as (i) Online Public Access Catalogue (OPAQ, (ii) Facility to search international Data-bases, Internet, or (iii) CD Rom system at the initial stage to make it more simple. In the beginning a decision to cover the whole collection or restart with a cut-off date can also be taken.

Practical Approach : Computer is being used in several libraries either partially for data storage and retrieval or fully covering entire library operations. It has been experienced that even partial use is helpful to a great extent with the help of a micro-computer and IBM compatible. Starting can be made with any library software. Data storage and retrieval operation will help in processing books and giving reference, bibliographical and CAS services. Activities can be expanded at a later stage as per the need and resources available.

A close look towards automation requirement of a college library having upto 50,000 collection reveals that it involves an expenditure upto Rs. 3 lakhs. This amount includes cost of infrastructure i.e., hardware, software, scanner etc., and all expenditure incurred upon data entry and bar-coding of the entire collection. Since college libraries do not have sufficient trained staff, the computerization project can't be handled without outside support. It is presumed that once the system is streamlined with the outside agency help, the existing staff would be able to handle the operations in routine as it requires only working knowledge, at a later stage. Hence, an initial financial assistance of Rs. 3 lakh to each College by UGC, will help start the process.

To keep pace with the fast changing modern time, the college libraries need reorganization. The application of computers in information retrieval is catching rapidly. The colleges cannot afford to lag behind. The problems associated with computerization should be identified, objectives defined in view of the resources and needs. A well organized information system needs to be provided to academic communities. In this way the resources of libraries will be used in an effective way. It will also be helpful in resource sharing and networking projects like INFLIBNET. In this manner, college libraries may be in a position to provide effective teaching learning information support to colleges in future.

School Libraries

If those who have been responsible, from time to time, for enunciating educational ideals and implementing educational systems, for us, had been a little less preoccupied with administrative difficulties, that is, if they had been more of educators than administrators, we could have hoped to make up for the lack of literary atmosphere in the majority of our homes, during the formative years we were at school. We would have had, then, in every school, a fully equipped, intelligently stocked library, where children could not only acquire valuable information, enrich the subject matter taught in the class-room, and thus acquire accuracy of thought and expression through the knowledge of fact, but would also have acquired and formed a habit of reading for pleasure, and enrich and foster intellectual interests assured in the class-room. We would not then have had to witness the appalling sight of a so-called highly cultured gentleman, which most often than not in India means how much he is worth every month-talking of nothing but of his personal and domestic interests. His outlook has not been, by education, enlarged enough to make him feel one with the universe. His little domestic world is all that matters to him. He has been educated only to a job, government or other; Colvin's ideal of education as 'a good citizenship in broadest sense' has not been inculcated in him. One could not expect a whit better from those who were taught for an examination, through books, no better than pre-digested bazar notes, by teachers not instinct with a spirit of their profession.

Watkin's observation as to the 'paucity of intellectual interests' among children in India is pretty largely due to there being no library in the school at a time when children, could, by tight guidance, form a reading habit. In India this instrument of education has been sadly neglected. The library room is conspicuous by its absence in schools in India. No room has ever been provided in any proposed plan for a school-building, in the province. The patrons and promoters of our schools, private as well as government, do not see any use for this one indispensable room, where children may grow into the culture and heritage that is theirs for the taking, unaided, may be unguided, and therefore unreproached. A headmaster's office may be a dispensable penitentiary, any old, shady, pipal or a banyan tree, may serve just as well as an elaborately furnished staff-room, but a library-room containing sufficient of interest to attract the young browser is an omission seldom pardonable.

When it comes to reckoning and to apportioning of blame, the teachers, I am afraid, shall come in for a good deal of it. Our children have few intellectual interests, not because they are in any way mentally inferior to children in other lands, but because we do not give them any thing beyond what they cram up for the spectre ahead, the public examination; and a textbook, I hope, you would agree with me, is the last thing for a child to be enthused with.

Again, those responsible for framing our educational system cannot escape the blame altogether; it has either been a wilful omission on their part or a short-sighted policy of minding the University examination, alone. The system is thus come to be an examination-ridden system. Teachers, therefore, could not be but what they are today-examination ridden, caring only for the passes and failures at a public stock-taking. The fault, dear sir, is then neither in our 'stars' who shine yearly at the University examinations nor in those who promote and patronise our schools, but in ourselves, in us teachers. During the last few years that there has been awakening of sorts among the teachers, I have heard of teachers combining and passing resolutions for the betterment of their lot, conditions of service etc., but not once have they raised their voice in demand for a library in every school. It shall be a great day for this province when our teachers shall wake to the urgency of the necessity for one. We are as much responsible for what our pupils lack in as we plume ourselves on what they achieve. We ourselves do not have a library-habit, much less could we be expected to impart it to our pupils. And all that is because most of us feel that we should not have been where we are, in the teaching profession. It is almost a truism in teaching that teachers are born and not made, but most of us are neither born teachers, nor have they been made teachers in spite of the tedious course at the Training College, but we are teachers out of necessity, this profession being thrust upon us, in the absence of nothing better doing. We, therefore make of this sacred calling, either a makeshift or a last resort. Most of us are almost always either looking forward to what looms on the horizon-Indian Civil Service, or Indian Audit Service or the Provincial Civil Service-or else pining for what we might have been. Whether it be fond hopes or vain regrets they do not let us be-we are less of a teacher for that attitude. I have indulged in all this raillery at the expense of my compeer in a classroom, in order to show that we are sick of our sacred mission, an angel weary of his charge. We, therefore, seem to have finished our education when we passed the degree examination. But a teacher, in order to be a teacher, has to be a student all his life; this might sound a little paradoxical and may be fallacious, but I would request the readers to recall the fact that all our great teachers in India, like Guru Nanak, Kabir, and Tagore, were students all their lives, and teachers only incidentally. A teacher has therefore, to be all his life a voracious reader, setting example for the young ones gathered at his feet.

It is no denying the fact that good libraries in middle, high or higher secondary schools in free India are largely non-existent, although the need for good libraries and reading rooms in supplementing and expanding the formal instruction of the classroom was affirmed by the Secondary Education Commission in its report in 1952-53. The position stated by the said Commission was as under:

In a large majority of schools, there are at present no libraries worth the name. The books are usually old-dated, unsuitable and usually selected without reference to the students' tastes and interests. They are stocked in a few bookshelves, which are housed in an inadequate and unattractive room. The person incharge is often a clerk or an indifferent teacher who does this work on a part time basis and has no love for books. What makes this situation particularly difficult is the fact that most teachers and administrators and authorities do not realise how unsatisfactory this position is and, therefore, they have no sense of urgency in the matter.

For a student, after home the next obvious place to start is the school and specially its library. It is, however, a sad fact that most of the schools, exception being public schools, lack library infrastructure facilities. In the name of library they only have a repository for the storage of a few hundred books collected from different means/sources. The library does not function as library in true sense of the term. It serves only as a window/counter where books are given for home on an appointed day and hour and received back in the next scheduled period. The Report of the Vth All India Education Survey conducted by the National Council of Educational Research and Training, speaks volumes of the sorry state of affairs of the library facilities and pathetic conditions as obtainable in our schools. While there were 7,35,771 recognised schools at various stages of school education, only 2,93,427 (=39.88%) had library facilities. 2,34,998 (= 80.09%) of these schools were housed in rural areas and 58,429 (= 19.9%) in urban areas. Only about 40% of the total number of the schools had some semblance of libraries. It was further observed that as against 58% urban schools, only 37.0 1 % of the rural schools had library facilities. Seen from the viewpoint of school stages, it was found that 1,38.413) (= 26.18%) primary schools, 93,094 (= 66.97%) middle schools, 14,550 (= 90.12%) secondary schools, and 94.08% higher secondary/intermediate/junior/pre-university colleges had library facilities.

The trend, however, indicates that as the level of education i.e., from primary to higher education rises, the library facilities also increase. On further analysis of these schools having library facilities, it was found that in as many as, 96,232(= 69.52%) schools the total number of books available was less than 100 and in 36,525 (= 26.39%) schools the number of books was less than 500. The number of schools having 500 or more books is just 5,656 (= 4.09%). Only 52,560 schools were found having services of full time librarian. Qualification wise there were only 2,885 trained librarians.

These figures themselves speak about the pitiable condition of libraries attached to our schools. The condition of primary school libraries is still worse, where as many as 1,25,679 school libraries were found to be in the charge of teachers or others who hardly found time for library from their other basic responsibilities. All these matters need serious consideration by all those who are sitting at the helm of affairs in school education. An all out and concerted effort will have to be made to bring in the desired changes. The post of librarian supported by necessary infrastructure will have to be created to initiate young pupils in the use of books and to inculate in them the habit of lifelong reading and learning. A minimum of two members of staff (Librarian + Attendant) are essential in a school library irrespective of number of books in stock and students on rolls. In a 'Close Access' system of library service even two staff members will not suffice. Moreover the book collection will be best used if the library follows 'Open Access' system. 'Open Access' system of library encourages better use of library resources, it has now been proven beyond words.

However, libraries in some of the public schools in several cities have got well equipped and well organized libraries with a collection of over 10,000 books. The students are required to attend a library period to get instruction regarding the use of the library and its resources. The librarians working there are professionally trained and impart library-use instruction to freshers in these schools. They also deliver lectures on general knowledge and current affairs during the week ends. For example Modern School in New Delhi, Senior Model High School in Sector 16, Chandigarh and two Kendriya Vidyalayas (Central Schools) in Chandigarh have functional libraries with professionally trained whole time librarians to administer and serve the student community, thereby making the library an integral part of the school education programme. Some of the other public schools in India have exceptionally good libraries. For instance, the Lawrence School at Lovedale in Nilgiri Hills near Oatacommand in South India enjoys the reputation of having an excellent school library. In the public school at national level, the Doon School at Dehra Dun, Mayo School at Ajmer, the Sainik School at Gwalior and Bishop Cotton School at Simla have excellent school libraries for their students.

The Development : The Secondary Education Commission in its report (195253), made the following recommendations for the development of school libraries:

1. As the proper use of a well equipped school library is absolutely essential for efficient working of every educational institution and for encouraging literary and cultural interests in students, every secondary school

should have such a library. Class libraries and subject libraries should also be utilised for this purpose.

2. Trained librarians who have a love for books and an understanding of students interests should be provided in all secondary schools and all teachers should be given some training in the basic principles of library work in the Training Colleges as well as through refresher courses.

3. Where there are no separate public libraries, the school libraries should, as far as possible, make these facilities available to the local public and all existing public libraries should have special session for children and adolescents.

To implement the recommendations of the said Commission, the Ministry of Education, Government of India, asked the state governments to appoint full-time librarians in all the secondary schools on salary scales equivalent to that of teachers and to provide for at least one period a week for students in secondary stage for self-study. They also directed the state governments to make arrangements for training librarians and teacher librarians in the Training Colleges through refresher courses. However, it appears that most of the states in India have not so far carried out the directions of the Union Government in this respect presumably for want of funds and lack of sense of urgency in the matter.

The Administration : With a view to carrying out the directions of the Government of India, and in particular to serve the requirements of the educational philosophy of the school and solve the problem of teaching the use and enjoyment of both, the library must be administered, staffed, equipped and organized in such a way that it becomes a contributing factor in the learning process of boys and girls in the school.

Adequate supervision at the state level is also necessary by having a State Supervisor of Libraries. The present need is that the existing school libraries should provide better library service and function in accordance with set standards. The support of the state as well as the district education authority is essential for the success of the library programme in the schools under their control. In the USA several states have the posts of Field Visitors for school libraries. Till such times as State Supervisor of Libraries is appointed by the Government, the District Education Officers may perform such functions with a view to seeing the actual functioning and suggesting ways and means for providing effective library service to the children in school. He should also ensure that the standards prescribed by the Department of Eduction are maintained by the schools inspected by him. A District Council for School Libraries with the District Education Officer as Chairman, and the District Librarian as the Secretary and representatives of headmasters and school librarians in the district may be constituted to coordinate service for stock of school libraries in the district in accordance with set standards as suggested by Dr. S.R. Ranganathan. The Secondary Education Commission has observed, as under, with regard to librarian for the school library:

> In the most schools, there is no conception of such (library) service. It would require the services of a highly qualified and trained librarian who would be on par with other senior teachers in pay and status and we definitely recommend that there should be in every secondary school a full time librarian of this type. If his function is merely to maintain a register of books, keep the library open at odd hours and occasionally issue books to a few students there would obviously be no need for a full time and highly qualified librarian. But if the library is to be the hub of academic and intellectual life of the school, if it is not only to meet but guide the reading interests of students, if it is to work as a centre of free and supervised study as well as group works on projects undertaken by them, if it is to do all these things, the librarian will surely have his work cut out.

In small schools there is no room for having a full-time librarian, but a full-time teacher-librarian for every school with more than 500 pupils is suggested. In the schools, with more than a thousand pupils and with a book stock eventually of five to ten thousands, the work of the library calls for full-time staff. The teacher-librarian win organize and develop the library, but the professional librarian will maintain and prepare it for use and do administrative tasks. In some states in India, e.g. Punjab and Haryana the subject of school library organization has been introduced in the curriculum of the Bachelor of Education course by the, concerned universities.

The Economy : Promoting any good library service in schools depends on finance. The school authorities must, therefore, be fully alive to the value of better libraries and willing to spend whatever is necessary for providing such a service. Recurring as well as non-recurring grants should be adequately provided for school libraries. There should be a definite annual appropriation for books and periodicals and to cover all the expenses inclusive of salary of librarian and full-time clerical staff and library building maintenance. The recurring library grant should be provided annually to cover expenditure on the books, other library material and equipment, etc. By mutual consultation between teacher and librarian, the book fund should be allocated to different subjects taught in the school. It is the duty of the state government or other educational authority or management administering the school to meet the cost of new building added for the library and initial expenditure on fittings and books covering the basic stock needed as a nucleus for library activities. There is also a need for development of book banks in secondary schools and for this purpose Education Department of the concerned state government should place funds at the disposal of the secondary schools from which they can take recourse to the establishment of book banks as recommended by the Secondary Education Commission.

Book Purchase : The school library must have well selected books to meet curricular requirement and need for recreational and inspirational reading. In addition, there should be one set of approved encyclopaedias and dictionaries and one or two good daily newspapers and about five periodicals suitable for pupils' use. The Secondary Education Commission had recommended that all the education departments should see to it that every secondary school has a small but select library of educational books and periodicals for teachers' use. The book selection should bo done heavily once in a quarter and lightly once in a month. A secondary school library should have an adequate number of textbooks so that the students can have an easy access to them, as recommended by the Education Commission (1964-1966).

Rules and Regulations

Physical Standards : The following are considered the main characteristics of a good school library in regard to its physical arrangement:

1. The Centralised Library is the best arrangement for a school library.
2. The physical arrangement should, as far as possible, comply with the minimum standards prescribed by authorities and, if feasible, exceed them. The following minimum standards may be set up in respect of physical arrangement:
    a. The library room should be centrally located so far as to be accessible to the largest number of pupils.
    b. It should be located where expansion is possible.
    c. The room should be placed where it receives the maximum light and where there is a minimum of disconcerting noises.
    d. It should be placed where there can be an entrance independent of the rest of the building, with suitable arrangements for heating, lighting and sanitation.

3. Space and equipment should be adequate. There should be at the minimum space enough to seat the largest class in the school.

Quantitative Standards : Quantitative standards for libraries should also be laid down by Education Authorities in each State. The All India Seminar on School Libraries held at Bangalore in 1962 recommended as under:

The Personnel : The annual expenditure for each school in its library staff should be equal to that on reading materials.

For a school of 560 pupils with 2 sections for each of 7 classes the minimum full-time library staff to work the library in single shift during the days on which the school work should be:

(i) One graduate-librarian with B.Lib.Sc. Degree or post Graduate Diploma in Library Science;

(ii) One semi-professional; and

(iii) One unskilled person.

If the library works, as it should, in 2 shifts a day and all the days of the year, the above staff should be multiplied by two.

The status of the trained graduate-librarian should be the same as that of the trained graduate teacher. He should be a member of the teaching faculty of the school and his salary scale also should be the same as that of the trained graduate teacher. Similarly, the semi-professional librarian in the school should be on par with that of secondary trained teacher.

Until there is a sufficient number of trained school librarians, it may be useful for a visiting librarian with a Bachelor's Degree in Library Science to be appointed to have charge of the school libraries in each specified area, each of which may employ for the time being semi-professional or part-time teacher librarians.

Whenever a teacher is employed as a part-time librarian he should be relieved half time for work in the library and he should be paid a special allowance.

Books Etc.

(i) Each school library should endeavour to provide not less than 20 books other than the prescribed textbooks for pupil.

(ii) Each school should acquire each year not less than 2 books other than the prescribed textbook per pupil.

The Finances : To give efficient library service to school children, to cultivate in them the reading habit and to make individual instruction possible, a school library should provide a minimum of Rs. 14 per pupil per year – Rs. 7 for reading materials and Rs. 7 for the service personnel.

In the present tax-pattern in our country, the annual library fund of a school should be borne by the proceeds of the management and the annual grant from the State Government in the ratio of one : one : four (1: 1: 4) and the Union Government should provide all the capital expenditure of a school library.

Qualitative Standards : In planning and evaluating a programme for a school library, the following qualitative standards may be prescribed as has been done in America:

1. In evaluating the service of the school library the teachers, the pupils and the librarian must plan together the use of material already available and the selection of materials to be added.
2. The school library has a distinct contribution to make to the social and cultural development of pupils.
3. The librarian, working with all pupils and teachers in the school, is able to give valuable assistance in curriculum making.
4. The school library should serve as a laboratory for reference work in school.
5. The library must have a wealth of materials of all kinds – books, pamphlets, pictures, prints and other

audio-visual aids organised with the educational needs of the particular school in view and directed by the staff keenly interested in young people knowing the materials and sources of materials.

6. The selection of materials should be the joint responsibility of all those who participate in using them-pupils, teachers and librarian.

7. Satisfactory school library service is dependent upon definite financial resources. The school administrator cannot expect maximum results with minimum expenditure. Provision for financing the school library should be included in the school budget.

8. The school library building should be designed and equipped with the functional purposes in view. The school librarian should be invited to work with the Architect or Engineer when plans are drawn for such a building.

9. A supervisory school library service at the State level should be provided by having an Inspectorate with qualified personnel in the Education Department with a view to promote more adequate library facilities for every school child. That office will issue directions and instructions to all school libraries in the State in the matter of better administration of libraries.

Essential Services : The following services are considered essential for having an effective school library.

1. It must build up a well-balanced collection of books, pamphlets and audio-visual aids appropriate to the objectives and needs of the school.

2. It must make readily available its resources and those of other libraries to pupils and teachers.

3. It must recognise children's interests and help them to expand the interests through reading.

4. It must help boys and girls broaden their fields of knowledge through use of books.

5. It must teach and encourage the use of library tools and materials.

6. It must provide assistance in finding instructional materials and share with teachers the guidance and stimulation of children's reading.

7. It must relate the school library to the public library and encourage pupils to build personal libraries.

Indispensable Factors : The following are considered indispensable factors in providing essential services:

1. A collection of books carefully selected to supply children with a variety of reading experiences with sufficient budget provision for additions and replacements.

2. A library room with suitable furniture, adequate lighting, necessary shelving and reading space sufficient for at least one-half more than the average number of children in one class.

3. A full trained librarian who has also had teacher's training and whose salary is commensurate with training and ability.

4. Opportunity for children to use the library at any time throughout the school hours.

5. The Headmaster or Headmistress and staff alive to the possibilities of an active library within the school and who utilize classroom work through the wide resources of the library.

Librarian's Role : The school librarian can aid the teacher and the administrator in the following ways:

1. Making them aware of the library and its facilities;

2. Helping with curriculum development;

3. Soliciting and accepting suggestions for the books;

4. Sending notices of new books and materials;

5. Helping prepare lists for units iii courses;

6. Reporting student interests and reading habits;

7. Providing an up-to-date professional collection of books and magazines;

8. Visiting classes and being interested in the method of presentation of materials; and

9. Meeting with and talking to subject-groups about their needs.

Mutual Consultation : Mutual consultation and joint effort is necessary between teacher and librarian in the following areas of work:

1. Allocation of the book-fund to different subjects.

2. Allocation of the amount for each subject to different classes.

3. Allocation of funds to reference books and periodicals.

4. Annual selection of periodicals and review of the list of current periodicals.

5. Book selection to be done heavily once in a quarter and lightly once in a month.

6. Preparation of reading lists in different subjects and for different classes from time to time.

7. Sharing the help to be given by the library to the pupils individually.

8. Evaluation of the library diaries of each pupil and the follow-up work suggested by such evaluation.

Five

Public Libraries

Library for All

According to Roanald Benge Public Library concept consists of four elements. First, the Public Libraries are available for the loan of materials and for reference purposes to all citizens. Second, that the public Libraries are mainly supported from public funds either on a local or on a national basis. The third element is their services as far as the individual is concerned should be free. The fourth one is that all material should be available as an integral part of right.

The Setup

The services performed by the modern Public Library are as follows:

1. It collects the printed and audio-visual materials.
2. Logical organization of materials for convenient use.
3. Provision of information service so that they may be used.
4. Guidance to individuals in the use of educational and recreational material.

5. The materials are provided

   (a) To facilitate informal self education of the people in the community.

   (b) To enrich and further develop the subjects on which individuals are under-taking formal education.

   (c) To meet the informal needs of a particular section.

   (d) To support the educational, civic and cultural activities of groups and organizations.

   (e) To encourage the constructive use of leisure time.

UNESCO's Role : The UNESCO produced a manifesto on Public Libraries in 1949. The "Manifesto proclaims UNESCO's belief in the public library as a living force for education, culture and information and as an essential agent for the fostering of peace and understanding between people and between nations."

The UNESCO manifesto emphasises that the Public Library service should be established under clear mandate of law so that public library service is available all over the nation. On the question of free access, the manifesto says to fulfil its purposes, the public library must be readily accessible, and its doors remain open for free and equal use by all members of the community regardless of race, colour, nationality, sex, religion, language, status or educational attainments. Discussing the public library in the community the manifesto says that the public library should be active and positive in its outlook, demonstrating the value of its services and encouraging their use.

The aims and objectives of the public libraries according to the UNESCO manifesto and revised by the IFLA are:

Educational : To foster and provide means for self development of the individual, group at whatever stage of education, closing the gap between individual and recorded knowledge:

1. To promote the use of Public libraries as educational institution for the individual;

2. To supplement formal educational programmes;
3. To promote the creation of specialized resources.

Information: To bring to the individual or group accurate information quickly, in depth, particularly on topics of current interest:

1. To promote the use of Public Libraries as information centres.
2. To promote the use of the public library as a referral contact points to specialized sources of information.

Culture : To be one of the principal centres of cultural and promote keener participation, appreciation of all arts:

1. To promote and encourage the use of public libraries as centres where individuals can take part in the arts in a positive way;
2. To encourage the public librarian to assume the role of initiator and organizer of cultural events;
3. To encourage the public librarian to liaison with the local societies and cultural organizations, fostering the creative use of leisure in the field of arts;
4. To promote and encourage the use of a public library as a 'special library' agency for local allocations and cultural organizations;
5. To promote and encourage the use of public libraries as cultural information centres.

To play a part in encouraging the positive use of leisure and providing material for change and recreation:

1. To promote the provision of general leisure material for the individual.
2. To promote the provision of leisure to special groups in the community.

In India the phrase Public Library is used in a very loose sense; it applies to any library which permits members of the public to use its materials for reference or borrowing on payment of fees or rent. In this sense all kinds of libraries National, University, School and Subscription libraries would be Public libraries.

According to the Advisory Committee for Libraries the internationally accepted definition of a Public Library is that it is a library

1. Which is financed for the most part out of public funds.
2. Which charges no fees from readers and yet is open for full use by the public without distinction of caste, creed or sex.
3. Which is intended as an auxiliary educational institution providing means of self education which is endless.
4. Which houses learning materials giving reliable information freely and without partiality or prejudice on a variety of subjects which will satisfy the interest of readers.

IFLA Definition : Public library is any library free to the public of community creed, sex, age, social and educational status, free of charge and either a govt. controlled or govt. aided, or any other library notified by the govt. or any local self govt. as public, supported by public fund. IFLA defines (1985) Public Library as:

> "A Library established and financed by a local or in some cases, central government body or by some other organisation authorised to act on its behalf available without bias or discrimination to all who wish to use it." The draft revision of UNESCO's Public Library Manifesto (1992-93) (i.e., 3rd revision in 1994) proclaims its belief in Public Library as a basic instrument in promoting peace and understanding and as a vital force for education, information and culture; ensuring free and direct access to knowledge, information and culture, independent decision-making, individual development

and freedom of expression; providing lending of collections; supporting reading and ensuring literacy; making available all forms of documents and all kinds of information to which the general public has access; making the gateway to the world of information and cultural experience at a local level; ensuring continuing life long educational communicating knowledge and awareness of cultural heritage; promoting dialogue and cultural exchange among people, regions and nations.

The Origin

Public Library Movement in India : The contributions made by Maharaja Sayajirao III of Baroda to modern public library movement in India is really remarkable. He was an enlightened person. During the course of his visit to the United States of America, he felt greatly impressed by the role played by public libraries in the advancement of education. Therefore, he decided to establish public libraries throughout his state. In order to organise libraries along modern lines, he invited W.A. Borden, Librarian of Young Men's Institute, New Haven, Connecticut. During his tenure of office, (1910-13), he established the Central Library and initiated a public library system. He also conducted library training classes to train staff in 19 10. The modern public library movement in India is said to have begun in Baroda during the first decade of the century.

"By the time Borden left the state, on May 15, 1913, Baroda city had its Central Library, comprising Reference and Lending Departments with a book stock of 40,000 volumes. Twenty-five thousand more books were awaiting addition as soon as more space was provided. Two of the three prant libraries had been established and thirty-six of the thirty-eight towns had provided their own libraries. Two hundred and sixteen of the four hundred and twenty-six large villages had founded their libraries. Even the small villages had come forward and had initiated their own libraries. There were 140 travelling libraries as well." By the time Borden left Baroda, he had achieved a great deal, in the form of planning and establishing a network of public library system in

Baroda. Due to the farsightedness of Sayajirao III, Baroda state was able to provide free library facilities to citizens of the state. The Maharaja passed away in 1936. It is a pity that an excellent library system developed as early as 1910 could not be sustained, due to lack of support on the part of the state government. The library system had deteriorated greatly by 1947.

After Independence : The Government of India constituted the National Central Library Committee in 1948. Dr. S.R. Ranganathan presented for consideration of this committee a draft Union Library Bill with a 30 year development.

The transformation of the former Imperial Library into the National Library of the country (1948), the establishment of the Delhi Public Library with the assistance of UNESCO (1951), the passing of the Delivery of Books Act in 1954, amended to cover periodical publications in 1956, all these constituted acts of great foresight of the young Government of Free India. The Central Government has also been making efforts to start a chain of libraries through its Five Year Plans. The Sinha Committee appointed by it in 1957 favoured introduction of library legislation in all the states. As a follow-up of the recommendations of this committee the Union Government set up in 1959 a committee, under the chairmanship of Dr. M.D. Sen, to frame a model public libraries bill. The committee submitted its report with a model bill in 1962. In 1963, the Union Government circulated the draft library bill widely among the states and library associations. In spite of all these efforts except nine of the 22 states and all the 9 Union Territories are without library legislation so far.

Under the Five Year plans, the Planning Commission, Government of India has included library development. In the first five year plan (1951-56) the objective was to set up a National Central Library, a State Central Library in each state, along with a network of circulating libraries consisting of deposit stations and mobile vans in villages. By the end of the plan period, there were nine state central libraries and about 100 district libraries.

In 1954, Government of India passed the Delivery of Books (Public Libraries) Act. The same was amended in 1956 and included newspapers. Under this Act, every publisher is obliged to send book or newspaper published by him to the National Library at Calcutta as well as to each of three public libraries at Delhi, Bombay and Madras.

During the Second Five Year Plan (1956-61), an amount of Rs. 140 lakhs was provided to the states for library development. The objective of the plan was to establish district libraries.

In 1957, Advisory Committee for Libraries was set up by Government of India under the chairmanship of K.P. Sinha. The committee submitted its report in 1958. It recommended 25 year library plan, levy of cess of 6 paise in a rupee on property tax. It suggested Government of India to contribute matching grant equal to cess collected by a state, each state should enact State Library Act and Government of India should enact Central Library Act. However, no action has been taken on these recommendations to a large extent. On the recommendations of the Library Advisory Committee in 1959, the Ministry of Education, Government of India, took the initiative to draw up a "Model State Public Library Bill". In 1967, Government of India passed the Press and Registration of Books Act.

During the 3rd Five Year Pan, the goal was to cover the entire country by means of a network of central state, district, branch, village and mobile libraries. The working group set up by the Planning Commission set a target of setting up of a network of libraries, reaching up to village level having a population of 2000.

In Five Year Plans, there was provision for improvement of libraries and some progress has been made. States have established state central libraries, large number of district libraries and quite a large number of rural libraries have been set up.

Raja Rammohun Roy Library Foundation: The year 1972 was the year of celebration of the bicentenary of Raja Rammohun Roy. The Government of India decided that a Library Foundation carrying library service to the towns and villages should be the best homage to the memory of Raja Rammohun Roy. Thus the Raja Rammohun Roy Library Foundation was established with its headquarters in Calcutta, to promote and support library movement in the country. It has played a significant role in the growth and development of public libraries in India by providing grants for purchase of reading materials, and for construction of library buildings. Recently, it has taken active part towards formulation of draft "National Policy on Library and Information System." Since its inception in 1972 till March 1986, the Foundation received total grants and contributions of Rs. 607.64 lakhs, out of which Rs. 382.19 and Rs. 225.45 lakhs were accounted for by the Government and the State Governments, respectively.

Other Initiatives : National Adult Education Programme (NAEP) was inaugurated by the Ministry of Education and Social Welfare (Govt. of India) on 2nd Oct., 1978. The programme did not succeed because of the half-hearted efforts.

A Planning Commission Working Group was constituted to give a report on modernisation of library services and informatics for the 7th Five Year Plan 1985-90. The report has been submitted.

National Policy: In 1985, a Committee on National Policy on Library and Information System was appointed by the Government of India, Department of Culture, to advise the government on the formulation of national policy under the chairmanship of D.P. Chattopadhyaya. The report of the Committee was submitted to the Minister of Human Resource Development, Government of India, vide letter of May 30, 1986.

Legal Matter : Due to the efforts of S.R. Ranganathan, the Madras (Tamil Nadu) Public Libraries Act, 1948 was put on the statute book on 29th January, 1949. Madras was the first state to provide the public library system through library legislation. Hyderabad state enacted Hyderabad Public Libraries Act in 1995. Andhra Pradesh Public Libraries Act, 1960 came into force in 1960. Mysore (Karnataka) Public Libraries Act, 1965 came into force on April 1, 1966. Maharastra Public Libraries Act, was passed in 1967. In the year 1979, the West Bengal Public Libraries Act was passed and enforced in the same year. Manipur Public Libraries Act, Kerala Public Libraries Act and Haryana Public Libraries Act were passed in 1988, 1989 and 1989 respectively. Mizoram, Goa, Gujarat and Orissa enacted Library Legislation in 1993, 1994, 2001, 2001 respectively.

Public library may function as a regular support for informal, non-formal as well as formal system of learning. Public library should function as the people's university, a community information centre and a nucleus of community's intellectual life. Existing institutional formal system of learning prevalent in India is not in order to reach out to every individual and satisfy the total educational need of the individual as well as the society. In spite of 'Operation Black Board' project aiming at universal literacy and other projects under non-formal education system adopted by Govt. of India, many a boys and girls relapse into illiteracy particularly in rural areas as they could not continue formal schooling for some reason or other to a higher level. The ill effects of "Downward Filtrating Theory" of the British Govt. in education, propagated by the "General Committee of Public Instruction" formed in Calcutta in 1823 could not be still wipe out resulting in literacy rate in India even in 1991 Census not more than 52. 11 %. On the other hand, the formal system does not meet the entire educational needs of the individual as well, specially due to emergence of increasing demands for various educational requirements of today's world in view of exponential growth of knowledge and technology. Besides, in spite of several Education Commissions' Report and lately the New Education Policy (1986) adopted by Govt. of India, the prevalent formal education system originated in the British model for producing necessary clerical office staff could not yet develop in order to fit in the present socio-cultural and socio-economic environment of Indian society. Lately, the perspective of formal education seems to change from personality development to academic performance. It is also found from experience that the existing formal schooling system rather alienates a large number of young people particularly in the rural areas from reality and makes them unfit to cope with real life situations.

Secondly, the informal learning of the individual based on environmental culture and family traditional skills requires to be examined and moulded time to time in non-formal way in the light of new knowledge and changed environment and situation. Folk culture which was one of the dominant elements in informal learning for mass education could no longer become commensurate with the need of a competitive industrial society.

Under such circumstances, it is only continuing non-formal system of learning under programmes with developmental, educational, cultural, welfare, agricultural, publicity, literary interests which ought to be devoid of both the rigidity of formal system as well as the aimlessness of informal system and which alone could complement and reinforce the inadequacy of formal as well as supplement the informal system of learning. The role of the public library is, on the one hand, to support the formal education particularly in schools and colleges by making provision for students' demands and keeping the library open during evening hours when schools and colleges close and thus providing scope for teachers' co-relating the class-teaching to the recorded knowledge in the library; on the other, the existence of a comprehensive permanent infrastructural network of urban and rural multi-purpose free public library system interwoven into the very texture of the social and cultural life of the people based on legal mandate under the umbrella of a State Central Library System is indispensable as a non-political, non-religious, culturally interwoven social institution in order to provide the appropriate permanent meaningful and very effective support both for organisation and follow-up activities of community need oriented and properly co-ordinated continuing non-formal educational programmes, followed up seriously in a continuing processes; and to support the informal learning as well as of one and all and achieve universal mass literacy and continuing to update of one's education freely. It is being continuously confirmed by anthropological enquiry that human behaviour may be shaped to the extraordinary extent by learning. As such public library system with the objective of free dissemination of knowledge and information irrespective of caste, creed, sex, age and standard constitutes a basic component of human resource development apparatus and its impact is effective, enduring and deep rooted in order to usher in a social and cultural renaissance.

New Trends : In the light of experiences gained in the states through library Acts and without Acts and in the context of present situation prevailing in the country, the approach towards the matter of public library development benefiting every citizen of the country requires to be made afresh. The first thing to be noted is that by 73rd amendment of the Indian Constitution in 1992, the Panchayats are given statutory duty to establish and maintain library service. Accordingly the Assam Panchayat Act, 1994 provides for establishing and constituting of "Gaon Panchayats" as body corporate and the functions including "Promotion of 'Adult Literacy," "Organisation of Villages Library and Reading Rooms" vide chapter IV section XIV and XV respectively are made mandatory. The "shall" has been replacing the term "may" of the Assam Panchayat Act of 1972 as amended upto 31st December, 1978. This Act is not yet implemented as the panchayats are not elected as per the provision of this new amendment, the regulations also are yet to be framed. Block Panchayats may be made viable library authorities along with branches and deposit centres in Gram Panchayats. As per already prevailing trend, there should be govt. run hierarchy of public library system, the State Central Library consisting of different sections at the apex, followed by District and Sub-divisional libraries under the Directorate of library services. Corporation and Municipality Act may also be amended creating mandatory provision for library service. The proposed state public library bill should incorporate the existing mandatory provisions; the existing library Acts may be amended in the context of the provisions of Panchayati Raj in India. Indian Public Library Association in its All India Library Conference held in Chandigarh from 5-8 Feb. 1996 recommends amendment of Library Acts by concerned states including tiniest of panchayati system. As the panchayats share in financial as well as organisational and administrative burdens of creation of comprehensive network of urban and rural public library system will be certain and spontaneous. District Committees may be formed for co-ordination, cooperation and development of resources and services among different categories of libraries district-wise.

Economic Side

Mandatory provision for regular financial resource is indispensable for fulfilment of provisions of any Act for public library services. Instead of Library Cess on surcharge of local property Act, surcharge maybe taken on state products and industries and deposited in the state library fund. In this case there will be no variation from area to area. Secondly receiving of the matching grant from RRRLF in this way will be easier. At present many public libraries do not receive the grant due to non-fulfilment of the formalities. In Assam, State Library Fund may be created out of surcharges on sales of local products like oil, tea, timber, etc., say three paise per one kg. tea leaves that means upon more than 400 million kg. tea leaves per year. In Goa it is already enforced on the sale of liquor bottle. Govt. of India may increase the amount of matching grant through RRRLF to the state governments. Any other special grant from any source 6% from Operation Black Board Programme, any service-charge like photocopying document delivery, exhibition of video cassettes, referral service, on-line bibliographic retrieval and information service, etc., may be added to the state library fund. Although all basic services must by kept free and the access of the children, the old and the disabled may be made free to other services also. Endeavour to develop other services would contribute something to the library fund.

The Working

The legislation is to provide for a State Library Board of Management as a statutory, autonomous body corporate, headed by the Minister of Education as Chairman exercising effective executive control of policy in library and information services and in its financial administration, accountable to the state Assembly. Legislative provision should define the constitution, composition, function, powers and responsibilities of Board of Management the Director of Lib. Service being full-time chief executive as Deputy Chairman along with full time and part-time executive members. The Board is to be advised by a broad based state library council headed by the Minister of Education. Statutory provisions are essential in order to empower the Board of Management to manage the affairs of the different units of state library service without much bureaucratic and political interference. Different sections of the State Central Library System also be, advised by respective advisory committees. In this respect, the provisions of the British Library Act of 1972 may be consulted along with provisions of the Public Libraries and Museums Act of 1964, passed by the British Parliament in order to draft a single Act creating facilities both for generalist and specialist readers.

The Suggestions **:** The public library development has been slow and sporadic. This is mainly due to lack of library legislation in some of the states and union territories and also at the national level. Already nine states have enacted public library legislation. A library law, if well formulated, provides adequate provision for financial requirements regarding establishment and proper maintenance of the public library system. Adequate public library services to rural and urban population can be achieved only through a sound library legislation, making it obligatory for the government to undertake financial responsibility to provide reasonable library services to the rural and urban population. However, librarians should not insist on levy of library cess in any such enactment.

It is essential that the Parliament of India should lay down the 'National Policy on Library and Information System.' The document on it has been debated by the professionals. Even the action plan for its implementation is ready. It will make it possible to strengthen public library movement and also achieve a network of public libraries. This will strengthen the public library movement.

There is a need to change the attitude of the government and those of various individuals and agencies involved in the decision-making, towards public libraries. The decision-makers need to be educated that public libraries have an important role to play in the growth and development of a community. A public library can serve as a cultural centre of the community. It should be regarded as a social force which can help in bringing social change, necessary for the welfare and advancement of the society.

The Evaluation

In India, there has been an uneven growth of public libraries in different states/regions and even within a local library system. Public libraries at different levels have multiplied in terms of quantity. The number of public libraries is vast but there is much to be desired regarding their quality of services rendered, book stocks are inadequate. There is lack of qualified personnel. A large majority of so-called libraries are nothing but mere reading rooms providing newspapers and magazines and are open for short hours. Those states which have enacted the public library legislation have to do much better than other states. Even in those states that have library legislation, implementation of the provisions of the Act has been inadequate and tardy. It may be pointed out that those regions, which are economically backward, are badly served by public libraries. The rural areas need to be given special attention. The needs of special groups like blinds, elderly, etc. have been neglected and need to be looked into by the public library systems.

Six

Largest Library

A national library is the most comprehensive library which serves a particular country's citizen. It is governed and funded by national governement.

The National library, in the 18th and 19th centuries, was usually a reference library only and its services consisted of making seats available, bringing materials to its readers for studying in its reading rooms, and producing a catalogue of its collections. The British National Library has added a lending function over the years, piece-meal; the US Library of Congress is also the main library of that legislative body, but has developed specialised information services in other subject areas; the Director-General of the Bibliotheque Nationale plays an important part in the administration of French public libraries; while the National Library Service of Botswana directly provides that country's public library services.

The encouragement of the development of effective national library services has been one of the main tasks of UNESCO's Library's program. It has held a number of international conferences on the subject, has fostered cooperation, provided money and expert advice, has drawn up criteria for national library services.

The essential services for National Library are following:

1. A reference collection of all the publications of the particular country, achieved by compulsory legal deposit (i.e., the requirement that all publishers deposit at least one copy of everything which they produce with the national library).

2. A current national bibliography of the country's output of publications (the comprehensives of which can be best assured by the legal deposit requirement), which in time will cumulate into the country's definite retrospective bibliography.

3. A lending service, consisting of a store of multiple copies of the whole of the country's publication, plus as much of the publication of the rest of the world as is economically feasible, so that-

   (a) any individuals or groups within the country concerned, through their own local or specialised library services, may be sure that a copy of an information-containing material, which they require, may be made available through the national library service as quickly as possible;

   (b) so that libraries in other countries may have a central point that they may approach to borrow material which may not be available in their own collections.

Other services of national libraries include :

(i) A national information service, or at least a national referral service, i.e., an office which can reliably and speedily refer enquirers to, sources of information which may not be available from the national library itself.

(ii) A national translation centre, where new and proposed translations are recorded, copies of completed translations held, and translations made of foreign material which is of great interest or importance, but is unlikely to be translated elsewhere.

(iii) A national publishing house. This might, e.g., republish out of print material and give opportunity to authors who cannot achieve publication elsewhere.

(iv) Librarianship and information work research and development.

(v) Librarianship and information work education and training.

National Library

There are two broad classes of staff employed in libraries- those involved in library and information work and those who provide back-up services. These categories can be sub-divided:

Library /information Staff

Non-professional

Pre-professional (trainee)

Professional

Specialist

Managerial

Support Staff

Manual care-taking

Clerical secretarial

Technical and computer staff Specialist

Library information staff

Non-professional: Unqualified staff are usually educated to 'O' level standard; should be able to understand national language and English language. They may have 'A' level or even higher qualifications which will enable them to take professional examinations.

Non-professional staff are expected to undertake most of the routine work so that professionals can afford more intellectually demanding duties. Some librarians have recognised the Reed for a career ladder for non-professional staff.

Pre-professional: Broadly speaking all non-professional staff are pre-professional, but strictly the term relates to trainee librarians. The distinction is worth making, for trainees should be given some practice at professional duties and an attempt should be made to introduce them to a wider perspective of librarianship than they see in their immediate job. The use of trainees as a cheap source of high quality labour is unfair and on a par with the use of library science students on field work as convenient extra hands, available for clearing long-standing work and doing unpopular jobs.

Specialist: Professional librarians can specialise in many ways, by type of library, i.e., national, public, academic, special; by function, i.e., reference work, children's services, bibliographical services etc.; or, perhaps, by subject interest, as in university libraries where graduate qualified staff specialise in an area of the stock-selecting, cataloguing, classifying, and taking general responsibilities in that area. In special libraries the knowledge of a particular subject area is very useful. Professional staff also carry out indexing, abstracting and translation work.

Managerial: Very senior posts in large libraries require more than bibliographical skills. Chief librarians are professional librarians with wider than average responsibilities, or professional managers comparable to industrial executives. Irrespective of the classification, it is evident that managerial expertise is now necessary for more senior posts in the profession.

Support Staff: Manual/caretaking libraries are expensive warehouses of knowledge. Equipment, stock, the buildings themselves are valuable. It makes good economic sense to employ people specifically to care for the library and its physical assets. Caretaking staff need to have qualities of realibilities, responsibility and resourcefulness-many caretaking problems arise outside normal hours of work when senior staff cannot be consulted.

Clerical/Secretarial : Many libraries employ secretarial and other clerical staff. Increased use of 'media resources' in libraries of all types, and the installation of computerised processes, have made technical knowledge essential. Although all staff concerned with handling new media should be trained in their use, large collections will require specialist technical staff. Computer processing in libraries has led to a need for trained operatives and, for libraries with in-house systems, some technical expertise; such posts are often designated 'Technical Services Librarian'.

Big Treasure of Books

In India, the National Library is situated at Calcutta. It has the highest collection in the country. Fabulour collections like the Asutosh Mukhopadhyay collection, the unparalleled and unique Buhar collection of Arabic and Persian manuscripts and printed books of international importance, the Vaiayyapuri collection of Dravidian manuscripts. The unique historical collection of India's greatest historian Jadunath Sarkar, and the collection of this contemporary Dr. Surendra Nath Sen, are among its precious holdings.

The National Library evolved out of the Imperial Library of British days, located in Calcutta. This Imperial Library was the result of an imaginative initiative taken by the famous proconsul and viceroy of India Lord Curzon, to whom India also owes a great deal for the preservation of its ancient monuments, especially the Tajmahal, The Imperial Library was conceived as housing the best of European thought, with an emphasis on English. The notion was that the Indians had to be acquainted with European civilization, which itself was partly an efflorescence of Greek and Roman thought. At the basis of this concept Babinton Macaulay, whose assessment of Indian literary tradition and achievement was deplorably short sighted.

The Imperial Library came into being as the result of a consolidation of the book collections in the old Fort William library at Calcutta. The Imperial Library was opened in 1903 by Lord Curzon and in 1948 it was shifted from the downtown, cramped location to the present spacious context at Belvedere, once a winter residence of the viceroys of India. Credit for this imaginative housing goes to the great Indian and international statesman Jawaharlal Nehru, and the elder statesman of India C. Rajagopalachari, who was also the first Indian Governor General after Independence. Jawaharlal Nehru in his famous comment on this question, observed, "I do not want Belvedere for the mere purpose of stacking books. We want to convert it into a fine central library where a large number of research students can work and where there will be all the other amenities which a modern library gets".

Seven

Particular Libraries

Libraries are universally recognised important social institutions. No community is considered complete without a library. The gradual spread of education, the intensification of research activities and rapid increase in production of recorded knowledge have led the expansion of libraries and the development of their services. A public library is an important element in the life of a community: an academic library is an essential part of an educational institution (School, college or university): a special (business or industrial or research) library is an indispensable in govt. departments, large business and industrial organisations.

Libraries with Purpose

Libraries are nerve centres of documentation and information activities, these are recognised as indispensable organs of research. This profession had started in the 1940s, in India, has now reached its zenith. With the advent of time, this profession has undergone drastic changes in thought and its contents and has developed into a major subject of study, branching off into several specialization, like medical librarianship, academic librarianship and Special Librarianship etc. Special libraries are the product of twentieth century to promote research and development activities, with limited subject coverage. In 1909, the Special Library

Association in U.S.A. was established in U.K., Association of Special Libraries and Information Bureau was established in 1924 and in India, Indian Association of Special Libraries and Information Centres (IASLIC) came in existence on September, 1955. After World War II due to tremendous increase in the budgets for research and development, special library movement grew rapidly in various countries. Due to continuous acceleration in research development in various countries, the future of special libraries is bright.

The Perception

While other types of libraries serve multiple objectives such as education, research, recreation, cultural and social activities, the major and perhaps only objective of a special library, is the provision of information, in support of the objectives of its parent organisation. Special libraries exist in a wide variety of organisation, most of them being units of larger organisations. Their purposes are usually other than provision of education or conventional library services, but invariably they meet the information requirements of the organisations to which they are attached. Special libraries are formed in research and development establishments, government departments, directorates, bureaus, industrial and business undertakings, learned societies and professional associations, trade and business associations, hospitals and health services, social and welfare organisations, museums, national gallery of arts, etc. However special libraries are established to serve a particular group of users or an activity or specialists working on a subject or a group of subjects or a particular type of documents, etc.

These distinguishing features identify special libraries although their functions do very often overlap. Special libraries also assume different names like technical library, business information centres and research information service, etc.

The Origin : Special libraries first began to appear in the United States (U.S.) in the first decades of the 20th century. They were a new form of library, quite different from other types of libraries in their functions and purpose and in their new methods of collecting and organising materials. In the later decades of the century, organisations increased in number, size and complexity, as business and industry began to grow rapidly. A large number of government organisations also sprang up to meet various activities of the government and libraries began to grow in all these organisations. World Wars I & II accelerated the process of industrial development backed by scientific and technological research; research and development became increasingly institutionalised that naturally led to the growth of special library collections and new services.

The growth of special libraries in Europe as well as in many of the developing countries also was modelled on the patterns of U.S. special library movements. As nations continued to industrialise and increased their research efforts, special libraries were established in research organisations and other agencies. Growth and development of special libraries in India also has been on the model of the Western Countries.

The Concepts : According to J.E. Wright the "Special Library" means a library which is concerned almost exclusively with the literature of a particular subject or a group of subjects. According to Jamieson and Foskett the activities of a group of readers in a special library should be directed to a common purpose. Dr. Ranganathan defines it as the 'Special library', which is built up to supply detailed information in respect of some limited subject field. According to him, "the difference between general library and a special library lay only in the nature of the clientele and the material or the documents served."

Characteristics of a Special Library

1. Special libraries are generally setup by govt., learned professional societies, business and industrial organizations etc., and they exist as an unit of their parental organizations/bodies.

2. Generally they are small libraries as compared with a large public/university or educational institutional libraries.

3. Their subject of coverage is very limited and serve specialist readers, who are also in small numbers.

4. Sometime they are designated as map library, film library etc., according to the form of material possesed by them.

5. Special libraries are mainly concerned with the supply of information to their readers, expeditiously for which they have to use some unconventional methods too.

6. The special library has to serve its parent organization for promotion of research, in order to make more and more money to stay in business.

The Organisation

The main principle in setting the library building is, of course, the convenience of users, since every employee of the organization, especially research personnel uses the library resources, so a central position is more suitable for library building. However, a library must be nearest to those, who will make the heaviest demand on its services, probably the research personnel. Regarding the space required for a special library, several standards have been quoted in several standard handbooks. But all of them are only guides and each individual library will have to make its own decisions based on its particular requirements.

Binns has provided a useful checklist of desirable equipments which includes shelving, desks (for staff and readers), filing cabinets (for reports, pamphlets, trade catalogues etc.) catalogue cabinets and drawers, chairs, typewriters, photocopying machines, microfilm reader and a wide variety of stationery. Now-a-days a computer is often a vital piece of library-equipments but this is usually available in some other departments.

The Functions

All the activities of a special library are derived from two basic types of information service that are provided by them. In fact, the reason for their existence, as stated earlier, is to provide such information services. The first service is provided in response to users' requests for information covering reference and literature search. The second is information service in anticipation of need and includes indexing, abstracting services which are designed to keep the users updated on new and current information. Decisions about collection development of the library, processing and organisation of documents, appointment of staff etc., are determined on the type and volume of services to be provided.

Book Purchase

Special library collections are working collections to support their information services, with an emphasis on current information and retrospective material, determined on the basis of the projects and programmes taken up by the organisations. Besides the traditional forms of materials such as books, journals, technical and research reports, other typical and significant material includes patents, specifications in scientific and industrial libraries, business records, trade information and news clippings, etc., in business libraries. A particular feature of a collection in a special library is that it is never static but dynamic and changing as new activities and programmes develop in the parent organisations. The library also gets affected by changes in the parent organisation and the scope and nature of the library collections and services also get changed suitably. Therefore, the staff of the special library must be constantly alert to possible new areas and the changing interests of the organisnations so that the library collection can respond to changing demands of information. Generally speaking the special library collections have three major components; the first is published information, the second internally generated information and the third, information available from sources, outside the organisation.

In most of the special libraries, periodicals provide the most updated information. Therefore, periodical collections are perhaps the richest of the library sources and the maximum funds are provided for subscriptions to periodicals. Specialised reports form the second category of published information. Information collected through newspaper clippings, pamphlets, statistical compilations, sales literature, trade catalogues, financial statements, government documents, etc., form the other sources of information.

The second major component of the collection is information generated within the organisation, such as, research reports, technical memoranda, laboratory note books, working papers, correspondence, house organs, newsletters, sales literature, and company and competitive advertising etc.

Use of resources outside the organisation is the third component of the special library collection. Usually, the special library has to depend on external resources for information and materials outside its scope of activities. In fact, special libraries quite often use public, academic and research libraries through formal inter-library loan procedures.

The Setup

Special libraries employ a wide variety of methods in organising their collections. The physical storage of its collection is determined on the basis of use. Catalogues, indexes, abstracts are prepared on the basis of ease of use, scope of the activities of the parent organisation and coverage. Classification, Cataloguing and Indexing systems also are simple in their design but are chosen to meet their requirements effectively.

The Staff

It is said that a good staff can do wonders with small stock, a large stock is almost useless without an adequate and qualified staff. To produce a dynamic and efficient library service, the person who is both a subject expert and a professionally trained, is the best proposition. Viscount Caldecote suggested that professional qualifications are more important than subject knowledge. Since too much specialisation can narrow one's range and a special librarian must be prepared for inquiries covering a very wide area of knowledge. Jones admits the importance of subject specialist qualifications but lays great stress on such personal qualities, such as personality, a high standard of background education and intellect, analytical skill and a sense of service. Ashworth himself a subject specialist and professional librarian, organises the value of both kinds of qualifications but points out that they do not need to be combined in one individual.

The ideal library and information staff will in fact, consist of a qualified librarian, subject specialists, translators, experienced shorthand and copy typists, clerical assistance and trainees. The total number of staff depends on such conditions as the size of the company, the number of research scholars and other major users.

The library collection may be of the following types, irrespective of the size of the collection in a special library.

Reference Materials: May include:

1. Dictionaries (General and Technical)
2. Encyclopaedias
3. Year Books
4. Hand Books
5. Manuals etc.

Specifications

1. Indian Standards (BIS)
2. British Standards (BSI)
3. International (ISO), etc.

Conference Papers

1. Reports
2. Proceedings
3. Preliminary publications
4. Discussed papers of conferences or seminars etc.

Periodicals: Periodicals are messengers of the latest developments and new inventions. Mainly technical periodicals, mostly from foreign countries are more useful to a special Industrial library. Even the back issues are quite useful.

Standard Text Books: Mostly foreign books and some Indian useful books are included in the library stock.

The Provisions

General Library Services : The library has three main functions as under:

*Acquisition-*Acquire the needed material.

*Preparation-*To prepare them ready for use.

*Circulation-*To provide for the reading.

Reference Services : In order to make information successful, various type of information services may be introduced in a special library.

Current Awareness Services: To keep the user informed promptly of all the nascent thoughts created in their fields of work as well related fields, the following methods may be adopted.

Rotating of Periodicals: Every new periodical on its receipt is sent to the clientele with the instructions to pass it to the next person on routing list and not to retain it more than three or four days (as required) and periodical may be received back, after circle is completed.

Reproduction of Table Contents: The contents of the newly arrived journals may be duplicated or cyclostyled and sent to the readers. The periodical should be kept in library for consultation.

The selective or full abstracting and indexing of documents can be done and printed or cyclostyled copies can be sent to each reader for information.

List of Current Acquisitions: The newly acquired materials should be brought out daily or weekly basis and should be frequently distributed to the readers.

Library Bulletin: The large libraries with adequate resources may bring out the library bulletin for internal circulation only and may be published monthly, quarterly or at any regular interval, containing the following informations.

Accession List of newly added reading materials and Journals etc.

Article List : Indexing the articles of acquired with or without abstract.

Reading List: A bibliography compiled on a certain topic/ subject.

Information Circulars: General information about library request to return of books, change of library rules etc., may be published in the bulletin.

Books Reviews: Books reviews on important and useful books may be published to catch the eye of the executives of the industry. So they may call the librarian immediately and request him to procure the same for them.

Miscellaneous: The minutes of the library committee, copy of important clipping, important features of annual report etc., may by brought out through the bulletin.

Translation Services : Since the technical language is not limited to any one/ single language. A language is said to be vehicle of thought. To solve the language barrier, translation service is essential. So translators may estimate the value of foreign literature in their respective fields.

Bibliographies in Specific Subject : Subject bibliographies of topics of current interest to users should also be prepared either on demand or in anticipated demand.

Literature Search : Librarian is responsible as a partner in research projects of the organisation. He will find out relevant literature on a subject for a new project or project in hand. He will be engaged in the current as well as retrospective search for the materials, preparation of reports, special charts and diagrams and data services etc. The subject specialization and technical knowledge, both are essential to achieve this objective.

Newspaper Clipping Service : Since the chief executives have hardly few minutes to see the newspaper and digest them, it is the librarian, who get through the long columns of the newspaper and make the important news and prepare clipping and file them neatly. These clippings will be perused by the chief executives. The librarian preserves these clippings for future references. He may prepare an index of available clippings for reference.

Reprographic Services : Due to the fact that enormous literature is published every day, it is beyond the capacity of any library to procure each and every published literature for the users' use. Moreover increase of scientific and technical publications including periodicals are so high that every year restrictions in acquisitioning them are required to be imposed to meet the budget of the organisation. As it is well known that considerable time of a research worker is wasted in noting down the reference literature, required and hence every possible efforts should be made to provide photostat/xerox copies of the references to research worker, so that they can devote more time for their research work.

Publishing of Journal : Now-a-days every reputed industrial organisation releases its journal proudly, which is the messenger of its organisation, proclaiming the policies performance, profits and the future programmes. The librarian will be assigned to look after this work and he will add few pages for the sake of the library news.

Inter Library Loan : No library can claim to be self sufficient. In case, if the material is not available in the library, that should be acquired on inter-library loan from other library. In addition to it, the arrangement of photo-reproduction of material, translation of material for readers will have to be made on demand.

Sources of Information

We have noted earlier in this unit that the emergence of special libraries at the beginning of this century and their subsequent growth and development were due primarily to the need for library and information support for business, trade and commercial enterprises, research organisations and for various functions of government departments. These activities were very much intensified and expanded after World War II, and were organised and operated through mission-oriented national research projects, innovative research for new product and process development, and vastly expanded activities and programmes of governments towards socio-economic development. As a natural consequence of these activities, information services are organised through specialised information centres with a new orientation and fresh approach. These centres which grew in different dimensions, were not necessarily tied down to any single parent organisation but were catering to a wider circle of users who were working in the fields in which these centres were operating. Thus new types of information centres began to evolve and shape. Today we have a variety of such centres operating in diverse fields at regional, national or international levels.

These trends were initially witnessed in industrially advanced countries of the West in the fifties and sixties of this country. These models naturally were influencing the development of specialised information centres in developing countries. For instance, in India, in 1952, a national documentation centre (INSDOC) was established to take care of documentation and information services to the research community in the entire fields of science and technology. But in the next two or three decades, a number of specialised information centres, have sprung up as no single centre can any longer serve a wide spectrum of research activities.

The Comparison : The difference between information centres and many special libraries is one of degree with reference to the services they organise. Three functional levels of service are presently offered by these two types of information institutions. At the minimum level, the special library disseminates information and materials acquired by them, answers reference questions, directs users needing details on research information to appropriate sources and handles routing of periodicals to keep their users informed of current developments in the field. At the intermediary level, a special library or an information centre, offers complex literature searches in specific fields, compiles extensive retrospective bibliographies, selects and transfers relevant research material in anticipation of demand, produces current awareness bulletins in specific disciplines, new products or new processes, or SDI services based on group of individual profiles. At a higher level, an information centre offers highly specialised consolidation and repackaging services which involve analysis, synthesis and evaluation of information and present them in a form required by users.

The final output may be a critical bibliography, evaluative and comprehensive state of art reports or a repackaged report for a specific used category etc. In fact, this range of service has necessitated the formation of different types of information centres, such as data centres, information analysis centres and information dissemination centres. The higher level of information service requires staff with subject specialisation and communication abilities. However these services can be offered by a special library, depending on their staff strength and material acquired and organised. A general difference between these two types of information institutions, is that while the special library offers services only to the staff of their parent organisation, an information centre often serves a widely distributed group of users whose only link being the common subject interest.

India has been quite active in developing her special libraries and information centres in the last forty years. In this section of this unit, we shall give you a quick overview of the main trends of current development in India in this area. This section, however has to be studied in conjunction with the other units wherein this topic has been discussed.

The trends witnessed in the industrially advanced countries of the West, influenced the design and development of special libraries, documentation and information centres in India also. Although India has been vigorously pursuing scientific and industrial research, backed by a positive government policy in the last forty years special libraries had grown in India from the beginning of this century alongside research activities of organisations such as the Geological, Botanical and Zoological surveys, academic and professional institutions like the Indian Institute of Science and the Indian Agricultural Research Institute and government councils like the Indian Council of Agriculture Research and the Indian Council of Medical Research and similar others. However, it is only after the advent of freedom in 1947, that research complexes such as the Council of Scientific and Industrial Research began to be organised and research activities became established institutional activities with government funding.

UNESCO actively promoted and provided technical assistance for the establishment of national documentation centres in many developing countries during the fifties and sixties. With the assistance of UNESCO, the Indian National Scientific Documentation Centre was established in 1952 as a constituent of the Council of Scientific and Industrial Research.

The next two decades saw several special institutions and documentation centres coming up in specialised fields such as atomic energy, defence, agriculture, medicine, social sciences and similar others. In the seventies, with the establishment of the National Information System for Science and Technology (NISSAT) under the Department of Science and Technology, sectoral information centres in fields such as leather, drugs and pharmaceuticals, machine tools, and food were established to meet specific information needs at national levels. Today three more national sectoral information centres are in operation offering specialised library and information services in textiles, chemistry, and chemical technology. In addition there is a data centre in crystallography.

The eighties are witnessing national information system developing in environment, non-conventional sources of energy, ocean sciences, space, biotechnology, electronics etc., under various departments of government, constituted for promoting research and development. Besides these, public sector undertakings such as heavy electricals, steel, drugs and pharmaceuticals, fertilisers etc., are also establishing information centres in their respective fields.

In all these special libraries and information centres, most of the types of library and information services mentioned earlier in this unit, are being offered. A beginning has been made to modernise their library and information services using computer and communication technologies (in many of these institutions). The next decade is crucial for India as demands for information services would increase with information technology offering unlimited opportunities for integrating information systems and services. This will necessitate a more sophisticated institutional infrastructure for information services in the country.

Eight

Mobile Library

In order to satisfy the laws of library science, libraries have to reach out to its users who are deprived and at a distance.

Popular Service

Personalised Service: Public libraries have to serve to the needs of all sections of the society-normal and abnormal, male and female, young and old, children, women, rich and poor, literate and illiterate, city folk and rural folk, etc. Libraries have developed various tools and techniques to help the readers that come to the library to help themselves. With little guidance, the readers can know as to how to use the catalogue, how to locate the books on the shelves, how to get a book issued, what are the rules and regulations of the library etc. In case of a fresh reader, who comes to the library for the first time, the Reference Staff will initiate the reader into the library mechanism. Even when a regular reader has some difficulty either in locating a book or locating a piece of information, the Reference Staff will provide personalised service to the users.

Service to Absentee Readers: Many a time, the reader may not be able to visit the library for information. He may not be able to visit because he is not a member of the library, or else, the information needed is simple and a reference librarian can easily save his time by providing information either by phone or post.

Service by Phone: A reader may ring up to the library and ask the reference staff to provide a piece of information. Most of such queries the reference staff can answer by using the 'ready reference sources' available handy to them. If the information needed by the reader needs prolonged search, the reader may have to ring him back after some time or else, the Reference Staff may pass on the information by phone or despatch the same by post if the information is substantive quantitatively.

Service by Post: Sometimes, the reader may write a letter to the librarian seeking information. The reference staff generally gather such information and send it to the reader by post. Sometimes, the reference staff may direct the user to consult a specific source or contact a specific person/ expert. Such a service we call as 'Referral Service.' This type of service will save the time of the readers.

Alert Services: Some libraries are providing 'alert services' to their absentee readers. For example, a library may be publishing a library bulletin to provide information about new additions to the library, book reviews to help the readers to select the books, new services that are being introduced, information about library rules, timings, staff activities, etc. Some of the special libraries are bringing out documentation lists as a form of Current Awareness Service. Indexing and abstracting bulletins are of great value to the absentee readers. These will help in identifying latest as well as useful material. If there is a request, the library may send a photocopy of the document by post. New means of communication like fax, e-mail, conferencing etc., can be used with advantage to pass on the information quickly to the readers.

Some of national contact libraries of USA, UK, etc., are providing various alert services like-list of additions (of books), article alert service, photocopies of title pages of important journals at the choice of their members, etc. These services are highly useful to readers away from the library.

Inter Library Loan Service: Some of the public libraries, particularly in the West have been sending selected books on inter-library loan to hospitals, prisons, institutions for physically handicapped, to village libraries, schools etc. Books of selective nature are sent to these libraries whether they are part of the library system or not. Books are sent in boxes at regular intervals so that users like patients, prisoners, blind, deaf, dumb, illiterates, neo-literates, children can have access to new and useful books.

Hospital Library Service: The patients in hospitals with physical disorder or mental disorder; those who can move and those who cannot move; those who have a minor ailment and those who are suffering a major ailment can be provided library service.

Library service in hospitals can be provided in two ways. Either by establishing a permanent library in the hospital itself or by getting books on loan from the local public library. All big hospitals have their own libraries which provide service both to doctors as well as patients. The class of material needed for doctors and that for patients will be materially different. Doctors mainly need books and scientific journals for enriching their knowledge about diseases, medicine, treatment etc. Of course, they do need some recreative material. Books needed for patients can be classified into two categories-of recreative nature, which will help the patients to pass on the leisure time, to forget pain and agony and to have a peaceful mind. The second category of books are those which hasten the recovery process. Some books do help in building-up confidence in the minds of the patients to fight against the disease; give tips for quick recovery, the disease, its characteristics, the do's and don'ts for the patient, etc. Such a class of material that contribute for the cure or recovery of the patient used in the hospitals is called 'bibliotherapy.' The librarian of hospitals should possess high knowledge of the books and qualities of a doctor-patience, sympathy and understanding.

Prison Libraries : Earlier a prisoner was regarded as an outcast for life. Now the problem is viewed from sociological and human angles. Several reformist activities have been initiated in jails particularly where hard-core and long-term punishment prisoners are housed. Books are the first and still the best means for reformation of the prisoners.

Books are read in prisons for those who cannot read. Lectures are arranged to put them on the path of realisation of god, virtues and civilized life. Adult education classes are also organised for the benefit of the inmates of the prison. All big prisons are having good libraries. Reading books not only provide enlightenment but also take them close to the outside world, to the right path and to delight.

Some of the prisoners appear for examinations to get academic qualifications. For such of them, prison library is the main source of information.

Public libraries do help in providing suitable reading material to prisoners through their extension or outreach service point in the prison.

For Physically Handicapped: Physically handicapped covers, blind, deaf, dumb, other abnormal. Many public libraries aware of the social responsibility towards these under-privileged class of citizens, have been trying to help them to get the information they want.

1. There are a sizeable members of blind persons who can read large print. For such people books in large print should be made available. Also they can be helped to use visual aids.

2. The second method is that a normal sighted person reads out the book for the sake of the blind. In this method the blind has no direct contact with the book. However, a social contact is established between the reader and the blind. One difficulty in such a situation is the non-availability of suitable readers.

3. A talking book is one where the text of a book is recorded on the disc or a tape and played. But this method is expensive.

4. The common method by which the blind people may be helped to read is through the use of the two systems of embossed script-Braille or Moon. Louis Braille, a Frenchman invented his script in 1834. These are symbols for letters of the alphabet, punctuation marks and for, such common combinations of letters as *'at'* and *'th'*. The Moon system of embossed reading was invented in 1847 by William Moon and this is easier to read.

5. These days text-reading machines and Braille printers are available for the benefit of blind readers. The text readers can recognise the text and speak-out for the blind readers. These machines can read in different tones, at different speeds etc., suitable to the users. A computer attachment can readily print out the text in Braille script for further use.

***Books to Villages and Schools*:** There are many villages which are deprived of library service. In fact villagers need library service most. Because, there are no libraries, they cannot spend much on purchasing books; and they cannot go out for getting library facilities. Public libraries started sending books in boxes to villages and schools so that these people can also have access to books. These books in boxes are rotated among the villages in a particular region or among the schools in a particular region. This type of extension of library service to schools and villages by boxes is common all over the world and proved to be very effective.

Books at Doorstep

Mobile Library is also known as the 'Library on Wheels'; 'Bibliobus' and 'librachain'. Mobile library service is in practice all over the world and every possible means of transport is being used for this purpose. Mobile library is preferred to a branch library for various reasons. The population may be scattered at many points and it is very difficult as well as uneconomical to open branch libraries. In thickly populated cities it is sometimes very difficult to secure accommodation to open a branch library. The mobile library service is meant to benefit those who are scattered far away who would otherwise go without library service. The mobile library van visits places at particular intervals of time. In many cases, it lends books to the users directly and in some cases it delivers books to be taken care of by the delivery stations. Besides the driver, the mobile van has a qualified librarian who performs a number of duties like charging and discharging of books, answering enquiries etc. Sometimes a separate rural library van is run to carry boxes of books for delivery stations at the village centres. This has been found to be efficient, quick and economical.

The mobile library has greater use in the rural areas than in the urban areas. In rural areas, the mobile library forms the backbone of the rural library service. Books for mobile libraries should be carefully chosen. They should be of interest to a great number of people. One disadvantage in running the mobile library service in the rural areas is that some villages are not connected by roads and many others have rugged roads. The vans should be preferably small and well-built. In cases where there are bad roads and motor vehicles cannot be used other modes of vehicles may be pressed into service, like bicycles, rickshaws or carts. The ultimate aim should be to provide books for all.

Nine

Librarian and Staff

Traditionally there are three main branches in the profession-archivists, librarians and documentalists, within which certain specialisations such as bibliographer or indexer have become occupations in their own right. Today, however, people are more willing to accept that the information occupations all belong to a single profession. Before going into the details of the present information profession, let us look into some of the basic issues of our profession.

Head of the Institution

There is a long standing dispute, whether librarianship is a profession or vocation. In order to resolve this, let us see what characterises a profession and as to what is vocation.

Profession : A Profession warrants :

(a) A specialised knowledge of the field-scientific, historical or scholarly;

(b) Intensive preparation for acquiring needed skills and methods to put the knowledge to work;

(c) A set of principles, a social code or ethics;

(d) An organisation that will bind all the numbers together for:

   (i) Concerted opinion.

   (ii) To achieve high standards in performance;

   (iii) To act as a force to achieve common good and work for collective thinking; and

(e) Working with the prime purpose of rendering a public service.

Vocation : A vocation involves :

(a) An activity of some kind-routine, physical or scholarly;

(b) A craft, trade or profession;

(c) Need certain or no skills; and

(d) Mainly an activity involving service against fee or free.

From the above discussion we can safely conclude that librarianship is a profession rather than a vocation. Because:

(a) It needs a specialised knowledge-imparted in various library schools;

(b) It needs intensive training and continued practice to gain mastery over the skills needed for successful librarianship;

(c) A set of principles professional ethics have been drawn;

(d) A large number of organisations at various levels and of different groups are in existence; and

(e) It is service oriented.

Gradual Development

Librarianship may be regarded as the one, as old as the book. But librarianship as a profession is just a little over hundred years old. Earlier it was only an occupation. The organisation of librarianship as a profession started with the establishment of the American Library Association in 1876. The imparting of specialised knowledge started with the establishment of the first library school in 1887 by Dr. Melvil Dewey. Most of the national library associations drew a set of professional ethics. During the last hundred years, it has grown rapidly and established itself as a notable profession.

The choicest few working in special libraries, who enjoy a status on par with the executives or scientists have been trying to keep themselves away from the common core of the profession. Mr. J. Farradane in Britain started advocating since 1953 that "information work is distinct from librarianship and should in no way be confused with it." He took initiative to form the 'Institute of Information Scientists Ltd.' as distinct from The Library Association in 1958.

The Library Association Record of 1953 and 1954 carried a spate of letters for and mostly against the arguments of Mr. Farradane. Some described that "Farradane was thumping a rather lonely tub."

***Unified View* :** Many librarians in UK and USA, and Dr. Ranganathan and others in India were of the opinion that the difference between librarianship and information work was one of degree not kind. Information activity is rather an extension of library activity.

Specialist's Role

Messrs Guinchat and Menou says that the current term for the unified profession of librarians, documentalists and information personnel, for want of a better, is 'Information Specialist'.

The general type of work of all information specialists is similar. They are :

(i) Process documents and information and must therefore master the technical skills involved;

(ii) Serve users and hence needs a gift for and interest in human relations; and

(iii) Need to work effectively on orderly and methodical turn of mind, a sense of organisation and imagination.

Common Utility

Service: An information specialist works nearly always for other people and this can occasionally be frustrating. He should continue to be useful.

Communication Skills : Personal relations of the information specialist with the users and producers of information have more decisive influence on the effectiveness of the service. Information specialist must be capable of understanding other people, mixing socially and inspiring confidence-in short of communicating.

Judgement : There are many factors that influence information and communication. These factors change so rapidly that there is never a readymade solution or a simple rule-of-thumb for every situation. An information scientist should take decisions on taking into acount of all the criteria and visualising all the implications of his judgement.

Curiosity : The information specialist should have curiosity to know people, organisations, things, facts, ideas and techniques so that he can make use of the right means and method for providing service.

Adaptability : The needs of the users change from time to time. So too are the knowledge and techniques employed for dissemination of information. The information specialist should have an adaptive and flexible mind.

Perseverance and Modesty : Information work is always demanding: yet its immediate results are often far from impressive; besides, it is frequently the user who reaps the benefit and the praise.

Important Aspects

Sound Theory : Librarianship for long was based on rules of thumb and practices were involved or improved on trial and error basis. Practical librarianship was by way of apprenticeship or by observation and adaptation of practices in vogue in popular and big libraries. Some of the librarians started publishing manuals and guides on several library practices for the benefit of their fellow professionals. Establishment of library associations gave opportunities for professionals to meet and discuss matters of mutual interest. Some of the leaders in the profession started bringing out basic works of guidance. The establishment of library schools gave sound and well rounded theory. Research in librarianship was initiated. Laws, rules and regulations were framed so as to assist in the day-to-day management of libraries.

Work of documentation brought-in scientists from diverse professions into the library and documentation profession. This helped the profession to understand the users better and to evolve new systems and services to meet their demands.

Information science enhanced the boundaries of the profession and disciplines. The demands of the users started changing fast. With the result there has been a great thrust on library, documentation and information professionals to understand users needs better, understand the technology, adapt and refine them from time to time to provide pin pointed information in an expeditious manner.

Library and information science (LIS) has attained due status in the universe of subjects at par with tradition disciplines. Education in library and information science is offered at various levels from school to university. At school and college level LIS is offered as an optional subject alongwith traditional disciplines. Special courses are also offered after school leaving certificate, post-degree programmes; as well as postgraduate courses in LIS. Research in LIS has also picked up and several areas in the discipline are being investigated with great emphasis and vigour.

Apart from the regular courses, in-service refresher courses, orientation courses into the new areas of the discipline etc. are also being organised on regular basis. New technology brought in specialists in computer, communication, repro and micrography and several other fields into information activity. Some of the subject Specialists are also involved in processing data; information analysis, condensation, repacking, etc.; providing liaison, referral and other services.

A set of moral principles and a code of conduct is a necessary guide to professional behaviour. Many of the countries have evolved written codes or ethics. Special codes were also drawn for some of the special branches of the profession. It is desirable to have a written professional code. These codes cover from general principles of dedication, devotion, determination and commitment to the profession; General social ethics of understanding the users; Social obligations of the library; Social behaviour, equality before service, etc.; Moral responsibilities of the professionals; Professional goals and objectives and means of achieving them.

The code of ethics should be prefaced with the nobility of the profession and responsibilities of the professionals.

These ethics time and again remind the professional his role, responsibilities and social commitment. The professional should keep the code of ethics before him so that they remind him the expectations of the profession. If possible an oath be administered to the new entrants in the profession to live up to the code of ethics of the profession.

Today almost all countries, regions and states have professional organisations-not one, but many. Sometimes, unhealthy competition and rivalries are also observed among the various associations. Objectives of professional associations are also different. There is a need for unified approach among various organisations. The dichotomy between library and information workers should be removed. These organisations should strive to achieve high standards in service; service to the society/nation by way of providing right information to the right user, at right time;

and bring the professionals together for close association and collective thinking.

Duties and Functions : Tasks in the professional work are defined by level of complexity, the general and technical knowledge required and their related responsibilities.

There are fairly elementary routines of manipulative tasks usually performed by subordinate personnel or assistants.

Technical tasks calling for professional qualifications and in certain cases for a general one too-cataloguing, indexing, bibliographic searches, etc.

Supervision, control and organisation of the various functions of the documentary chain. These tasks require a sound professional and general training together with some experience.

Technical tasks requiring high level training and social experience in the fields or disciplines concerned. e.g. Evaluation of information; Liaison with users, etc.

Overall design and management of the unit; teaching and research; training, internship etc.

In all information units there is a natural tendency for these divisions to overlap, with the result the profession contains a large number of generalists.

The Standards : Broadly speaking there are four grades of professionals;

(1) Para-professional (assistants);

(2) Professional Juniors (Minimum qualification of graduation in LIS);

(3) Professional Seniors-grade II (Generally postgraduates in LIS with minimum 5 years of professional experience);

(4) Professional Seniors-grade I (Managers).

There are quite a few who enter the profession at the lower level and gradually climb up to the higher levels.

At professional junior level, the entry may be direct. They need proper orientation into the system, services and professional ethics.

At the professional senior level, the entry is by selection among experienced professionals. Their entry and their success will depend upon the maturity which they may demonstrate in their work and behaviour.

Quite sometimes, people in other professions particularly those with computer science, reprography, publishing and book trade, audio-visual media, etc. background enter the LIS profession. They undergo initial training at the appropriate level in an educational institution specialising in LIS or receive in-service training in conjunction with adhoc courses. Some of them may enter the profession at the fag-end of their career into library and information field. Sometimes their experience, their competence as specialists can be an asset to the organisation. But often they may not be able to cope up with the work and the demand of the profession.

In this profession specialist skills reflect the type of information unit; the functions of the documentary chain which it covers; and its subject fields. These criteria can, of course be combined.

The major specialisations are archival administration; library administration; information management; documentation services, etc. Particularly in the fields of information and documentation (I&D) persons with the special knowledge in the concerned discipline are preferred.

Another area of specialisation is teaching and research in LIS. Lately with the development of large information systems and networks; and the creation of complex agencies to formulate information policy, a new specialist field has emerged-the planner or manager of information. Some of the retired professionals have started offering consultancy service and liaison service.

The new occupation requires an excellent specialist background, advanced training in information science and powers of synthesis.

Officer's Role : The status of the profession is the reflection of rules which define levels of responsibility, qualifications, career prospects, duties and rewards of each position and the level of training and amount of experience required.

A few countries have established rules at the national level for a particular branch of activity or for particular organisation. In the majority of countries, unfortunately, they are either not defined at all or only partly defined at the three levels.

A recognised professional status is very important since it clarifies the relative standing of the profession and makes it possible to attract and keep staff with requisite qualities. Without such a formal framework, there is the risk, especially for new occupations, that each individual will be dealt with a haphazard fashion with a natural tendency to diminish his socio-professional standing. The danger of this is increased by the fact that the profession is too small to form a sufficiently powerful pressure group.

The Personnel

There are two broad classes of staff working in libraries-those involved in library and information work and those who provide back-up services. These categories can be sub-divided:

Library Information Staff

Non-professional

Pre-professional (trainee)

Professional

Specialist

Managerial

Support Staff

Manual/ care-taking

Clerical/ secretarial

Technical and computer staff

Specialist

Library/information staff

Non-professional : Unqualified staff are usually educated to certificate or diploma in library science; national language as well as English should be known. They may have even higher qualifications which will enable them to take professional examinations. Non-professional staff are expected to undertake most of the routine work so that professionals can spend more time on intellectual work.

Some librarians have recognised the need for a career ladder for non-professional staff. Some libraries have three levels of library assistants : library assistants, senior library assistants, principal library assistants,

These levels allow experienced and competent staff to progress to positions of responsibility, even though they don't wish to qualify.

Pre-professional : Broadly speaking all non-professional staff are pre-professional, but strictly the term relates to trainee librarians. The distinction is worth making, for trainees should be given some practice at professional duties and an attempt should be made to introduce them to a wider perspective of librarianship than they see in their immediate job. The use of trainees as a cheap source of high quality labour is unfair and on a par with the use of library school students on field work as convenient extra hands, available for clearing longstanding work and doing unpopular jobs.

Specialist : Professional librarians can specialise in many ways: by type of library, i.e., national, public, academic, special function, i.e., reference work, children's services, bibliographical services etc.; or, perhaps, by subject interest, as in university libraries, where graduate qualified staff specialise in an area of the stock-selecting, cataloguing, classifying, and taking general responsibilities in that area. Some public libraries also employ subject specialist staff. In special libraries the knowledge of a particular subject area is very useful. Professional staff also carry out indexing, abstracting and translation work.

Managerial : Chief librarians are professional librarians with wider than average responsibilities, or professional managers comparable to industrial executives. Irrespective of the classification, it is evident that managerial expertise is now necessary for more senior posts in the profession.

Support Staff Manual/Caretaking : Libraries are expensive warehouses of knowledge. Equipment, stock, the buildings themselves are valuable. It makes good economic sense to employ people specifically to care for the library and its physical assets.

Caretaking staff need to have qualities of realibilities, responsibility and resourcefulness-many caretaking problems arise outside normal hours of work when senior staff cannot be consulted.

Clerical/Secretarial : The use of library assistants for clerical and secretarial work is inefficient: they are rarely trained clerical officers or typists and will not be effective at such tasks; they will be removed from library duties whilst undertaking other work. This is wasteful of their own skills; the work itself will be less accurate and will not have a professional finish.

Many libraries employ secretarial and other clerical staff for these reasons; some libraries employ specialist receptionists.

Increased use of 'media resources' in libraries of all types, and the installation of computerised processes, have made technical knowledge essential. Although all staff concerned with handling new media should be trained in their use, large collections will require specialist technical staff. Computer processing in libraries has led to a need for trained operatives and, for libraries with in house systems, some technical expertise; such posts are often designated 'Technical Services Librarian'.

Specialist : Besides technical/ computer staff, libraries employ other classes of specialist. Some of these are:

- Large libraries often employ people with artistic talent to work on displays and exhibitions.
- Other specialist staff in libraries include advisory staff.

Status of Librarian

Non-professional : The certificate Course after the school or a graduate is required.

Professional : The usual first step to professional degree from a university or college in library and information science. This degree should be followed by a postgraduate course from university or institute.

Fellow : Associates of five years' standing may be admitted to Followship by submission of a thesis in librarianship (a significant and original contribution to the literature); by professional distinction; or by submission of published work in librarianship and information science which has made sustained and significant advancement in the field.

The Management : As a reflection of tile increase in demand for management skills, some library schools offer management emphasis. These are usually intended for experienced and qualified librarians, librarians with courses of advanced level, intended for exprienced and quallified librarieans.

Process of Recruitment

Recruitment is the process of seeking and finding suitable people for jobs available in an organisation and includes the drawing up of a person specification for a job; the placing of advertisemente and all those activities which aid the receipt of a number of applications from people qualified and experienced in the skills, knowledge and attitudes required. The prerequisites are job analysis and specification.

Person Specification: A person specification is the blueprint of an ideal employee; candidates for the job will be compared with it and close matches will be put on a 'short list'. There are seven headings under which a job and the ideal jobholder are judged, as given below:

1. Physical make-up
2. Attainments
3. Skills
4. Work interests
5. Work attitudes
6. Personality
7. Personal background.

Physical Make-up: Specifying physical requirements is harder than it first appears: vague statements like 'someone is needed who is fit'-do not actually describe standard levels of capability. For example, many people would consider, and describe, themselves as fit if they are capable of attending work and carrying out their duties: the job might, however, need someone who was strong enough to lift weights and carry them for distances-perhaps, a library assistant in a house bound readers' service with book boxes for users' individual choice, many of whom might live in flats with unreliable lifts. This heading also includes consideration of the impression :the jobholder makes-i.e., personal manner, bearing and speech. Usually such features must be left to a personal interview when the general impression made by the candidate on the interviewing panel is taken as a measure of their impact on people in general.

Attainments : The job specification will usually define the knowledge and experience required to do the job adequately and so the question of qualifications and amounts of time spent in various types of work can be often answered direct from that specification. Jobs in libraries rarely leave this category blank, even the most junior of the library assistants in the smallest library must have a certain minimum standard of education.

Skills: There are various types of skill, for example, verbal influence is one, literacy another. It might be thought essential for anyone working in a library to be able to accurately file in alphabetical order. There are not many libraries who conduct tests of candidates' capability for alphabetisation all that is needed is a set of '5X3' cards with terms on them or authors' names which applicants could sort into either letter-by-letter or word-by-word order. Any skill required should be of specified standard, it is not an easy task as can be illustrated by looking at the difficulty of establishing a standard of verbal fluency.

Work Interests: It is not an invasion on personal privacy to enquire about a candidate's interests both at work and away from it, as personal interests compatible with tasks performed at work are strong sources of job satisfaction. It is also sensible to appoint someone to a job as readers' adviser who expresses a personal interest in books and their contents.

Work Attitudes: Besides the importance of an individual's attitudes to work and the organisation, there is the question of aspects of job and the working situation which might cause dissatisfaction to the post holder. The negative aspects of the job must be recognised and specified and attention must be paid to the characteristics of a person who would be least inconvenienced by them and happiest at work.

Personality: It is unrealistic to specify personality characteristics too closely, not only because terms are so imprecise and ambiguous, but also because we should only be concerned with those characteristics needed for adequate performance of the job. It is more useful to specify that 'flexibility' is sought, and to seek to establish this by investigating candidates' previous adaptability, that to rely on lists of traits like open-mindedness, honesty etc. It is one of the paradoxes of the recruitment and selection process that personality, perhaps the most important of the variables, is the one least capable of identification prior to interview. Application forms do not give many clues to it, even references are unreliable.

Personal Background: Care must be taken with this category that unrealistic requirements are not set and that, in the subsequent selection process, candidates' privacy is not infringed. It is reasonable to specify that the candidate must live close to the work, or even occupy a service flat, if the job is a caretaking one which will need proximity. It is not reasonable to specify that the post holder must be single and have no dependent, just because the panel feel that this will lead to better attendance at work. It is becoming rarer for application forms to require information on applicants' children and home circumstances. The wish expressed by some people that one's sex should not be asked for it is understandable, but the problem of gender and its possibility of impaired job chances is only postponed to the interview by such means.

One of the cheapest and most reliable ways of attracting candidates is by recommendation from present employees, at least this method is much used in industry and commerce. Libraries together with most other public service organisations, consider such methods incompatible with the aims of a fair recruitment policy and seek to fill posts by open competition.

Advertising: Professional posts are usually advertised in national papers, to ensure a wide audience.

Local papers are the best media for junior posts. It is unlikely that anyone would move to a new area for the post as a library assistant, and the expense of national coverage would be wasted.

Many libraries send application forms to prospective candidates. Reasons for doing this are:-

(i) Personnel records can be standardised, it is easier to fill and compare applications on a standard form.

(ii) Incomplete applications can be avoided; the form can include all relevant headings.

(iii) Application forms are fairer to candidates-each receives an identical form and has, theoretically, an equal chance of success.

(iv) An application form is useful for cross checking in an interview.

It is wise to ask candidates to bring documents proving qualifications etc. to the interview. There is a risk of loss when original documents are sent by post, and obtaining copies is expensive. Documents which could be required include:

- Birth Certificate
- Marriage Certificate
- Degree or Qualification Certificates

Selection : If recruitment is the process of casting the net and trawling for applicants, then selection is the stage of narrowing down the search; of discarding patently unsuitable people and investigating further those who seem to fit the person specification.

Short-listing : Short lists should be short. As a rule it is pointless to interview more than, perhaps, six candidates for anyone post. Interviewing time is expensive, especially when several senior staff comprise the panel, and there is a temptation to cut interview short when there are too many candidates to see.

This is unfair to the applicants themselves and does not allow the panel time to make proper assessment.

It is important that a personal meeting should take place between an employer and a future employee. The mix of personalities will affect working performance and relations more than any other factor. The important qualifier to this is that the person doing the interviewing should be the one who will work with the post holder otherwise the benefits of assessing the personality mix do not accrue.

The interview as a method of selection has been heavily criticised; it is subjective, short and necessarily pressured occasion. Candidates who perform well at interview may not perform well in the job and, conversely, a bad interview is no true indicator of poor job performance. Interviewers are rarely well trained and adopt at the art of asking pertinent questions expertly, unless they have received specific training or are professional personnel department staff. Unfortunately, the interview is a popular and common feature of the selection process so that the best hope seems to be to limits its worst failings and maximize its benefits.

Panel Interview : A panel interview requires two or more people acting as interviewers at the same time. Panels are used for several reasons; bias can be lessened by a mix of opinions on a candidate; better information on the job is possible when several staff can answer questions; candidates are given an opportunity to meet a number of their future superiors. Disadvantages are: large numbers of interviewers can make candidates unduly nervous by creating an 'on-trial' atmosphere; as numbers on the panel increase the scenario becomes more difficult to stage, e.g., who will ask what?

A personal interview is conducted by one interviewer. Advantages are: a more relaxed style can be adopted, both by the candidate and the interviewer; the interview is easier to plan and the progression of topics likely to be more natural. Conversely, there is a possibility of bias as the interviewer must rely on his own personal opinion without the need to justify his reasons.

Serial interviews are sequential interviews with any number of interviewers. They can be arranged into a series of personal interviews, if informality is required, or they can be used to break up an unwieldy panel into digestible chunks. The main advantages depend on the particular structure of each interview i.e., candidates will feel relaxed only if each serial interview is informal-and the longer one taken up by this form of interview can be conducive to either increased relaxation, or anxiety. The problem of bias is avoided by this method.

Training Facilities

Systematic Framework: Training is expensive, not only must the cost of the trainer's time be calculated, but the trainees' as well. Materials, premises used and the cost of any library equipment damaged also should be added to the total. In terms of the library's objectives, the only real justification for money spent in training is that it should contribute to the aims and purposes of the service and that the same objective could not have been achieved in any cheaper way. The most useful way of ensuring that training is cost-effective is to utilize a framework like the one outlined in figure.

The Diagnosis: This stage, although seeming far removed from training, is the vital first step. The manpower plan for the service is derived from long term objectives— a library planning to install a complete system of computerised charging in two years' time might be wise to specify some suitable training programmes for its staff well before the event and to plan for the recruitment of relevant staff if training were seen to be only partially a solution.

Conversely, a library intending to subscribe to an on line system for bibliographic control and processing would be foolish to recruit and train librarians in cataloguing skills, under the old system.

Basic Conditions : With training the key to success is to put last things first. The simple equation for analysis requires first a statement of the knowledge, skills and attitudes needed in staff for adequate performance of the particular task. The setting of standards for these three components is a necessary and skilled part of professional training. Put very simply, the trainer must ask, 'What would I like the trainees to be able to do, or know, before?' This question addresses the crucial problem of training; the answer to it will often show that training is not the best solution to the library's problem. An example will clarify:

A library is having problems with long lunch time queues of borrowers at the books-returned desk. Furthermore, borrowers have been complaint that the counter staff are abrupt to the point of rudeness.

One approach might be to train all counter staff in interpersonal skills with emphasis on courtesy and also to train them in processing of books and manipulation of files. This approach assumes that the staff are the problem and seeks to solve training.

Another could be to replace the Browne charging system manual filing of tickets by a faster, mechanized or even auto one. Job design approaches would also include looking methods employed by staff when dicharging books to see if better ones could be devised, without significant loss of accuracy studying the actions and reactions of staff and the movements by them to ensure that poor counter layout is not contributing problem.

When terminal behaviour has been decided upon, the trainer set the standard of skills, knowledge and attitudes required as behaviour in each trainee. This does not mean-'What knowledge skills and attitudes does each trainee have?' but 'What is the minimum level of knowledge, skills and attitudes we wish trainee to have before they are considered suitable for training entry onto the programme?'

The training need, or gap, is simply the difference between the standards. The range of methods for training is almost as wide variety of phenomena that could be learning to take place-the essential difference being that training is purposive, i.e., that someone structured a learning experience for the benefit of someone.

Methods include lectures, demonstrations, programmed learning experiential earning (where the trainee experiences at first hand) role playing and other forms of simulation (case studies being intellectual equivalent), and, of course, reading staff manuals other texts. If the audio visual media are also included it becomes very long. Evidently trainers do not have a problem of limited range of methods for training.

The method chosen will depend on the component of the knowledge, attitudes mix being developed as well as on the available funding. Lectures are cheap, for example lecturer and many listeners, but not noted for their value in training-you do not learn how to operate a computer keyboard by hearing about the layout.

One of the vexed questions is whether or not to trail house. Libraries with very customised processes are obliged to train, their own staff internally. This does not often happen at professional level; it is assumed that the output of library schools meets at least the initial basic requirements of libraries.

Evaluation and Measurement : Training is evaluated by measuring the total value of the training programme to the attainment of the library's objectives in terms of the cost/benefit equation. The validity of a training course is assessed in terms of its success or otherwise in attaining the objectives for it evaluation differs in that it must include an assessment of the costs of the training.

Libraries can test the value of their training programmes by observation of employee performance afterwards by testing formally the skills and knowledge learned; by conducting systematic performance appraisal and by various forms of follow-up investigation.

There is no firm distinction between the terms training and education, but the difference can be explained as follows: Training should develop certain skills, knowledge and attitudes in the employee which will be useful in job performance. These skills can be practical, e.g., filing, or intellectual, e.g., handling users enquiries. Education should develop wider potential in the student by opening up new fields and perspectives without immediate relevance to any particular job. Teaching of practical skills is often incorporated in education; these can be necessary as a foundation for further learning but are only means to an end.

Induction Training : A new member of staff needs to be introduced to the library as an organisation and to understand what part his own job plays in achieving library objectives. Induction training begins before new employee comes to work and includes the information he is given about the library and the job he is applying for.

Many librarians feel that the early weeks in a job are very important; too important for new staff to be left to sink or swim, collecting experience and information where they can. In many government departments, large industrial firms, and some academic institutions all new staff, including library staff, are given a short induction course. The usual length of such a course is between 3 to 10 days.

The nature of induction training makes delay unwise. A programme of induction is pointless if left until the employee has worked in the job for six months. The amount of training appropriate for induction depends on the size and complexity of the library system and the age and experience of the employee. There is tendency to rush induction programmes, especially in library where staff are scarce. Rushed 'courses usually result in information 'flooding', and participants retain little of what they hear, usually the less-important details. Lengthy courses, on the one hand, can create impatience in the employee who is anxious to get to grips with his 'new job'.

In-service/Job Training : The most obvious training need for any employee is instruction and practice in the tasks comprising his job. Job training is a way reducing expensive mistakes and accelerating learning on basic skills. The usual method is for colleagues, or immediate superiors to instruct the new entrant in the manner known as 'watch Nellie'. This casual approach can have drawbacks:

(i) existing staff can pass on mistakes as well as experience;

(ii) not all staff are competent instructors;

(iii) traditional methods are not always best for present need rigidity of approach can result from such 'handed-down information.

On the plus side such training is the easiest, cheapest way of familiarising staff with new tasks. Existing staff are knowledged about the job in the context of that particular library.

Continuation/Development Training : As user's needs change so much library staff alter and the tasks they do and the ways they do them. Continuation trail aims to develop new skills in all staff-both newly arrived and more experienced-to prevent any divergence of purpose between library objectives and the tasks designed to achieve them.

Specialist Training : Professional staff may develop interests in specialist library work. Examples are:-reference service, children's services, real advisory work; not everyone is clear about their special subjects at Library School. Specialist training is beneficial to both library and staff career development. Large systems, especially those with professional training officers, can run such course house.

Management Training : It is not easy to pinpoint the stage at which management skills become necessary; the librarian in charge of even the smallest library has a staff to deploy and a service to manage. The more senior posts, especially in large libraries, involve management of large staff, stocks, and budgets and increasingly require professional management expertise.

Increasing size and complexity of library systems-and changes in the technology and products they employ-make management training more and more necessary. The large management schools have been slow to respond to the needs of the public services, although now there are a variety of courses geared to a non-profit making sector. Another problem for senior librarians is that time away from work is hard to obtain-the very people who most need management training are the ones least able to be spared. Part time courses minimise the problem, at least as far as retention of a job is concerned; it does not alleviate workload, though, but adds to it and, for this reason, part time management courses are recognised as endurance tests in their own right.

An organisation which recruits and selects people with the appropriate skills, knowledge and experience and which conducts training systematically is likely to do performance appraisal. Performance appraisal is normally done annually and by the employee's immediate superior. The process is subjective, even though it is often given a veneer of objectivity by the use of rating scales; bias can be minimised by the superior discussing the employee's strengths and weaknesses with him and explaining the basis of the assessment by having more than one person make the appraisal; and by ensuring that all employees undergo the same process and with the same documentation. Performance appraisal is used for probation, for employee training and development, and for promotion purposes.

Ten

Significance for Education

Education and libraries have an integral relationship. Libraries play an important role in all instruments of education—the informal, formal, semi-formal and non-formal.

Distance Education

Family : The first instrument that we can think of, that humanity had used from the very beginning, is the first institution in which ordinarily the child holds membership—the home. It is through the home that the child makes his first contact with the world and it is in the home that he learns his first lessons in the arts of life. We shall even concede that when his circle of experience widens so as to include other formal and informal instruments of education, the home does continue to exert some influence. But the limitations of the home as an instrument of universal education have now been, for long realised. In our present time, due to the crowded condition of our homes, the busy lives of the elders and the exacting requirements of the struggle for existence, the home is found to be more and more wanting in its capacity to discharge the duties of an instrument of universal education. The Utopian educationists have even gone to the length of condemning the home outright. They protest that parents would educate children wrongly and that in 99 cases out of 100 parents are altogether ignorant of the right method of teaching, nay, even of treating children. Hence Plato would abolish the home altogether. The Sevarites would renounce parental authority when the children attain the age of seven, so that they may not thwart their education.

Society's Influence : Another informal instrument of education that was very influential in the past is the community that mixed fabric of institutions and social groups with which individuals come in contact. It includes the neighbourhood and the families of neighbourbood, when functioning for the community as a whole. They were effective in the earlier days before the days of the rapid succession of inventions, before the days of crowded cities, when the village community was a compact body capable of knowing and shaping each of its individuals. But today, the crowded city life in which nobody cares to know his next-door neighbour, the lack of sincerity and harmony, the cupidity of the privileged few, the ignorance of the exploited many, the poor leadership which often leads mankind to disaster and the chaotic conditions of the occupational world, are rendering the community quite ineffective as an instrument for universal education.

College Education

In formal education, men and women receive education of a specified level based on a specified syllabi. This form of education is imparted in academic institutions, such as schools, colleges, universities, research institutions etc.

The library does occupy a significant place in academic institutions. Educationists and scholars hold that it is a "better proof of education to know how to use a library than to possess university degree." The UGC (UK) maintained in 1921, "The character and efficiency of a university may be gauged by its treatment of its central organ, the library... An adequate library is not only the basis of all teaching and study, it is the essential condition of research without which additions cannot be made to the sum of human knowledge." The library has become still more important in academic set-up due to change in the nature of education. During the past, formal education was based on dictation the teachers used to dictate and speak and the students used to listen to. This system has been done away with in Western countries and in India also we are following new methods with appreciable speed and success. The present-day education is no more an one way system in which the student had passive participation. In the changed system the student is expected to actively participate. The teacher mainly kindles the curiosity of students, makes them aware of basic facts, teaches them methodology and refers them to books to find detailed information for themselves which is discussed later in tutorials etc. Parry Committee wrote in this connection, "lecture and textbook method is no longer regarded as the sole method for teaching," and recommended, "if one of the main purposes of University education is to teach students to work on their own, reading by students must be preferable to attendance at a lecture unless the lecture is superior in presentation or contents to the available literature."

Universal Concept

One of the main purposes of the Library Movement is to educate the illiterate, diffuse knowledge amongst them and dispel their ignorance. In a country where large masses of the people are steeped in ignorance and illiteracy and consequently lead maimed and imperfect lives, the least part of our duty is to help them to lead more virtuous and perfect lives by educating them to that end. Those of us who, by the accident of birth or other cause, are placed in more fortunate situations in life, have to undertake the task and endeavour to carry it to a successful issue. We ought to realise it to be a religious duty which we owe to the Maker, who made us all alike, and whose children we all are.

Apart from this humanitarian aspect, there is also the national point of view which calls for active and strenuous work in this direction. Suffice it to say, that we cannot grow into a nation and claim to take an equal place among the civilised nations of the world, unless we educate our masses, make them understand the world movements and take them along with us. No lover of India, no Indian who desires to see his mother country occupy an honoured place among the civilised countries of the world, can afford to slumber any longer. He should wake up and do what he can towards the amelioration of the condition of the ignorant brethren. Herein have to be laid the foundations of national unity; for without the realisation of national self-respect engendered by education, the consolidation of our people into a nation is unthinkable.

The work we have to do in this direction has to reach the villages and the rural areas, as having to do with the masses. The task is no doubt a stupendous one, but one need not despair of success.

The Constraints: An aggregate of constraints on spread of universal education has left vast numbers in the country educationally, and consequently economically, under privileged. Though it would be quite erroneous to assume that an unlettered person is for that reason an ignorant person, but it is a fact that now illiterate adults are gradually getting conscious of their being secluded from the outside world. This consciousness may be less intense in small groups of people in the countryside living largely on subsistence agriculture but in the majority of the cases, they consider the illiteracy as a social stigma since they wish to live in close contact with the cities, made possible through trade and commerce and inter-play of various communication media. Results of a recent survey comprising more than 100 adults literacy projects all over the world show that in 30 per cent of the cases 'social prestige' is the reason given for joining the literacy class. The economic reasons weigh with the less than 25 per cent of the respondents and only 4 per cent of them indicate their interest in reading the scriptures.

The reasons for this non-impelling attitude towards literacy as a means for economic improvement may be their ignorance of the efficacy and implied advantages of functional literacy. Although it does not mean that literacy will automatically and necessarily lead to higher productivity in all the cases because other factors of development are also necessary to achieve better yields and outputs. But this much is sure that functional literacy brings change in the mental level of the worker and enables him to add accuracy and precision in method of his work which factors are the essential compliments for better production in both the areas of agriculture and industry. A universally literate society will be more responsive to adapt itself to change than one without access to formal knowledge. A UNESCO-sponsored study in Bombay finds positive factors present more generally among the literates than among illiterates where lapses like lack of safety consciousness, absenteeism or wastage of raw materials are more common.

The Methods: As regards the methods of work with the literate, we have to begin with lectures, talks, readings, story-telling, cinema shows, exhibitions and the like-things that will draw them in. We have first to approach them on topics which will interest them as affecting their occupations or trades. The details of the course must necessarily vary with the locality and the groups of persons who are to be instructed. But in every case it should begin with an intimate association of the teacher with the taught so as to lead to the creation of confidence in the teacher. The teacher must live and move with the villagers when he is on his programme and his lectures and talks may well be modelled on the lines of the familiar Kalakshepam of our Bhagavatars. The programme would begin with educating the villagers on matters relating to their daily life and end in the creation of a desire to seek the knowledge in books. The village school-master would legitimately be the person to start the work and he ought to be assisted by other suitable organisations. Each Taluk Board, for instance, might well appoint a teacher who should go round to the villages, like a Sanyasi and carry on the programme of educating them.

The institution of night schools with which we are familiar is a useful instrument of adult education. Experiments in this direction by social service organisations have proved a great success and teaching institutions of this kind ought to be organised wherever possible.

A small library would be a necessary auxiliary to the courses given by the itinerant lecturer or the night school teacher.

Centre of Literacy : Many Government and non-government agencies are engaged in the problem of illiteracy and they are working for eradication of the malady. But the magnitude of the problem is so high that a comprehensive and combined effort by all the individuals and organizations together is called for.

Libraries can lend their strong helping hand to tackle the problem. The first noticeable factor is that adults do have appetite for education and ability to learn. In a survey made by the Adult Education Department of the University of Rajasthan, it was revealed that making the facility of library open to them was considered to be the best help, the university could render to the community for continuing education. People also argued for better library provisions like branch and mobile libraries and improved library facilities. The library should, therefore, function as a centre for adult education; planning its activities in the following directions:

Setting up Literacy Class : The literacy classes should be held in the premises of the library, preferably in a room of the library building. The literacy teacher and the library staff should work in close co-operation on the various programmes in this regard.

Motivating the Illiterates : The illiterate adults should be attracted to the class through various audio-visual aids and literature. The entertaining programmes of music, drama and film show should be arranged frequently to allure the illiterates to the class. The nature and content of these programmes should identify with the individual and community needs of the people.

Follow-up Programmes: This is very important because even after achieving literacy, adults again become illiterates in the absence of any reading programme, The first task of the post-literacy programme is the adequate supply of reading literature-books and magazines to the neo-literates which may be easy for them to read. It is a vital role of the library to make provisions for such reading material, keep them in organized collection and supply them free of any charge to the neo-literates.

Besides the nature and the standard of the literature, the language is also important. The reading material should be supplied in the language of their (adults') interest. Therefore, it is the work of the library to know the subject and language preference of the neo-literates and thereby help the literacy teachers in selecting the texts.

Keeping Literacy Organisers Informed: A great deal of research is being carried out on the methods and techniques of literacy programmes in and outside the country, the details of which are published in various books and journals. The library should keep the literacy organizers informed in its area so that they may take advantage of such findings in planning their programmes. However, the limitations of the school as an instrument of universal education has come to the surface. We saw the need for life-long education, if education is to fulfil its generic purpose. Even with all the continuation classes and the extension courses it is impossible to put all mankind perpetually into the formal school. Thus, it is obvious that the reconciliation of the idea of life-long education and the impossibility of life-long stay in a formal school can be brought about only by the invention of a new instrument for perpetual self-education.

When the informal instruments of the home and the community proved ineffective and the formal instrument of the school proved to be inadequate, the semi-formal instrument in the library came to be recognised. No doubt libraries had existed ever since books came to be written, but they had been devised either to hoard books or, at most, to serve books to a selected few. It was not till our days that the library has been conceived as a tool for universal education for the education of all, at all time. This new role of libraries is the message of the modern library movement, which has assumed worldwide dimensions since the Great War. This new instrument of education is semi-formal in the sense that it does not enforce a curriculum, it does not enforce a particular time table, and it does not seek the help of the teacher's feature. At the same time, it does not leave everything to the casual education that may be derived from contact with the elders in the home or with the members of the community. Unlike the home and community, it sets apart special trained men for the sole purpose of helping each man in finding what will best suit his needs. In this, it has some resemblance to the formal help given by the school.

One great effect of the recognition of the library as such a semi-formal instrument of education, that should supplement the formal school, is that the State, which is responsible for the general welfare and of the general education of the masses, is beginning to wield that instrument, in a way which the State alone can wield. Practically in all the countries of the world, there is a Public Library Act in force which creates not merely stray libraries, however big, but also libraries in mass, libraries in myriads, throbbing with this new idea and radiant with the effulgence due to the possession of the new gospel, books for all.

Self-Education : To put it in plainer terms, we must develop in the students the capacity to find facts, ideas, and information promptly and accurately as and when required. The outlook on education should no longer confine the aim of education to the cramming of a tiny brain with more than what it can hold of the vast universe of facts, ideas, and information. According to the new outlook, work at the formal school should be mainly for educating the student for life-long self education with the aid of materials published from time to time.

Attached to every rural school there should be a reading room and a library accessible to the village folk. The former should contain some instructive newspapers and the latter, a decent number of useful books. The provision of these two adjuncts should be made a condition of the recognition of the schools. The reading room being a purveyor of news would be popular and would attract people and these would naturally be drawn to the associated library.

The reading room should be widely advertised and the library, properly classified and catalogued and made easily accessible. The rules and regulations for loaning out books should be drawn up in a sympathetic spirit. The two institutions should be started and maintained from public funds until the people for whom they are intended are got to realise their usefulness and contribute towards their upkeep. In order to ensure speedy fulfillment of their purposes they should be placed in charge of the most enthusiastic masters in the schools, who would enthuse the readers and help them to select books and papers suited to their tastes. The librarians should not merely maintain the usual library registers but hold periodical talks on the importance of reading and popularise the institution and get people to cultivate a habit of reading. The librarians doing their work with enthusiasm should be adequately rewarded. I have no faith in honorary workers; for, unless work is paid for, it is seldom done well. People's money finds its way out in ever so many ways in the name of efficiency and I fail to see why persons engaged in the beneficent library activities should not be remunerated. Specially is the need for remuneration the greater in the case of the poorly paid village schoolmaster who works for national uplift in an out-of-the-way place. At least for the first few years, honorary service in this respect must be ruled out, lest the salutary movement should fail of its purpose and stand condemned.

In urban areas there are indeed high schools and colleges provided with libraries and reading rooms, but they do not cater for the needs of the general public. The local bodies concerned should therefore be made to start libraries where none exists and to subsidise suitably those already in existence. The libraries should be properly and adequately staffed so as to accomplish the purpose in view. Private individuals or agencies, left to themselves, would start libraries for public use only on the Greek Kalends.

Expenditure on public libraries should be considered a proper charge on the revenues of the State as much as expenditure on elementary education. I quite realise that libraries must grow and require both an initial outlay and a considerable recurring charge; and furthermore, they have to be started all over the Presidency. The expenditure, heavy as it may appear at present, would, under wise direction, facilitate, in the long run, considerable retrenchment of expenditure on prisons and police, law courts and judiciary, medicine and sanitation and it need not therefore be grudged.

The Library Movement is indeed a well conceived, beneficent activity requiring discreet direction. Hasty, ill-advised, ineffective procedure would wreck it. *Festina lente* should be our motto in large, delicate undertakings of this kind. Would the public co-operate with the Library Association and make the movement the success that it eminently deserves to be?

Today non-formal education has become popular and has established a unique place in Indian Education System. This establishment has influenced the Public Library System. The services rendered by the Public Libraries cannot be underestimated; actually it is a parameter with which one can assess the literacy of a nation.

Government's View

Population explosion and education explosion takes place in two different lines. It is very hard to elevate the growth of education to the level of population. The existing traditional system of education will not help to bridge the gap. So, the traditional learning system would have to be reformed and the new Education Policy is to be introduced. As such, the Non-formal Education System was introduced to cater to the needs of aspiring citizens.

The Characteristics **:** The services of the Public Library to any system is related to the characteristics of the system. Hence it becomes essential here to study the characteristics of the Distance Learning System. So far ten characteristics are identified and they are as follows:

1. First, the open learning system is capable of eliciting, interpreting and analysing learned goals and abilities at the entry point and throughout the student's participation with the instructional and learning programme.

2. Second, the system encompasses two separate but related programmes, the instructional programme embodied in the institutional system and the learning programme carried on by learners with the assistance of the system.

3. The third characteristic is the system's ability to enable learners to participate in the programme of learning and instructions without imposing traditional academic entry requirements and without the pursuit of an academic degree or other certification as the exclusive reward.

4. Fourth, open learning goals are formulated in such a way that they can serve as the basis for decisions in instructional design, including evaluation. The learning objectives are also fully known to the students, so that students can participate in decision-making.

5. Fifth, as an operating principle the system is capable, after reaching a critical minimum of aggregation, of accommodating increased numbers of learners without a commensurate increase in the unit cost of the basic learning experiences, i.e., costs must not be directly and rigidly volume sensitive. After reaching the necessary level of aggregation unit costs should diminish in relation to total system costs.

6. Sixth observation is that the open learning system makes possible the use of sound, video, film, print and other communication diffusion technologies as vehicles and options for mediating learning experiences.

7. Seventh, the system uses testing and evaluation principally to diagnose and analyse the accomplishment of specified learning objectives, including that of self-directed rather than other directed learning.

8. Eighth, open learning is able to tolerate distance between the instructional staff and resources and the learner, and employs the distance factor as a positive element in the development of learner independence.

9. Ninth, the system accepts the learner and his surroundings as the environment for learning, and concentrates on enriching that environment instead of developing specialised teaching environments that intrude barriers of place, space, time and other direction in learning.

10. Finally, the system seeks, obtains and maintains the active cooperation of community and regional resources as important factors in enriching the learning environment, diminishing learner dependence on a single resource and returning learning as a natural and continuing activity to the indigenous learning environment. Thus, the open learning system is an essential step toward the "Learning Society."

A more appropriate and universally accepted definition of Public Library reads as follows: "....offering a wide selection of materials chosen to embrace as completely as possible the varied interests of the individual and the community, free from bias or religious, political or other motives." This definition clearly emphasises that the public library has to serve both the formal education system and non-formal education system without any biased view.

The introduction of open university system of education will have far reaching consequences on the nature and content of library services. Libraries will be required to tackle persons from different occupations and regions. They are the main source of the background readings. A fully enriched and up-to-date reference section of the library needs to be backed with an equally efficient reference service in order to help the students in pursuing their studies intensively. The students will also require the textbooks for longer period. Hence the textbooks section of the library may be equipped better to meet the requirements of the students. The readers will have to be made conversant with complicated tools of the library like the classification system, methods of library catalogues, encyclopaedias, dictionaries, handbooks, bibliographies and various other published guides to the literature on the subjects of their interest.

Eleven

Mutual Cooperation

The concept of 'Resource Sharing' involves two words 'Resource' and 'Sharing'.

Resource mean, wealth or available assets.

Sharing means giving, to have or use with others. Thus, Resource Sharing means sharing ones assets with others.

Resource Sharing in Libraries we mean sharing material, or function or services, any of the two; or all.

Libraries in the past had only written or printed documents. Written documents are manuscripts. These documents are always kept away and are not shared with other libraries. The users are expected to visit the library for consultation. The other category-the books were also not loaned to every one and they were seldom shared with other libraries. With the introduction of printing by movable types, books started appearing in good number and libraries have started accepting the concept of 'sharing' their books with other libraries.

Library Material : Today one finds a large number of other kinds of material (other than books) in the libraries. These include periodicals, thesis, reports, reference material, patents, standards and specifications etc. 'Document' is a comprehensive term used by library and information personnel to indicate the various kinds of material available in the libraries.

After the Second World War, a large number of non-book material also started entering the libraries. These included microforms, audio-visual aids, etc.

Advent of computers brought in several other documents like tapes, floppies, databases on CDs, etc.

Basic Needs

However, rich a library may be, it is impossible to acquire and store all documents within its four walls. In order to satisfy the needs of its users, it may have to depend on other libraries. Secondly, of late there has been specialisation in the collections of libraries. One has to approach such special collections to meet the special needs of its users. Thirdly, the library budgets are decreasing and costs of documents are increasing with the result the number of documents being added to the libraries is decreasing. Fourthly, some of the tools like union catalogues, location lists, including databases made it easy to resort to resource sharing.

The Sphere

1. Experience and expertise of library personnel;

2. Material-books, periodicals, patents, standards and specifications; audio-visual aids like microfilms, films, phono-records, audio and video tapes; computer floppies, tapes, CDs etc.

As a Measure of Economy

Cooperative acquisition of books and periodicals; sharing of processing costs of documents; cooperative storage of back volumes, periodicals; access of databases and database services; sharing of equipments like, computers printers, microfilm/fische readers and printers, ,etc., on tune sharing basis.

Aims and Objectives of Resource Sharing

1. To make available material not available in the library;
2. To have access to services not available in the library;
3. To economise the cost of organisation and management of libraries;
4. To have integration of library and information services of a system, or of a geographical area;
5. Reciprocity leading to better interaction among libraries;
6. Can have better and quality library services: etc.

Functions of Resource Sharing

1. Assist in selection, acquisition and processing of materials;
2. Inter-library lending, supply of copies of material;
3. Sharing of costs of storage and retrieval of documents as well as information;
4. Quality production of products and services;
5. Saving the time of the users in location, acquisition and use of material.

Forms of Resource Sharing

Acquisition : The process of acquisition involves selection, placing orders, chasing the vendors, passing of bills, payments, etc. All these activities can be reduced greatly by cooperative acquisition. This will also result in saving the costs in correspondence, earn a larger discount, save time and clerical labour.

Processing : Centralised classification and cataloguing services like that of OCLC [online computer library centre (Ohio)], MARC (Machine Readable Catalogue) project of the library of congress and also its shared cataloguing project proved how flawless, cheap and quality, services can be provided. Similar services are also available in UK, Australia and Canada.

Online cataloguing, retro-conversion using databases, etc., also lead to economy with quality.

Catalogue Card Service : Printed catalogue card services like that of the library of congress; The British National Bibliography; VINITI of Russia are also examples of shared catalogue.

Cataloguing-in-Publication (CAP) : The Cataloguing-in-Publication Program was initiated by the library of the Congress in 1971 with 27 participating publishers. Currently, the number is around 2,500 participating publishers. The process of classification and cataloguing of a publication is done before the book is released. The cataloguing data provided by the LC is printed on the reverse of the title page which helps the individual libraries in copying down the data on their catalogue cards. The LC Card Number and ISBN helps the American libraries in ordering printed catalogue cards.

Cooperative Storage : Most libraries are getting cluttered-up with less use or no use material on their shelves and creating a problem of space to new acquisition. Such material which is not in active use may be stored on cooperative basis at a central dormitory.

The storage facility can be created by mutual agreement and suitable record creation by participating libraries.

Inter-Library-LOAN : Inter-Library-Loan is the most common and age old form of resource sharing among libraries. Under this scheme a library can get a document from another library on loan basis for a certain period. This is being practised all over the world. There are certain pre-requisites for the successful implication of this programme. This includes

1. An agreed inter-library loan code;
2. A union catalogue for location of the document;
3. An agreed delivery system;

4. An agreement with regard to the transaction costs;
5. A common library card:
6. Cooperative delivery service; etc.

Sharing of Equipment : Equipment like computers, reprographic systems, scanners, microfilming devices, CD cutters etc. can be shared by a group of libraries with advantage.

The Limitations

(i) Fear of losing autonomy;

(ii) Inertia or indifference or both;

(iii) Lack of union catalogues and other location lists;

(iv) Lack of a code of understanding;

(v) Fear of loss during transport;

(vi) Lack of resources by majority of libraries;

(vii) Fear of bigger libraries that they will only be used and others may not have to offer anything in substance;

(viii) Failure to comply with the norms by some of the libraries may dampen enthusiasm of others;

(ix) Lack of knowledge of users and assessment of user needs;

(x) Lack of adequate funds;

(xi) Legal and administrative restrictions imposed by the authority or management;

(xii) Lack of technological backing and organisational structure;

(xiii) Heavy costs involved in resource sharing; and

(xiv) The success in resource sharing may affect the publishing industry, with the result cost of publications may go-up.

Cooperative Acquisition : The INSDOC, Delhi has initiated Centralised Acquisition of Periodicals (CAP) through which it is acquiring foreign periodicals for about 30 CSIR laboratories. This project is in operation for the last several years. Through this process, it is earning about 5% discount from the publishers, which is being passed on to the laboratories.

Cooperative Storage : With the initiative of NASSDOC (ICSSR), New Delhi and Jawaharlal Nehru University, ' Delhi an Inter-Library Resource Centre (ILRC) was established in New Delhi in 1975. Some 38 libraries of Delhi deposited their less used serials and government documents at the centre. Already more than a lakh of volumes of serials have been deposited at this centre.

National Catalogues : National Union Catalogue of Scientific Serials in India (1988) was the result of the work of INSDOC in collaboration with several scientific libraries all over India. It contains holding data of about 800 science and technology libraries. It lists about 35,000 serials.

Union Catalogue of Social Science Serials was compiled and published by the NASSDOC (ICSSR), New Delhi in 1980s. This need to be computerised and updated.

Cooperation with International Systems : India is a national member of international information systems like INIS (International Nuclear Information System); AGRIS (Agricultural Information System), FSTA (Food Science and Technology Abstracts) of CAB, UK. A list of international information systems and their focal points in India is appended.

Sharing of Equipment : Many libraries in India are sharing the computer network facilities available for information exchange.

The Organisation

Network can be defined as a group of individuals or organisations that are interconnected. The advent of computers and new developments in telecommunication technology made networking a global phenomenon. Library and information institutions are forming networks to achieve better resource sharing and to provide better service to the users.

Aims and Objectives of Library Networks

(a) To promote sharing of resources;

(b) Assist in acquisition and processing of material;

(c) Exchange of documents and data;

(d) Cooperation and coordination in collection development;

(e) Help in the establishment of referral service, online retrieval of information and online union catalogues;

(f) To build bibliographic databases;

(g) To build various other databases like that of projects, specialists, institutions, etc;

(h) Electronic Mailing;

(i) File transferring;

(j) Evolve standards and guidelines in techniques, methods, procedures, hardware, software, services and so on.

Uses : Library and Information networks help in

(i) Online retrieval of bibliographic, numeric, as well as full-text databases;

(ii) Compilation of reading lists, topical bibliographies, etc.;

(iii) To have bibliographic control by integrating national library catalogues, etc.;

(iv) Automatic book requesting systems;

(v) Use of CD-ROM products and services;

(vi) Remote data entry facility;

(vii) Downloading of information;

(viii) Library mailing, inter-library requests and lending, etc.;

(ix) Document delivery;

(x) Access to public domine information /data/software; etc.

Prerequisites for Network Organisation

1. Agreements for implementing cooperation;

2. Establishment of facilities for sorting little used materials;

3. Agreements on acquisition policies to ensure consistent development of holding to avoid redundancy;

4. Agreements to share the currently owned materials, with protocols, limitations and priorities carefully spelled out;

5. Schemes for intelligent organization of data/ documents;

6. Methods of adequate delivery of resources to users (the output media);

7. The subject interest area should be a common one among the centres being connected;

8. Compatibility between the computing systems available with the organizations to be netted is essential;

9. To ensure the ability of network among the resource sharing libraries, a compatible record format is highly desirable;

10. Standardization of policies and procedures across the network and adhered to by all participants in order

that these tasks could be performed and shared in efficient manner;

11. Adequate means of information dissemination;
12. Formal established organisational cooperation;
13. Established and functioning communication links (telephone, telex, fax, satellite communication channels);
14. An agreement should exist on acquisition policies to ensure consistent development of holdings and to avoid redundancy.

Twelve

Process of Classification

The philosopher, John Dewey, claimed that knowledge is classification. Aristotle, Bacon and other philosophers had given concepts of systematic classification of knowledge, which have been utilized in library for many years and also influenced the library classification system. Dr.Ranganathan puts classification under law of library science. He says, 'A library is a growing organism as knowledge itself is growing; it is necessary that classification must be comprehensive, embracing all past and present knowledge and allowing places for any possible additions to knowledge'.

Classification simplifies the process of thought. This is true of formal thinking or logic. When we design the course of study, pursue research or locate any information, we make use of classification, a kind of map of knowledge.

Classification is the process by which we group like things together. All the members of a group of like things share at least characteristics which members of other group do not possess. Characteristics are applied as the basis for finding out the likeliness between things. A characteristic is an attribute by which concept grouped or subjects divided. For example, we may keep lions, tigers and leopards close to each other by grouping them in a zoo; we observe that they are having a common characteristic of cat family which elephants, camel and hare do not possess.

The recognition of likenesses may be performed by machine by human beings. Human perception for like characteristics attributes may be intuitive or the result of conscious thought, for example we all are classifying things in our day to day life and we do in normal course. We never keep books and shoes together. We always separate each one according to their characteristics attribute, qualities and traits.

There is always a purpose behind all classification. The same thing can be classified by different persons in different ways. We go to grocer shop we mark that grocer arranges his coins in numerical order, but a numismatist arranges them in a historical sequences. So the arrangement or classifications are made for the convenience. A grocer also arranges his commodities in such a way that he can locate which commodity is kept in which place. He classifies things in his own ways, so that he can directly go to the commodity that is asked for. So the object of classification is convenience. Convenience that matters the, particular way in which things are to be arranged and classified.

Classification has everyday practical uses, for example supermarkets are organized so that all products of the similar nature are kept togethet whether it is meat or vegetables or dairy products or home appliances. Further they are subdivided into subgroups like mutton, chicken, potato, onion, garlic, butter, cooking oils, milk, cream, mixer, refrigerator, fan cooler and others. Without classification supermarkets would be unpleasant to use or carry on business. In the same way warehouses and factory stores arrange goods and parts together according to how they are used.

Classification is a mental process primarily. The idea or the concept of the thing is judged by experience of our mind, we develop a group or separate the dissimilar characteristic and create another group by our mental process. This mental process is an aid to our memory. This classification is an important work in library science.

When library professionals classify books, they arrange in the most convenient order. This convenience is always directed towards storage and sorting of the documents.

Classification gives the action of classifying and then result of classifying. The action of classifying indicates the physical action of sorting and the result of classifying indicates the mental process that dictates sorting.

Classification displays the relationships between things, and between classes of things. We see that members of the class PAINTINGS differ from the members of class DRAWINGS; but also that these two classes have a closer relationship with each other than either has with the class SCULPTURE, because they share the quality of being two dimensional. In the same way we appreciate that these three classes are related, because they are all kind of what is called Fine Art. The result of classification-is the display of network or Pattern of Relationships.

There are many possible ways of arranging books. Size, colour, binding, by press, by publisher, date of publication, by author, by title or by subjects are generally the factors. These factors are considered to determine the arrangement. But in practice this does not serve satisfactorily. Again we can say that the convenient way is to arrange by the thought content of the material. But this also can not be the basic principle, there are certain other factors to determine the arrangement of library material. These are children books; reference book; books of unusual size; date of printing; rare books; bound periodicals; fiction or non-fiction; local collections; magnetic discs and many other.

When one has to locate a book in the huge collection of volumes, can realize the value of classified arrangement of books. Libraries employ classification system to make easier for readers as well as staff members to locate the volume on the shelves.

The normal procedure in the library is to identify the subject of a book and on the basis of decision taken with respect to the nature of library; a class number is being assigned from the classification system. This number indicates the subject of the volume according to the system used in the library. If the library also arranges its books under each subject alphabetically by author, an author number is assigned. The class number and author number together are known as the call number, which is used to obtain the volume from the shelves for the reader.

The Devices

Classification is a tool for organizing the document stores or library. A document is the physical carrier of a message. A document may be in various forms like book, films, slides, periodicals, newspapers, cards bearing the names and addresses of local organizations in a reference library files and machine readable media. The messages that documents bear may be simple facts, views, interpretations of events or works of art. For example Gita is message, just as Yojna is periodical, The Hindu is newspaper or name and address record is directory. When the number of documents become too much for a person seeking a particular information to scan through all those, it becomes necessary to organize them. When these tasks become too great to be performed informally, it is institutionalized. Specialists are appointed to carry out the task. These specialists are librarians and other information workers, whose function is to mediate between their clients and the documents containing the message.

Librarian's contribution to society is very precisely. He enables clients to find any required subject of documents from the total set as quickly and easily as possible. He selects and collects documents, organizes his collection, cooperates with other librarians and information workers, and he helps as well as encourages his readers to use documents. The main task on which the user depends, is the organization of collection which means the arrangement of documents in some helpful order and the provision of catalogues and indexes which act as both-keys and complements to that order. We call the techniques developed to bring about this organization 'fixing'.

As indexing is concerned with the easy location of subsets or subclasses of documents. All the indexing techniques are application of classification. The characteristic which defines the different classes sought by a reader differ as the name of the author, the name of series of works (e.g. Library Science Series), the name of the translator, illustrator, composer, performer or film director; and the name of subject about which messages are required. In practice, we consider only classification by subject or in some cases forms of document.

The Perception

Concepts are the ideas and it can be distinguished from the names of things. The same concept may have many names, for example in different languages-book, buch, livre; or in the same language, synonyms-firearms/guns, adolescents/teenagers, panthers/leopards. A name may stand for many different concepts in case of homonym. In concept indexing, the indicter recognizes the concepts with which a document deals, rather than merely accepting the names he finds in the document. In practice, he provides the means for readers using the concept and not what is used the concept in the document and that he distinguishes the different meanings of homonyms, so that the client is not led to irrelevant documents by the indexing system. If we call the set of name or symbols which represent classes of documents the "index vocabulary", then we can say that in concept indexing the index vocabulary is controlled, because the indexer has controlled synonyms and homonyms. Failure to control the index vocabulary may lead to the failure to find material on a subject which is, in fact, available in a collection; or to the irritation of being presented with irrelevant documents.

Controlled vocabulary are usually structured that is they display the relationships between different concepts, either by means of references:

Systematic order between documents or records of documents in a catalogue is an order which displays the relationships between the subjects of documents it keeps together and works on the same subjects. This sequence illustrates the principle:

vertebrates

– fish

– birds

– mammals

– rodents

– rats

– mice

– insectivores

– hedgehogs.

Here we see the class RATS, kept with its closely related class MICE; these are preceded by the class which contains them, RODENTS, and followed by INSECTIVORES, which is related to the RODENTS; INSECTIVORES is in turn followed by the classes it contains, such as HEDGEHOGS. Systematic order is one method of displaying structure, so it brings the advantages of a structured vocabulary with the additional facility of easy browsing through the sequence.

Systematic order is the peculiar contribution of the classification scheme to indexing.

The common application of systematic order is the placing of books in order on the shelves of libraries, this is what most people think of as 'classification'. This use enables readers to browse for themselves among the stock, giving them greater autonomy, and making open access libraries possible.

Systematic order is used in the classified catalogue, obviously; but a classification scheme can also provide the basis for the display of structure in an alphabetical subject catalogue-the references:

Vertebrates see also Mammals

Mammals see also Rodents

Rodents see also Rats

Mice see also Rats

could be easily derived from the systematic sequence above. In fact, a classification scheme is the basis of any kind of controlled and structured vocabulary. Alphabetical subject indexes to classified catalogues are derived from the classification scheme. By the technique of chain indexing, thesauri for post coordinate indexes are often produced from classification schemes. So systematic order may be used for the records of documents on machine readable media, to save time in computer searches, and to make the broadening and narrowing of searches through the computer easier.

Hence classification is about the discovery and the display of relationships by means of systematic order.

The Oxford dictionary defines facet as 'one side of a many-sided body'. Subjects can be divided into constituent sides or parts and

the word facet may therefore be applied to a classification which can work on the principle of an analytico-synthetic method. Fundamental concepts are analysed and clubed together into facets. These concepts can be combined further to form more complex subjects. The following example should make this principle clearer.

A firm sells canned and bottled beers (mild, bitter, larger and stout) in various sizes from 330 ml to 31/2 liters. The firm wishes to devise a faceted classification scheme for coding items in its computerized sales system. In order to do this the relevant concepts, '330 ml', 'cans', 'bitter' and so on, are grouped into facets using the characteristics of 'capacity', 'container' and 'beer type', that is :

Capacity	*Container*	*Beer Type*
facet	facet	facet
330 ml	Cans	Mild
440 ml	Bottles	Bitter

Notational Symbol : Each concept within the classification scheme must be allocated a notational symbol which will enable the representation of that the concept by a 'shorthand' code or classification number. Numeric digits could perform this function.

The process of classification is achieved by first ascertaining notation for each constituent concept and then combining the, notations to form a coding or classification number for the complete subject. For example, to classify 440 ml cans of lager' the subject first broken down into its constituent concepts:

440 ml cans lager

and the relevant notations ascertained from the classification scheme

2 1 3

These separate notations are combined to produce classification number:

213

Similarly:

1 litre bottles of mild = 421

31/2 litre cans of bitter = 512

In order to avoid confusion, when using a notation such as the shown here the notational length (that is, the number of digits must be constant and concepts from facets must be combined or cited in consistent order. In the above examples the order is that in who the facets have been written down, namely:

Capacity	*Container*	*Beer Type*
1 Cans 2 Bottles		
1 Mild		
2 Bitter 3 Lager 4 Stout		

If a coding in a computerized system were all that was required then the above scheme would be satisfactory but for other purposes for example a manual filing system, it would be inadequate.

Let us now review the steps that have been taken in order compile the faceted scheme.

Step 1 Analysis into relevant concepts, that is:

440 ml

bitter

cans lager

1 litre

bottles

etc.

Step 2 Grouping into facets characteristics, for example:

Capacity	*Container*	*Beer Type*
440ml	Cans	Bitter

Step 3 Adding a notation, for example:

2440 ml

4 1 litre

Step 4 Choosing a citation order, for example:

Capacity	*Container*	*Beer Type*

A further decision, which has not been specifically referred to, also had to be taken. This relates to the way in which the scheme is to be written down or printed, that is, the schedule order. In the above example the schedule order:

Capacity	*Container*	*Beer Type*

Schedule order would therefore become Step 5:

Step 5 Deciding upon the schedule order

For very brief schedules a tabular form of presentation can be used, but for lengthier schemes a continuous form is more appropriate, for example:

Capacity facet

1 330 ml

2 440 ml

3 550 ml

4 1 litre

5 31/2 litre

Container facet 1 Cans 2 Bottles

Type of beer facet

1 Mild

2 Bitter

3 Lager

4 Stout

Classifying Subjects : It was possible to classify subjects by scanning the classification schedules. However, as the classification scheme develops into a more exhausive and more complex system, such a scanning process becomes difficult, if not impossible. The scheme will therefore require an alphabetical index to make it more intelligible; so that the place in the schedules of a particular concept, and hence its notation, can be ascertained. In addition an introduction to the scheme would have to be written. This introduction will explain how the scheme may be used and will provide examples to illustrate this explanation. In a faceted scheme, among the more important things to be dealt with are the citation order and the method of notational combination. The introduction however should be as brief as possible subject to clarity and explicitness.

The compilation procedure for a complete scheme, one final, important point needs to be made. It can be noted that after examining the illustrative, alphabetic notations, the citation and schedule orders could be given a strong influence symbols. Therefore this allocation could, in many instances, more usefully be undertaken after decisions relating to those orders have been made. Taking this into account, the full procedure, therefore, would entail the following eight steps:

1. Analysis
2. Grouping
3. Order in array
4. Citation order
5. Schedule order
6. Notation
7. Index
8. Introduction

As we have seen, all of these would not be essential in every case, for example in a simple scheme for coding entities in a computerized information system.

Where analysis is concerned, appropriate concepts or terms are selected by an examination of the literature of the subject field or fields. It may be sufficient to use sources such as glossaries, dictionaries, encyclopaedias, indexing and abstracting journals and other classification schemes but it might become necessary to look at actual texts when such sources are inadequate or for current terms. The scheme for the estate agent, for example, used terms taken from actual advertisements.

This is a faceted classification of machine bolts for use in a computerbased business system. It enables each type of bolt to be uniquely identified by a coding. Such bolts are available in different materials, in different thread sizes, in different head shapes and with different finishes.

Material

1 stainless steel

2 brass

3 steel

Thread size

1 0 BA

2 1 BA

3 2 BA

and so on

Head shape

1 round

2 flat

3 hexagonal

4 square

Finish

1 unfinished

2 chromium plated

3 zinc plated

4 painted

The citation order is the same as the schedule order shown above so that sample classification numbers would be:

Chromium-plated brass square-head bolts of 2 BA thread = 2342

Unfinished steel flat headed blots of 1 BA thread = 3221

General Classification : This is a general classification of the whole of knowledge for use in libraries. It was devised by S.R. Ranganathan, who was one on. world's foremost classification theorists, and was the first scheme to, be based entirely on faceted principles. Ranganathan introduct number of new ideas and terms, one of which was the term facet.

In the Colon classification a 'facet formula' for combining concepts is provided for each basic subjects field and this is followed by lists of the concepts (called by Ranganathan 'foci') in each facet within that field. Here, for example, is the beginng of Class Education:

T(P): (E), (2P), (2P2)

Foci in (P)

1 Pre-secondary

13 Pre-school child

15 Elementary

2 Secondary

25 Intermediate

3 Adult

31 Literate

35 Foreigner

38 Illiterate

4 University

An examination of the concepts (or foci) in (P) and the first part of the 'facet formula' for the class, that is, T (P), will indicate that the subject 'University education' will have the class number T4, the square brackets in the formula are ignored.

Foci in (E) cum (2P)

1 Nomenclature

2 Curriculum

3 Teaching technique

Again an examination of the concepts in (E) and a further 100 at the formula will indicate that the classification number for 'Teaching methods' is T:3 and that for 'Teaching methods in universities' T4:3.

The 'cum (2P)' tells us that the concepts in (E) should be linked whenever necessary to those in (2P) and the scheme states:

Foci in (2P)

1 2 3 to be got by (SD)

(SD) means subject device and this allows for the use of the classification number for any subject, from the whole of the Colon scheme, to be included here in parentheses. For example, 'Mathematics' is Class B and therefore the classification number for the subject 'The teaching of mathematics' would be T:3(B) and for 'The teaching of mathematics in universities' T4:3(B). The comma preceding (2P) is superfluous because of the parentheses.

Foci in (2P2)

1 Audio-visual

13 Audio

133 Gramophone

136 Radio

15 Visual

The concepts in the above facet would allow the classification of such subjects as 'The use of visual aids in the teaching of mathematics in universities', which would have the classification number T4:3(B),15.

Citation order in the Colon classification always conforms to the one formula, the PME5T formula, which stands for: Personality (relating to the most important facet which establishes the character of a subject)—Matter (relating to materials)—Energy (relating to processes, activities or operations)—Space (relating to geographical areas)—Time (relating to time periods). This does not mean that the maximum number of facets is five, which would be insufficient for many subjects and multiple 'personality' or other types of facet may be required. In the above Education class formula, for instance, (2P) stands for a 'second round' of the personality facet and (2P2) stands for a second, subsidiary level, of this second round of personality facet.

Hierarchial Classification **:** A 'hierarchy', as used in classification, is a series of classes or groups in successive subordination, for example:

Literature

English literature

Hindi literature

Punjabi literature

Poetry

Drama

Fiction

Thus each entity (for example English poetry) falls into a subgroup of a larger group (for example English literature), which in turn forms part of an even larger group (for example Literature).

Such a classification is built up by a processes of division, according to certain characteristic of language, that is, English literature, Hindi literature, Punjabi literature. Each of these classes can then be further subdivided by the characteristic of form of literature, that is, English poetry, English drama, English fiction; Hindi poetry, Hindi drama, Hindi fiction; and so on. This is sometimes referred to as a 'top down' approach.

The tree structure shown above could be presented thus:

- Literature
  - English literature
    - Poetry
    - Drama
    - Fiction
  - Hindi literature
    - Poetry
    - Drama
    - Fiction
  - Punjabi literature
    - Poetry
    - Drama
    - Fiction

As the process of division continues the hierarchical classification lists or 'enumerates' (hence 'enumerative' classification) complex subjects, for example 'English poetry', which comprises a language (English) and a literary form (poetry). This may be contrasted with the faceted approach, which would list 'English' and 'poetry' as separate concepts but not as a complete subject.

In a properly designed hierarchical classification each subject should have only one place where it fits into the system.

Order of the Subjects : In a hierarchical scheme the order of subjects at a particular level of division is important. This order corresponds to the order of concepts within facets and should be as helpful to the user as possible. For example, in literature, at the language level it would be helpful to place the 'home' language, for example English, first, then related European languages followed by other languages.

The citation order in a hierarchical classification is derived from the order in which the characteristics of division are applied. In the literature example, the first characteristic of division is language and the second literary form. The citation order is therefore:

Language Form

but this citation order' is 'in-built' to classification numbers for complex subjects listed in the scheme.

Notation : Here is the above scheme with a simple notation consisting of numeric digits added:

1 Literature

11 English literature

111 Poetry

112 Drama

113 Fiction

12 Hindi literature

121 Poetry

122 Drama

123 Fiction

13 Punjabi literature

131 Poetry

132 Drama

133 Fiction

This notation may be described as:

Pure Expressive	Only one type of symbol is used (the numeric digit). It reflects the structure of the classification; 111 'English poetry' is a division of 11 'English literature', which in turn is a division of 1 'Literature'
Hospitable	A decimal notation can be aided to indefinitely and therefore, in theory, is infinitely expansible.
Mnemonic	'Poetry' is always represented by the digit1; 'Drama' by the digit 2;'fiction' by the digit 3. This type of mnemonic aid is referred to as a 'systematic' mnemonic.

Index : The index to an enumerative hierarchical scheme lists complex subjects, for example 'Drama: English literature' Here is an to the above schedule:

Drama: English literature	112
Drama: Punjabi literature	132
Drama: Hindi literature	122
English literature	11
Fiction: English literature	113
Fiction: Punjabi literature	133
Fiction: Hindi literature	123

Punjabi literature	13
Hindi literature	12
Literature	1
Poetry: English literature	111
Poetry: Punjabi literature	131
Poetry: Hindi literature	121

The index brings together aspects of a subject which are separated in the scheme, for example poetry in various languages. It is therefore a relative index; it collocates distributed relatives.

New Schemes

The process of classification, in an enumerative scheme achieved first by consulting the index and then by proceeding location pinpointed in the schedules. Although the index lists subjects rather than concepts one should never classify of index alone as this can lead to error. The relevant schedules examined in order to find the correct number. To take a example, if a book which deals with the work of famous such as Shakespeare, Dinkar and Nehru were to be classified, index entry for 'Literature' might be referred to and the class obtained. However after proceeding to in the schedules it apparent immediately that 'Literature' is divided by language the question whether all the authors dealt with are English authors must then be classified. Thus the structure classification scheme itself acts are as classifying.

If the classification of machine bolts were copied in a hierarchical scheme, dividing first by material, then by thread shape and head shape and finally by finish, it would begin to the following, appearance: brass bolts stainless steel machine bolts steel

Round

Unifinished Chromium

plated Zinc plated Painted

Flat

Unfinished Chromium

plated Zinc plated Painted

Hexagonal

Unfinished Chromium

plated Zinc plated Painted

Square

Unfinished Chromium

plated Zinc plated Painted

1 BA

Round

Unfinished Chromium

plated Zinc plated Painted

Flat

Unfinished Chromium

plated Zinc plated Painted

Hexagonal

Unfinished Chromium

plated Zinc plated Painted

Square

Unfinished Chromium

plated Zinc plated Painted

2BA

Round Unfinished Chromium

plated Zinc plated Painted

Flat

Unfinished Chromium

plated Zinc plated Painted and

so on. Several problems are apparent:

The extract from the scheme shown here has only progressed as far as the subject 'Painted flat 2 BA stainless steel bolts', yet already it is far longer than the faceted scheme.

As subjects, and not concepts, are being listed, constituent concept, such as 'unfinished' have to be repeated every time that they occur in a complex subject. However, it is still only possible to classify a subject if it is listed. For example, the subject 'Chromium plated stainless steel bolts' (that is, omitting the size) cannot be classified nor can the subject 'chromium plated bolts'.

Because of the problems (1) and (2), a hierarchical, enumerative scheme tends to become a compromise, and enumeration is not carried to its logical conclusion. Therefore the finished scheme it often very complex in nature and the basic principles of construction are difficult to identify.

Classification for Office Organization : The following are illustrative extracts from a possible enumerative classification for the organization, by subject, of off in files.

16	TRAINING
16.1	MATERIALS
16.11	Visual aids Supplies
16.12	COURSES
16.2	Clerical
16.2.2	Management
16.2.3	Engineering

The index entries to the above schedule would be:

Clerical courses	16.2.1
Courses	16.2
Engineering courses	16.2.3
Management courses	16.2.2

Materials	16.1
Supplies	16.1.2
Training	16
Visual aids	16.1.1

A system might be suitable for the products, supplies, services and functions of an organization. As an advantage the flexibility which the system offers, in that it is easy to subdivide and add topics, but, a disadvantage is the fact that an index is essential. Therefore a combination of systems for storing and retrieving information in the office and recommends 'direct filing', that is, alphabetical sequences by name, subject, and so on, where an index is not required.

A hierarchical enumerative scheme has the further problem that a subject can only be classified if it is enumerated, or listed. To take a simple example from the above scheme, the subject 'Visual aids for clerical courses', cannot be classified. A choice would have to made between 'Visual aids' (16.1.1) and 'Clerical courses' (16.2.1).

***Dewey Decimal Classification*:** This is a classification which covers the whole of knowledge was devised over a hundred years ago for shelf arrangement libraries. It has simple decimal, expansible notation. Here, is example, are some parts of the Literature class, which the reader '" see equate closely to the scheme shown above although the notations different:

800	Literature
810	American literature in English
811	Poetry
812	Drama
813	Fiction
829	Literature of English and Anglo-Saxon languages

821	English poetry
822	English drama
823	English fiction
830	Litnature of Germanic (Teutonic) languages
831	German poetry
832	German drama
833	German fiction
840	Literature of Roman languages.French literature
841	French poetry
842	French drama
843	French fiction

With a decimal notation each subject is capable of division into nine subsidiary subjects, for example 821, 822, 823, 829, all of which are theoretically co-equal. As very few subject divide intonine parts naturally distortion is bound to occur, nevertheless this is an easily understood system and offers hospitality and expansibility The Dewey scheme utilizes a three figure 'minimum' base, a illustrated above; further division continues after the decimal period for example:

822.3 English drama of the Elizabethan period where the '3' represents 'elizabe than period'. A fifth digit may then indicate a particular dramatist within this period, for example:

822.3 Shakespeare

If an item which deals with a work such as 'A criticism of Shakespeare's Macbeth' were classified by the above scheme, the classification is by subject, but if the actual text of Macbeth were to be defined, classification in this case would be by form, that is, literary form, it will be necessary in general classification to cater for this classes.

641.5	Cookery
641.52	For breakfast
641.53	For luncheon, brunch, elevenses, tea, supper, snacks
641.54	For dinner
641.55	Time and money-saving cookery
641.552	Money-saving cookery
641.555	Time-saving cookery
641.56	For special situations
641.561	For one or two persons
641.562	For persons of specific ages
641.5622	Infants and children
641.5627	Adults aged 65 and over
641.563	For health, appearancepersonal reasons
641.5631	For sick persons
641.56311	For persons with heart diseases
641.56314	For persons with diabetes
641.5632	Cookery with specified vitamin and mineral content
641.5634	High-calorie cookery
641.5635	Low-calorie cookery
641.5636	Vegetarian cookery
641.5637	Health-food cookery
641.5638	Protein, fat, carbohydrate cookery
641.504	For various specific times of year

641.506	For Christian church limitations and observances 641.507 For religious limitations and observances
641.508	For special occasions. Holidays, birthdays, etc.

The above extract illustrates the great detail of this scheme but it is also somewhat confusing and illustrates the problems of enumeration. A compromise has had to be reached and hierarchical process of division has not been continued at each step. For example, division by 'Meal' is not further subdivided by'Special situations' and then by 'Health, etc.', but division by each of the characteristics is carried out separately. Thus it is impossible classify the subject 'Cooking dinner for one' or 'Cooking for aged 65 and over who suffer from heart disease'. A choice has to made in these instances between 'Cooking for dinner' or 'Cooking for one' and 'Cooking for adults aged 65 and over, or 'Cooking persons with heart disease'.

What is known as 'cross-classification' alsc occurs. This happens when different characteristics are applied at the one point division. For example, 'For special situations' is divided by characteristics of 'number of people' and' age' at the one step.

The index to the Dewey decimal classification is a very detailed often praised indeed and its relative nature, which was devised all lauded by Melvil Dewey' (the scheme's creator), has had considerable influence on many other indexes. Here is an illustrative example:

Sadism

Gen. med.	616.85835
geriatrics	618.97685835
pediatrics	618.9285835
psychology	157.7

statistics 312.385 835

other aspects were see Sexual deviations

This indicates that various aspects of the subject 'Sadism' can be found in five different places in the schedules, and the cross reference informs the user that additional aspects may be found bconsulting 'Sexual deviations'.

Dewey classification numbers can become quite lengthy and the digits after the decimal point are sometimes split into groups of the for greater convenience and ease of use.

Library of Congress Classification

This classification was constructed at the turn of the century for the US Library of Congress and it reflects knowledge as represented in the books which are included in this great library's stock. The following extracts are taken from Class T 'Technology'. Classes published in separate volumes and Class currently contains close 01 400 pages. This is only one of upwards of thirty volumes in the complete scheme, which gives some indication of the vast size that a classification which attempts to enumerate all subjects can reach.

Within Class T, Class This 'Building construction', and The 6000 onwards is concerned with 'Building fittings and their installation'. Here is a brief outline of this section of the scheme:

Building Fittings and their Classification

6010-	GENERAL WORKS
6100-	PLUMBING AND PIPEFITIING
7000-	HEATING AND VENTILATION
7700-	ILLUMINATION LIGHTING
8000-	DECORATION AND DECORATIVE FURNISHINGS

9000- PROTECTION OF BUILDINGS

Each of these divisions is further subdivided, for example:

PROTECTION OF BUILDINGS

6488 6489 6490

9025 General works

9031 Against damage from natural causes 9100 – Protection against fire

9700 Protection from burglary, sabotage, etc..

The above extracts illustrate the hierarchical nature of the scheme but fail to do the scheme justice in that Class TH from division 6000 onwards actually takes up 21 pages of complex schedules and the principles of construction become hidden in a wealth of enumerative detail. Here, for instance, are the divisions of one very small section, 'Plumbing of the bathroom':

Plumbing of bathrooms, Toilet rooms, Lavatories

6485 General works

6486 General special. Specifications, etc.

6487 Systems Details Fixtures

6488 General works

6489 Catalogues of bathroom fixtures

6490 Basins Baths

6491 General works

6492 Shower baths, Sprays

6493 Tubs

6494 Foot baths

6495	Sintz baths
6496	Bidets
6497	Soil fixtures
6498	Water closets. Toilets
6499	Urinals
6500	Flush tanks and auxiliary valves, etc..

The subject 'Plumbing of a bidet', for example, would have the class number TH6496. Despite the detail displayed here, the true nature of the Library of Congress scheme is still not fully revealed. Here is a further extract from 'Heating of buildings':

Heating of buildings

7201	Periodicals, societies, etc.
7205	Congresses
7207	Collected works (nonserial)
7209	Dictionaries and encyclopedias Directories
7212	General works
7216	Special localities
7215	History
7216	Country divisions, A-Z General works
7221	Early to 1860
7222	1869

The process of classification in an enumerative scheme, achieved first by consulting the index and then by proceeding to the location pinpointed in the schedules. Although the index lists subjects rather than concepts, one should never classify from the index alone as this can lead to error. The relevant schedules must be examined in order to find the correct number. To take a simple example, if a book which deals with the work of famous authors such as Shakespeare, Dinkar and Nehru were to be classified, the index entry for 'Literature' might be referred to and the class number obtained. However after proceeding to 1 in the schedules it will be apparent immediately that 'Literature' is divided by language and the question whether all the authors dealt with are English language authors must then be classified.

It is possible to introduce an element of synthesis, or 'number building into a hierarchical enumerative scheme, in several different ways. This helps to reduce the length of the schedules but improves efficiency.

One method is to provide auxiliary tables of terms which may be applicable throughout the schedules. These tables may include, for example: Common subdivisions, such as those of form of presentation, for example 'Encyclopaedia' or 'Serial'. Geographical tables for specifying 'place', for example 'United States' or 'United Kingdom'.

Permit tables for specifying 'time', for example 'Twentieth century' .

Another method is to include instructions within the schedules themselves for dividing one classification number in the same manner as answer. All plants, for instance, may suffer from 'injuries', 'disease' and 'pests'. Instead of enumerating each of these concepts under every individual plant, they can be listed once and instructions given for the division of each plant in, the same way.

Bibliographic Classification : The 1940-53 edition of this general classification scheme for library materials by HE. Bliss is essentially enumerative but a certain amount of synthesis is provided for by 'systematic schedules', some of which may be applied throughout the scheme but others are applicable only in specific classes. Below are shown extracts from two schedules of the former variety:

Numerical Divisions of Any Class or Section

1. Reference books (including dictionaries, glossaries, encyclopedias, indexes, handbooks)
2. Bibliography....
3. History....
4. Biography....

Geographical Division

a	America
aa	North America
ed	Europe
ea	Great Britain

'Education', in the Bibliographic classification, is J, and by use of the above schedules:

A history of education in Great Britain == J3ea

This number has been derived in a very similar way to the way in which classification is achieved in a faceted scheme. The subject is analyzed into its constituent concepts and a notation assigned to each:

History = 3 Education = J Great Britain= ea

The instructions for citation order and method of combination given in the scheme must now be followed. Usually, classification would be first by subject then by 'place' and then by 'form', but when 'form' is 'history', as in this case, 'place' is cited last. As different symbols are used, a linking device is not required.

Bliss was a firm believer in brevity of notation. He thought that the economic limit should be three or four letters or digits. Perhaps because of this, he did not emphasize sufficiently what he refers to as 'composite notation', a general method of number building for complex subjects which he admitted might be necessary for specialist classification. He advocated the possible use of a hyphen to link numbers. Using this method, the classification number for the subject. 'The influence of politics upon the history of education in Great Britain', could therefore be:

J3ea-R where R is 'Politics'.

Dewey Decimal Classification

Like the Bibliographic classification, the Dewey scheme makes use of generally applicable special tables for standard subdivisions, areas, and so on. In addition, in more recent editions, there is a great deal of provision for synthesis, or number building, in many specific places throughout the scheme. The instructions at 636.8 'Cats', for instance, are:

636.8 Cats

636.800 3-7 800 9	Standard subdivisions Notations from Table

General principles

636.801-.808	Add to base number 636.80 the numbers following 636.0 in 636.01-636.08, e.g., breeding cats.

From Table = 'Encyclopedias' and therefore, following the first instruction above:

An encyclopaedia of cats = 636.8003

Referring to 636.0, which is the general number for 'Animal husbandry' :

636.801-.808

636	Animal husbandry
636.081	Selection and acquisition
636.0812	Judging

636.0811	Ownership makrs
636.082	Breeding
636.084	Feeding

It can be ascertained that the classification number for:

Feeding cats = 636.8084

The above number is derived as follows:

Base number for cats	=	636.80
Add numbers following	=	636.0
Number for feeding	=	636.084
Add '84' to '636.80'	=	636.8084

The example given in the scheme, 'Breeding cats', is obtained in similar fashion.

Various Models

There are two major examples of synthesis being grafted on to an enumerative scheme. The first dates back to the turn of the century when the Universal decimal classification was formulated. This scheme, which has been issued in a number of different languages and has progressed through a number of editions, was based upon the every decimal classification but a number of signs of combination and abbreviation were introduced to allow for number building. The second scheme is of much more recent origin and is the ongoing mission of the Bibliographic classification.

Universal Decimal Classification (UDC)

General number building is allowed for by signs of combination, for example:

+ Addition

/ Extension (used for consecutive numbers)

= Relation

Here are some examples of UDC classification numbers. They are the same as their counterparts in the Dewey decimal classification except that the figure minimum is abolished, therefore

310 in Dewey becomes 31 in UDC:

31 Statistics

51 Mathematics

53 Physics

54 Chemistry

63 Agriculture

Applying the sings of combination to the above numbers in order to build up numbers for composite subjects would achieve results as illustrated in the following examples:

Mathematics and physics	= 51 + 53
Physics and chemistry	= 53/54
Statistics relating to agriculture	= 63:31
	or 31:63

There is no stipulated citation order in UDC, hence the possible alternative for the last number. This provides for great flexibility, if necessary, a double colon may be used to 'fix' the order of the constituent elements of a compound number, especially when UDC is used in a computer-based information system, for example:

Statistics relating to agriculture	= 63::31

Unfortunately UDC retains a great deal of enumeration and this can result in conflict with the synthetic facilities. For example, a common auxiliary table for 'persons' (Table 1(k)—05) is applicable throughout the main schedules:

-05 Persons

-053 Persons according to age or age groups

.2 Children and infants

6 Young persons. Adolescents. Teenagers

.8 Adults. Grown ups

.9 Old persons. Persons in old age

-55 Persons according to sex and kinship

.1 Male persons. Men

.15 Boys

.2 Female persons. Women

.25 Girls

The subject Accident statistics' is classified at 313.12 and therefore, by applying the above table:

Accident statistics relating to women= 313.12-055.2

However, the table is not used consistently but is sometimes replaced by enumeration, for example:

343.91	Kinds of criminal
343.914	Women as criminals
362.8	Care of young persons
362.86	Care and welfare of girls and young women

However, that the number listed, or enumerated, in the schedule is shorter than the number that would have been obtained through the use of synthesis, for example:

343.91-055.2 Women as criminals

Bibliographic Classification Revised Edition

A new revision of the Bibliographic classification based upon facet analysis, began to appear in 1977 and is still in progress. It is the work of Jack Mills and his colleagues at the Polytechnic of North London. Within Class U Arts/ Useful arts, UVC in both the original scheme and the revision is 'Clothing industries'. Given below (some extracts from this class, on the left the original and on the right the revision, which illustrate the difference between the two.

UVC Clothing Industries

Original scheme	*Revision*
UVD Men's and 'boys' clothing	UVD Products
UVDN Men's and boys'neckties, gloves, hats, caps	By mode of manufacture, e.g. UVD C Knitwear
By material, e.g.	
UVE Children's clothing	UVD E Textile
(No enumeration)	By occasion when worn, e.g.
UVF Women's and girls' clothing	UVD KL Industrial
UVFL Women's and girls underwear, lingerie hosiery, gloves	'By sex, e.g. UVD Q Unisex. UVDS Female
By sex, e.g.	
UVDV Child	
By part of body covered , e.g.(Trunk and arm)	

Faceted : A faceted scheme lists concepts only-classification numbers for complex subjects are built up by means of synthesis.

Advantages : Because complex subjects are not listed, such schemes are easier to compile.

The schedules are shorter for the same reason but, despite their brevity, they permit the classification of both very simple and very complex subjects.

New subjects can very often be catered for by the combination of already existing concepts.

Disadvantages : The notation can become long and complex and why be unsuitable for the arrangement of documents on shelves as in a library. The problem of citation order can cause difficulty.

Enumerative: An enumerative scheme attempts to list all possible subjects, both simple and complex, within the defined subject field or fields.

Advantages : Such scheme have been generally accepted and widely used with considerable success throughout the world for a long period of time. A fairly short and uncomplicated notation can be used. 'Notationally', it is easier to display the structure of the scheme.

Disadvantages : It is impossible to list every conceivable subject.

There can be a lack of accommodation for even simple subject.

New subjects cannot be accommodated and regular revision may be required.

In relation to the use of general enumerative schemes in libraries, standardization is facilitated because classification numbers may be included in centralized records. For example, Dewey decimal classification and Library of Congress classification numbers, are included in eye-readable and machine-readable records supplied by the Library of Congress and the British Library. With schemes such as the Dewey decimal classification there is also the possibility of 'integrity of numbers', that is, the stabilizing of existing numbers, a policy initiated by Dewey.

However, general schemes may be unsuitable for certain purposes. For example, in libraries and information services which specialize in particular subject fields, they are not detailed enough specific areas. Special classification schemes, restricted by subject are therefore required. Although these may be enumerative faceted, the latter is now more common. Special schemes are useful for the manual filing of office papers and for the coding entities in computerized systems.

Policies of Notation : Each concept within the classification scheme must be allocated a notational symbol which will enable the representation of that concept by a 'shorthand' code or classification number. Number digits could perform this function.

A common error is to think that choice of notation is the first in the compilation of a classification scheme. It should now be apparent that this is not so; the allocation of a notation is one of final steps.

Notation is, however, a very important feature. Poor note can reduce the value of even the best constructed scheme. Some of the policies which might be booked.

Uniqueness : There should be taken that one concept or subject cannot be mistaken for another. In a machine-based system, for example could be disirous if the coding for a component, say a ball-bearing were the same as that allocated to a completed product such gear box. A distinction must however be made between unique identification of a subject and identification of an actual item example, in a library the subject 'Use of artificial satellites telecommunication' might have the number XX 007 but there well be a great number of cooks dealing with this subject, all with the same class number. For unique identification of each book some must be added to this number, so that in effect it becomes a book number. This addition could consist of letters and digits could represent author, copy number, volume, and so on. A is situation exists in a computer-based system where a code used as the sole key for identification and location of a data record If several records have the same classification number then further coding must be added.

Simplicity : Notation should be easily comprehensible and must have ordinal value as it reflects and 'fixes' chosen orders, therefore:

1 A

2 or B

3 C

not

$

&

*

Confusion should be avoided, for example the use of both the upper case letter '0' and the digit '0', or the lower case letter 'I' and the digit '1'. It is advantageous if notation is easily memorized, written and spoken.

For classification and coding in industry, 'in order to assist the many functions of manufacture by providing a logical and meaningful system of identification for information, data and components '" the best type of symbolisation is generally considered to be purely numerical and of uniform length'.

Brevity : Notation should be as brief as possible. Note that the longer the base, the shorter the classification numbers. . For example, using letters, with a base of 26, it is possible to allocate class numbers no longer than two letters to 676 subjects (that is 26 x 26). Using numerals, with a base of 10, only 100 subjects (that is, 10 x 10) can be allocated numbers no longer than two digits.

Hospitality : Notation should have the ability to accommodate new concepts or subjects as necessary. It should allow for the insertion of both subordinate and coordinate subjects. The former is catered for quite easily by the decimal use of numbers (or the use of letters on the same principle). If 1 represents 'Fiction' and 2 'Poetry' then further expansion is possible in this manner:

1 Fiction

11 Historical fiction

12 Romantic fiction

13 Science fiction

2 Poetry

21 Lyric poetry

The insertion of the coordinate subjects is more difficult but i could be provided for by leaving gaps, for example:

1 Construction

4 Testing

7 Maintenance

but the gaps may not be in appropriate places and therefore could interfere with the required order.

Flexibility : It may be useful to be able to alter citation order according to the needs of a particular set of users. Facet analysis lends itself admirably to variations in preferred citation order.

Expressiveness : This means that the notation reflects the structure of the scheme and such a notation may also be known as 'structural' or 'hierarchical', for example:

I Military ordinance

II Artillery

III Field artillery

Although sometimes considered helpful (the user can understand the systematic order more easily and it can be effective tool in hierarchical computer searching), expressiveness is not essential if it results in longer classification numbers and limits hospitality.

Although the above features may be desirable, it is obviously going to be difficult to incorporate them all into a single scheme. It is particularly difficult in a faceted scheme for synthesis does not lend itself to brevity, simplicity, or expressiveness.

Retroactive Notation : One device which is sometimes used in faceted schemes in an attempt to shorten numbers is 'retroactive' notation. 'Retroactive' simply means 'backwards'. In notational terms a change of facets is indicated by a reversal of alphabetic or numeric direction from forwards to backwards. A classification number such as :

ABCD

shows no change of direction and therefore is derived from one facet only. However the classification number:

CDEBCDABC

shows a change of direction, and therefore a change of facet, between the E and the B, and the D and the A. It could have been written as :

CDE/BCD/ ABC

but the ' /' is superfluous because of the retroactive nature of the number.

In allocating such a notation, it will be seen that the first letters of the alphabet are used to introduce those facets which are to be cited last and not for the primary facets. The letter' A', having been used once, must not be used again in any earlier facet. Similarly 'B', having been used once, must not be used again. Thus the notational base, which is available, is progressively reduced. Care must therefore be taken that when the primary facets are reached, there are still sufficient notational symbols remaining. It is usual to ensure that an adequate amount of the notational base is reserved for the primary facets before allocating a notation to other facets.

Example: Hospitality-from the Library of Congress classification in the fifth edition of Class Q Science will be found:

QD CHEMISTRY

ORGANIC CHEMISTRY 241 Periodicals

243	Yearbooks
245	Collected works
248	History

'Encyclopadeias' are not enumerated or listed, and therefore An encyclopaedia of organic chemistry' cannot be classified. In the sixth edition of Class Q, however, appears:

246 Dictionaries and encyclopedias

This class number has been neatly slotted into the appropriate place in the scheme by making use of the gap left, for hospitality pruposes, in the notation between 245 and 248.

'An encyclopaedia of organic chemistry' can now be classified, the number being:

QD 246

The notation is 'mixed' comprising upper case letters and digits.

Example: Flexibility: From the London education classification. In this scheme the facets are arranged in an order of in CI concreteness, for example:

Lab Teaching methods

Mim	Mathematics
Ras	Primary schools

The recommended or preferred citation order is there for reverse of this, for example:

Ras Mim Lab = Teaching mathematics in primary schools

It is pointed out, however, by Foskett, the compiler individual libraries or information services may wish to vat; order: 'One of the greatest advantages of a faceted classification is that. . . the facets can be arranged in any sequence, to suit particular user'. If it were desired to bring together all items dealing with 'Teaching methods' and to sub-arrange first by subject and by environment, then the citation order could be altered to come to the schedule order and the classification number would become—

Lab Mim Ras = Teaching mathematics in primary schools

Note the 'pronounceable' notation. This led to some interesting mnemonic classification numbers, for example:

Bux = Documentation Pil = Sex education Ror = Choir schools

Unfortunately in the second edition four letter notation had I introduced and the pronounceable element was therefore reduced.

A change of facet as consistently indicated by a change from lower to an upper case letter. The upper case letter therefore as a facet indicator.

Example: Expression-from the Colon classification

X Economics

X7 Public finance

X72 Tax

X724 Income tax

X7244 on salary

Note the way in which the structure of the scheme is reflected in the notation.

Example: Retroactive notation-from the Dewey decimal classification

Perhaps without realizing it. Dewey included a 'flavour' of retroactive notation in his 'History' class:

42	History of England
42.05	History of England in the Tudor period
42.1	History of London
42.105	History of London in the Tudor period

Note that whenever the notation returns to '0', that is goes backwards to '1', then the characteristics of division changes from 'Place' to 'Time'.

***Colon Classification*:** The Colon Classification owes its name to the fact that the notational device first used by it to demarcate facets in Class Number was the symbol 1/:1/ (colon). Hereafter the word 'facet' will be used instead of 'dimension' or 'zone' in accordance with the terminology of the Colon Classification.

In the first three editions of the Colon classification, the implied assumption was that the number of facets in a universe of discourse is constant. Of course, among the fixed number of facets several arrangements are possible, some of which may be 'more or less helpful'. Of the 'more or less helpful' arrangements one is forcedly preferred for adoption. To mechanise the arrangement of facets in the preferred order, a rigorous face-formula is given for each universe of discourse called a Main or a Canonical class.

An important contribution of the Colon classification, the Library classification: Fundamentals and procedure (1944) and the Elements of library classification (1946) is the isolation of the concept of Universes with Loose Assemblage. They have introduced the term 'Phase' in describing an existent which is loosely assembled. In the first edition, the Colon classification (1933) prescribed the digit "0" (zero) as the symbol to connect the class numbers corresponding to the constituents of an existent with loose assemblage. Of course the resulting number is itself a class number. It may be called a Phased Class Number. Each constituent of a Phased Class Number is itself a Class Number. The second edition of the Colon classification (1939) recognized two species of phase-relation for which it prescribed zero and colon as the respective connecting symbols. The Fundamentals made an objective analysis of the problem. The Elements isolated one more species of phase-relation. The Agile has indications that the projected work in India includes a thorough analysis of phases, isolation of different species of phase-relations, and prescription of distinctive connecting symbols for them. It is hoped that this investigation will lay down a technique for handling new species of phases as and when they come to be known, though they may be unknown at present.

The Colon Classification is perhaps the first of the analytico-synthetic variety. It is a pure example of that variety. Its preliminary schedules include those of (1) Main Classes, (2) Common Subdivisions, (3) Geographical Divisions, (4) Language Divisions, and (5) Chrono-logical Divisions. Then follow one chapter for each 'of the Main Classes. In each chapter, if the Main Class is not broken down in the first instance into Canonical Divisions, there are usually one or two schedules corresponding to the one or two trains of characteristics which are relevant to its classification. In other words, the facets of the Main Class are mentioned and the foci in each of them are enumerated. If the Main Class is broken down into Canonical Divisions in the first instance, such of the Canonical Divisions as admit of them are provided with similar schedules based on the trains of characteristics relevant to their classification. Generally speaking the divisions in each of the above-mentioned schedules are enumerated in a 'more or less helpful' order. There are however regions where alphabetical arrangement is prescribed in the form 'Divide by Alphabetical Device'; and there are definite rules which prescribe the minimum arrangement is prescribed in the form 'Divide by Alphabetical Device'; and there are definite rules which prescribe the minimum arrangement is prescribed in the form number of the initial letters which should be used to secure individualisation. An example of this will be found in the Full Crop Schedule worked out for Agriculture in the Abgila of March 1950. It will be found in the Full Crop Schedule worked out for Agriculture in the Abgila of March 1950. It will be found that the international name of crops is prescribed to be used for Alphabetical Device. The Alphabetical Device is used only when there is strong evidence to show that there is no other arrangement which is at all helpful. The point is that when none of the possible arrangements has more of the element of helpfulness than the purely alphabetical one, the alphabetical arrangement scores because people are more familiar with it.

The first part of Colon classification is entitled 'Rules of classification'. It gives objective definition of Class Number and of most other concepts. In the preliminary chapters it describes various devices by which class numbers should be constructed. What are called Facet-and Phase-Formulae are defined. These formulae enable one to analyse a given specific subject in a systematic manner and rearrange the words in the name of the specific subject filling up ellipses if any, as a preliminary to the construction of the class number. The facet-formula of the main class or canonical division to which the specific subject belongs helps in this analysis and breakdown of the specific subject into its fundamental constituent elements. Connecting symbols are prescribed by the rules and also indicated in the facet-and phase-formulae for synthesizing the fundamental constituent numbers, got by translating the fundamental constituent concept, into the derived composite class number as the translation of the name of the specific subject. It is this process of first analysing the specific subject and at the last stage synthesizing the class number which makes the Colon Classification an analytico-synthetic classification.

The potential vocabulary of the Colon Classification is infinite. Its infinity is of a higher order than that of the Decimal Classification. The order of infinity of its potential vocabulary is that of the number of facets and phases its notation can accommodate. To take the example given in section 1521, we saw that it is impossible to get a Decimal Number for the specific subject 'Curriculum in secondary education'. But we can provide a Colon Number. It is T2 :44. Here

T = Education is Main Class

2 = Secondary education is a division in the Education schedule

44 = Curriculum is a number in the Problem schedule is the connecting symbol prescribed

The facet-formula prescribes the order in which the above symbols should be synthesised. Thus we get an individualizing, coextensive number, i.e-., a precise translation for the name of the specific subject. To use the old analogy of visitors and chairs, the Colon Classification can produce a greater abundance of chairs than the Decimal Classification. The occasions when two visitors will be obliged to sit on the same chair will be few and far between. Indeed the ideal is to eliminate such an occasion altogether.

There is one danger in an analytico-synthetic classification when viewed as language. Since an enumerative classification gives a ready-made translation (class number) made by the classificationist himself, it is ensured that no two different translations are made for the same original (specific) subject. But it is well known that when different translators translate with the aid of a dictionary, they may produce different translations. This is perhaps a desirable feature in literary translation. But it will be disastrous in classificatory translation. For, translating the name of a given specific subject into two different class numbers will mean inconsistency in arrangement.

That is why it has been stated that an essential quality of a classificatory language is that it must have no synonym and two different translations for the same original passage should not be allowed or possible. It is the facet-formula which protects Colon Classification from this potential danger. It is that formula which gives the necessary rigidity. But we have to beware that the facet formula does not introduce more rigidity than it is absolutely necessary for avoiding synonyms. If it introduces a greater amount of rigidity than it is necessary, to that extent it will restrict the potential vocabulary of the classificatory language.

To get a view of the map of the field of knowledge provided by the Colon Classification one must take into consideration fully worked-out class numbers, past, present and future. If that is done it will be found that a good map is provided. The conscious implementation of Hospitality in Chain and Hospitality in Array in the methodology of the Colon Classification, keeps co-ordinate classes and subordinate classes quite apart as and when new areas (specific subjects) are explored and have to be marked on the map. The facet-notation enables the Colon Classification to carry out these obligations of cartographers even more thoroughly than the Decimal Classification is able to do.

Viewing the problem from the angle of analogy with transformation, the facet and the phase-notation of the Colon Classification enables to avoid the fault of the Decimal Classification described in section 1523. It is not merely the end sub-cell in the multi-dimensional space of the field of knowledge, which is transformed into the end sub-interval in the linear space of class numbers, which is fully represented. But everyone of the sub-cells in a cluster constituting a compound cell is rightly transformed.

In using the terminology of the Boolean Algebra the field of Colon Nu Numbers is a closed one in the sense that the product of any two sub-fields is contained within the total field. By throwing the search light of Boolean Algebra on the Colon Classification, it is expected that some of the subtler faults which are escaping unnoticed may be brought to light.

The notation or the Colon Classification is even more resourceful in its counter-tactics than that or the Decimal Classification. It has been able to withstand the grosser attacks of the field of knowledge. But in our days the field of knowledge has started, as it were, bacteria warfare. It has begun to play Hanuman's tactics as described' in section 1515. It is playing these tactics unendingly. Just as the vocal muscle of the witch in the Ramayana episode became too stiff at a certain stage for the jaws to be easily moved, we have been experiencing that the rigidity of the facet-formula is causing trouble in putting up the necessary counter-tactics. It is to take away this rigidity that the work on Optional Facets is being pursued.

The Colon Classification has virtually no patent medicine. Every mixture has to be compounded according to prescriptions written out by a competent doctor to meet the exact requirement of the disease diagnosed. This does not mean that mixtures in frequent demand should not be compounded and stored in advance to be handed over readily on demand.

Similarly the Colon Classification has virtually no ready-made toys. Every toy should be built up to suit the exact fancy of the child needing it. This does not mean that the toys in frequent demand should not be assembled in advance and kept in readiness, to be handed over readily on demand.

The Colon Classification has closely followed the optical analogue in the design of its terminology, there is no need to elaborate further the statements made in that section. The structure of the Colon Number discloses more fully than any other classification number the structure of the specific subject.

A new feature of the Colon Classification which, however, needs to be mentioned here concerns the method it uses: (1) to secure theoretically infinite Hospitality in Array and in Chain severally.

To secure Infinite Hospitality in Array the Colon Classification uses not only the Octave Notation but also other devices like Subject Device, Alphabetical Device, Geographical Device and Chronological Device. These are all described and illustrated in the Colon Classification. Of these, it is the Chronological Device which has usually facility to provide truly Infinite Hospitality in Array. It has stood the test admirably in accommodating Authors in Literature with neat individualising class numbers, no matter how many they are. It is also showing its capacity in individualising any number of special schools of thought in any region of knowledge. In the former, it consists in representing an author by the year of his birth. This makes classification of the authors belonging to any particular form of literature in any particular language chronological. This arranges the works by and on them in a manner which is not only helpful, in the ordinary sense, but also suggests the evolution of the literary art.

Thus Hospitality in Chain is got by the decimal-fraction-notation which imitates the denudation process by which the links in the chain are successively derived.

When a link begins to throw forth its links of higher order, it often happens that all the links in the array of the next order are not thrown out at one time. If they are, it may be easy to determine a 'more or less helpful' arrangement among them and allot the extra digit or digits needed to represent them according to the octave notation or any of the devices mentioned above. When they are not thrown out at one time, it is difficult to surmise which place the first link which is thrown out should be given in the array – which octave and which place in the octave. It is here that the Colon Classification has contributed what has been described in the Prolegomena as Unscheduled Mnemonics. It is a subtle device and is therefore a powerful one. It gives a greater degree of autonomy to a classifier in sharpening Simple and Dependent Foci. It is difficult to explain it in general terms though it has been attempted in the Philosophy of library classification. Unscheduled Menmonics consists in using an ordinal digit to represent a primordial idea which is not often represented by any term in a natural language, when it is taken in isolation, but is represented by different terms when it is put in the context of the different subjects. For example, the digit 3 represents Physiology in Biological Sciences, Social practices in Sociology, Functions of State in Political Science, Teaching Technique in Education, Distribution in Economics, Contract in Legal System and so on—all at bottom analogous at least in a thin or distant way. This mnemonic quality enable a classifier to form new foci in any facet without reference to the classificationist. What is more he need not wait to give numbers to these foci until all of them have appeared. Even when only one appears, he can number it with a high probability that it need not be changed and that very other classifier and the classificationist himself would be numbering it in the same way. The organisational set up on national and international basis for removing the effect of the small probability for inconsistency in fixing numbers by unscheduled mnemonics, has been described in Library classification and international documentation of the F.I.D. I have some vague information that there is a tradition of such unscheduled mnemonics current in the Tantric school. I wish something is done to collect, record and study this tradition of unscheduled mnemonics. Even among the common folk in western countries there is some trace of this which is brushed aside as sheer superstition. But scientific outlook requires that we should not brush aside anything on the sole ground that we cannot fit it into the rational matrix which intellect produces. We should be prepared to postulate and even grant trans-intellectual existents, though it is necessary to be on our guard not to become credulous subjects of fraud.

Universal Decimal Classification : In late 19th century there was an increasing concern for the problems of documentation. In earlier years cataloguers had concentrated on the problems of describing and recording books mostly in a bibliographic tradition, with a wealth of detail but with a corresponding delay in the dissemination of information. In the early 1890s Paul Otlet and Henri La Fontaine, in Belgium, translated the earlier cataloguers' efforts toward a universal catalog into the world of documentation. They proposed a' universal index to recorded knowledge which must include non-book materials and ephermera as well as conventional material. In 1895 the First International Conference on Bibliography, for which Otlet and La Fontaine were largely responsible, approved their plans and established the Institute Interna ional de Bibliography (IIB). Otlet and La Fontaine had already agreed that such an index, and bibliographies based on it or contributing to it, must be organised systematically rather than alphabetically. They looked to the Dewey Decimal classification as the basis of a truly international scheme.

Otlet and La Fontaine negotiated with Dewey to use his scheme for the IIB's index. They wanted three things: to translate it into French, to expand its subject schedules and make it truly international in scope, and to allow arrangements to include non-book materials. Dewey was impressed and inclined to agree, but his assistants (in particular Dorcas Fellows) could not tolerate such changes to his original plan. Negotiations dragged on until in despair the Belgians went their own way. Without that reluctance of members of Dewey's staff we might now have only one decimal classification, and a realisation of Dewey's plan: a scheme of universal scope for documentation, a scheme for general use (as in DOC now), and an abridged scheme like the abridged DDC.

The adapted scheme was published for the first time in 1905 by the IIB as the Manual due repertoire universal bibliographique and became known in the English speaking world as the "Brussels classification". Even then it had more detail than the contemporary edition of the DOC, and it had most of the synthetic features peculiar to what is now the Universal Decimal Classification. It was quickly adopted by libraries in Europe, particularly special libraries with a scientific and technological orientation where nonbook materials are common.

Probably the greatest impact of UDC on libraries has been through the abridged editions now published in some 16 languages. The first of these was not an official UDC abridgment but was a version used by S.C. Bradford in the Science Museum Library in London. Bradford was an early and enthusiastic supporter of UDC who attempted an index in English similar to the original index of the IIB. Bradford is the Science museum

Library before the British Standards Institution became the official British publishers responsible for organizing UDC revision and communication of changes as well as publication of English versions.

The first scheme with an analytico-synthetic element was the Universal Decimal Classification. Though the Universal Decimal Classification was not accessible at the time when the Colon Classification was designed and consequently it has not been possible to use it as a model in the designing of the Colon Classification, there is no denying that the latter appeared in the field only a generation later. In spite of it, it had been taken first for description because it has developed the features of an analytico-synthetic classification in a more pronounced and fundamental manner and the auxiliary books and writings centering round it have developed a terminology which makes communication easier. It was a good in disguise that the schedules of Universal Decimal Classification were not accessible for several years after the Colon Classification was designed and developed up to the third edition. If it had been, the pressure of its tradition would have inhibited free thought, even as the Decimal Classification had done. Indeed, it is being realised that many of the faults of the Colon Classification are due to the pressure of the tradition of the Decimal Classification.

In 1931 the IIB became the Institue Internationel de Documentation (II D) and in 1937 changed its name again to the Federation International de Documentation (FID) its present name. In the preparation of the 1927-1933 edition, Otlet and La Fontaine were joined by Frists Donker Duyivis of the Dutch Patent Office, who was to look after the natural science schedules. He became secretary of the II B in 1929 and stayed until his retirement in 1959. He was one of the principal influences on the development of UDC as we know it. The offices of the institute moved to the Hague, together with the master card file of the UDC. From these offices is conducted international coordination of the revision and development of the UDC.

The ultimate coordinating body of the UDC is the Central Classification Committee (CCC). Originally this was made up of the editors of UDC and the secretary-general of FIC, but these members were joined in 1964 by representatives from the national committees responsible for publication of native-language editions and for the coordination of the work of special subject committees within each country. In addition there are international subject committees that report directly to the CCC.

Comment and criticism concerning existing schedules and proposals for revision or new classes travel up this committee structure, ultimately to the CCC. It is common for comments or draft schedules to be circulated at each level for future comment, so the process can be lengthy one, but it is also a process that involves the users of the scheme more directly than with any other major scheme. When draft schedules reach the CCC they are considered in the light of the scheme as whole, and after any modification to avoid clashes with any other schedules, they are issued as P-notes. At one time P stood for projects, and there were two kinds: projects provisions that had to be discussed and debated fully before official acceptance, and projects d' extensitions' that would become part of the UDC automatically if no objection was heard within 4 months. After a period of proliferation of different kinds of P-note, the system was simplified to the second of the original projects. After 4 months without objection the contents of P-notes are cumulated in Extensions and Corrections to the UDC published every 6 months and then cumulated triennially.

Revision takes place in three ways. The first is the obvious and natural extension of topics by more detailed subdivision. The second is by minor alternations of existing subdivision notation. The third and most important, since it is almost unique to UDC, is the "starvation policy" introduced by Donker Duyvis. This policy attempts to deal with a problem of particular significance to UDC that it is used mostly in scientific and technical libraries and is strongest in these dynamic and rapidly changing subject areas. It is difficult to apply a policy of changing the internal structure class as it stands-as LC has long done and as DDC now does " its II phoenix schedules'- since this policy assumes fairly static collections and the opportunity for fairly leisurely reclassification.

UDC is a synthetic scheme, using punctuation marks, auxiliary schedules to link and add to the basic notation derived from the DDC. The content of the schedules derived from UDC changed significantly over the years, but the basic outline is similar enough to DDC to assure anyone who knows the outline of DDC. They are dealing with a familiar scheme, at least for subject content. For most users, however, the characteristic feature of UDC is its v wide range of auxiliary signs and schedules, to allow for addition and extension of class numbers and for subdivisions of language form, place, time, etc. However, the main contribution in the auxiliaries is the use of nondecimal punctuation marks to signal use of DDC or DDC based decimal notation.

Auxiliaries : There are two kinds of auxiliaries: general, affecting the whole scheme; and special, affecting only specified parts of the scheme The general auxiliaries can in turn be divided into two groups: those that are simply signs that join other notational elements together a those that are signs that introduce explicit tables of subdivision.

To the first general group belong the signs of addition, extension and relation. The addition sign + is used to join together two subjects not adjacent in the schedules..

54+ 66 CHEMISTRY AND CHEMICAL TECHNOLOGY

It is an awkward combination to index and to file (54+66 shot file before 54 since it covers a larger subject area), and UDC does whole heartedly recommend its use. The extension sign/ is used join consecutive notational elements, either two adjacent elements the beginning and end of a sequence.

537/538	ELECTRICITY AND MAGNETISM
22/28	THE CHRISTIAN RELIGION

When the extension sign is used with lengthy notation sharing common higher level, the notation for the higher level may omitted.

621.396/.397	THE EFFECT OF HOT-AIR CENTRAL HEATING ON INDOOR PLANTS
635.695:632.38	VIRUS DISEASES OF INDOOR PLANTS
635.695:582.675	INDOOR ANEMONES

The entity 635.695 INDOOR PLANTS, three laments have been added successively: notation from another class to indicate an effect on the entire notation from within the same class to indicate a problem of the entry, and notation from another class to indicate a kind or subclass of the entry. In other words, the colon is performing three separate functions. Notice also that the order listed here is an ideal arrangement for documents on shelves or in index files of general-to-special type. But the use of only the colon as a relational sign means that UDC numbers must be filed by the notation that fellows the colon, thus reversing that order-at least in this case; in fact the order will be arbitrary, depending on what notation follows the colon. There are further problems with the use of the colon. A collection on mathematics and its subdivisions written for engineering students might include:

51:62	MATHEMATICS FOR ENGINEERS
511	ARITHMETIC
511:62	ARITHMETIC FOR ENGINEERS
512	ALGEBRA
512:62	ALGEBRA FOR ENGINEERS

making it impossible to keep together all the textbooks for engineering students. For a long time, principally in the English editions of UDC, brackets were used to "intercalate" the related notation:

51 [62]	MATHEMATICS FOR ENGINEERS
51[62]1	ARITHMETIC FOR ENGINEERS

51[62] 2 ALGEBRA FOR ENGINEERS

511 ARITHMETIC

512 ALGEBRA

The official use of brackets is now as a grouping device, for example:

54 + 66 (05)

might mean A JOURNAL (05) ON CHEMISTRY AND CHEMICAL TECHNOLOGY or CHEMISTRY AND JOURNALS ON CHEMICAL TECHNOLOGY

But UDC now offers

[54 + 66] (05)

to make it clear that the meaning is JOURNALS ON CHEMISTRY AND CHEMICAL TECHNOLOGY.

A more serious problem with the single colon as a relational all sign is that no order is specified or even recommended in DC for the elements that it joints. Thus using 633.491 POTATOES and 632.3 PARASITIC DISEASES, both 633.491P:632.3 and 632.3:633.491 may mean PARASITIC DISEASES OF POTATOES. UDC recognized the potential conclusion and took away most of the value of the sign by instruction to use both combinations in indexes or catalogue. This instruction effectively limited the relational sign to a link between only two components and prevented the exploration of assemblies of more than two components.

The use of the double colon can resolve the problem, by indicating that only the combination as expressed ::.may be used: 633.491 :: 632.3, but not 632.3:: 633.491.

Even with the later developments of : and :: the problems cited earlier remain the use of the relational sign in whatever form to indicate effects or influences (phases), problems (facets), and kinds can result in confused file order.

The remaining general auxiliaries are all tables of subdivision with distinctive punctuation marks to indicate their function.

Auxiliaries of Form and Language : The first two concern only the physical document: the common form auxiliary (0...) and the language auxiliary. Both are derived from the ADDC but with an interesting development that is echoed in some of the other auxiliaries. In DDC the list of common form subdivisions is a mixture of what Berwick. Sayers described ,as' inner' and' outer form' on the one hand, the internal point of view or approach to the subject an, on the other hand, the physical arrangement or form of the material, for example, the philosophy of a subject and an ENCYCLOPEDIA, respectively. UDC was able to recognise the distinction and to offer: 1 for the PHILOSOPHY of a subject, leaving the common subdivisions mostly for 'outer form'. It then enclosed DDCs 0... in parentheses to give it a clear indicator of its separateness from subject numbers. Such a concentration on 'outer form' freed notation used in DOC for 'inner form' for further expansion in UDC.

A similar development took place with the language auxiliary. DOC had no such facility; UDC included it because of its international and multilingual applications. Detail was taken from DOC's class 400 LANGUAGE and given the equals sign as an indicator of this separateness from the subject schedules. A further refinement took place when UDC ignored DOC's notational structure of three integers followed by a decimal point and decimal fraction notation. Instead, UDC regarded all notation as decimal and used a period after every three digits, breaking up a number in order to make it more mnemonic. This practice, together with the introduction of parentheses to introduction form and other subdivisions, free the 0 from its use in DOC only as an indictor and allowed it to be used as a specifying digit:

=42	THE ENGLISH LANGUAGE GROUP
=420	ENGLISH

• Auxiliaries of Place, Time Race, and Persons time, and race found in varying degree in most major classification schemes. Like the group already discussed, the next group of general auxiliaries includes the common subdivisions of place, these too enjoy a development freed from the national constrictions of DOC.

The general auxiliary of place () took what was earlier the divide like' device of DOC (employing subdivisions of 940-999 to subdivide any other number) and is now the DOC Area Tables, and used those digits in parentheses. Because the parentheses indicated only place, the hitherto inaccessible 91 GEOGRAPHY and 92 BIOGRAPHY were now available as (1) and (2) for new meaning. UDC used them to indicate geographic or topographic detail not tied to politoco-geographic areas: rivers, mountains, seas, and even ideas like central, bordering, north, and south, rivers, mountains, and seas are listed and named in (2) as :

(237.15) SIERRE MADRE AND MEXICAN PLATEAU

Concepts like central, bordering, north, and south are listed at (1) as : (1-14) SOUTH

The (1) is simply a carrier digit to support the concept (-14) SOUTH; in fact, the concept may be added to any other geographical subdivisions in parentheses;

(468.1) ANDALUSIA

(468.1-14) SOUTH ANDALUSIA

For time subdivision UDC departed from all other traditions and used the date enclosed in quotation marks; "1976" means in 1970. The notation is decimal, so that "197" means the 1970s a "1970.01,.01" means January 1,1970.

Periods of time can also be indicated by the extension sing "196/197" means the 1960s and 1970s , and a negative sign-me, BC:

"-0055" 55 BC

The auxiliary for race is a combination of the auxiliaries of place and language, combining their signs. The language auxiliary sign= inside parentheses () indicates the race that speaks that language with form and place, the race auxiliary is able to expand beyond normal limits of the language specification by the freedom from p language numbers. For example, it is able to specify (=94: ESKIMOS, (96) NEGROES, and further, (1.493 = 40) WALLOONS by combining the race and the place specification using the carrier and a further subdivision.

The auxiliary-05 for person originated in class 3 social sciences but was clearly useful for general application:

62-055.2 WOMEN IN ENGINEERING

The only remaining general auxiliaries are the point of numbers .00 ..., and .000.' The first and original point view auxiliary .00 is used when many compounds joined by colons m; introduce confusion in a file, as in a collection of documents for business concern. It might be easier to organize the collection by the several aspects of the business and then subdivide b variety of subdivisions using colons. For example:

could be rearranged as :

635.965:582.675	INDOOR PLANTS :MARSH MARIGOLD
635.965:632.38	INDOOR PLANTS :VIRUS DISEASE
635.965:697.38	INDOOR PLANTS: EFFECTS OF CENTRAL HEATING
635.965.004:632.38	INDOOR PLANTS: MATERIAL MARSH MARIGOLD
635.965:002.3:582.675	INDOOR PLANTS:DETERIORATION/ WEAR:EFFECT OF CENTRAL HEATING.

The introduction to the UDC has more examples of these of .00

A fairly recent addition to the point-of view auxiliary is one to account for an author's point of view. The notation is .000 and may be used as follows:

635.965.004:632.38	INDOOR PLANTS:USE/ CARE:VIRUS DISEASE
162.6.000.335.5	DIALECTICS FROM THE MARXIST POINT OF VIEW

linking 162.6 DIALECTICS and 335.5 MARXISM

Special Auxiliaries : Special auxiliaries are subdivisions that deal only with limited ranges of subjects. They have the signs-, .0, and '. The-and .0 are equivalent and are so used throughout the scheme, occasionally being combined when more than one kind of special subdivision exists for combination, as in class VIII LITERATURE they may be applied anywhere in the area that they cover:

621-77	SAFETY DEVICES
621.039 5-77	SAFETY DEVICES IN NUCLEAR REACTORS
7.061	FORGERY IN ART
75.061	FORGERY IN PAINTINGS

There is no consistency in the use of and .0 in the scheme, as Dubuc points out (10), and proposals have been made to use only.

One other form of special auxiliary is the postrophe to indicate combinations of chemical elements :

546.33	SODIUM
546.13	CHLORINE
546.33'13	SODIUM CHLORIDE

Different Categories

The enumerated schedules themselves resemble the familiar decimal structure of the DDC, but the resemblance is more apparent than real. The same major classes are present and for the most part of the same divisions appear within these classes; but from that point onward (or downward) more and more differences can be seen, resulting from revisions within UDC. For example, RADIO ENGINEERING is represented by 621384 in the DOC but by 621.396 in DOC. This seems to be similar because both numbers begin with 621.3, but in fact the notation is distinctly different, as it is therefore for the whole of this large class.

Differences in the schedules are not limited to notational differences of this kind. UDC has also restructured classes from the form used by DOC; for example, the use in 8 LITERATURE of the two special auxiliaries-AND .to accommodate the facets of form and of literary science and technique. The facet of period, if necessary, can of course, be represented by the Common auxiliary of time.

To describe in detail the enumerated content of the classes of UDC would be to repeat in large part a description of DOC, which has been laid out elsewhere in many textbooks and is in any case generally well known. Instead, the major differences are described here.

Generalities : UDC accepted most of this class as Dewey had laid it out in DOC. The major exception was in the early development of 00 as a class devoted to fundamentals of knowledge. DOC has now developed this class, but its form remains distinct from UDC, which divides the class as :

001	THE SCIENCES AND KNOWLEDGE IN GENERAL
002	DOCUMENTATION
003	SEMIOTICS, SYNTACTIC'S, SEMANTICS, WRITING, SCRIPTS, NOTATIONS, SIGNS AND SYMBOLS

005	ORGANISATION STUDY, METHODOLOGY, ANALYSIS AND SYSTEMATIZATION GENERALLY.
007	ACTIVITY AND ORGANISING INFORMATION, COMMUNICATION, CONTROL THEORY (CYBERNETICS) INCLUDING 'HUMAN ENGINEERING'.
008	CIVILIZATION CULTURE PROGRESS
009	THE HUMANITIES THE" ARTS" IN GENERAL

***Philoshopy*:** With minor variations of terminology this class reflects the DOC from which it was originally taken, with the exception of the area of psychology. In DOC, 130 and 150 are devoted to the area of the mind; 130 concentrates on the ills of the mind and also on the occult and paranormal phenomena while 150 is concerned with the operations of the mind in its normal state. UDC anticipated DDC's re-organisation of these classes in using 13 for the occult and parapsychology, and 15 for the functions of the mind. Indeed, UDC introduced a new classification of the subject at 159.9, so as not to interfere with collections classified by the original 15. This new classification has since been reflected in DDC revisions.

***Religion*:** There are few differences here between DDC and UDC The organisation of this class is biased toward Protestant Christianity because of the persuasion of melvil Dewey and his assistants to the extreme point of the absence of a single notation for Christianity itself, on the assumption that religion was Christianity and anything else was either variation or heresy. UDC fares better than DDC because the synthetic nature of UDC allows the construction of detailed notation for concepts and problems in non-Christian religions denied by the more enumerative structure of DDC.

***Social Sciences*:** In many subdivisions of this major class there are minor differences between DDC and UDC occasioned, for example, by the ability of UDC to use the common auxiliary of place ( ) instead of DDC's "add" device, or by the allocation of specific notation for geographical extension, as in 310 STATISTICS. Otherwise the subdivisions of this class are the familiar ones, with the exception of LAW.

Law is always a problem for classification schemes; the library of Congress has yet to publish a complete schedule. DOCs class 340 LAW for many editions was the most confused class in the scheme, though the revised version in DDEC 18 improved beyond measure. UDC adopted some of the early DOC class, changed some, and relied on synthesis to modify the rest sufficiently to solve most problems of subject description. Part of the problem lies in the use of legal literature by lawyers: in the dichotomy of the literature organised by problem (or kind of law) or by legal system.

UDC subdivided 340 LAW as :

340	LAW IN GENERAL
341	INTERNATIONAL LAW
342	PUBLIC LAW; CONSTITUTIONAL LAW
343	CRIMINAL LAW; PENAL OFFENCES; PENOLOGY, CRIMINOLOGY
344	SPECIAL LAW; CRIMINAL LAW.
347	PRIVATE LAW; CIVIL LAW
348	ECCLESIASTICAL AND CANONICAL LAW

This subdivision avoided the DDC inclusion of US and UK STATUTES AND CASES as major subdivisions of the class LAW, and of LAW OF OTHER COUNTRIES. These inclusions violated the fundamental laws of classification and caused severe confusion in the class and its practical application in law libraries.

As in so many cases, this approach by UDC, based on the analytico-synthetic philosophy, resulted in the later modification of DDC's class to a very similar overall organisation.

PHILOLOGY LANGUAGES

This is a nonclass, since LANGUAGE has now been moved to class 8, to form LANGUAGE, LINGUISTICS, LITERATURE.

Mathematics and Natural Science : UDC kept close to the original DDC outline of this class, though it made minor changes that anticipated later DDC developments. Most developments were in extensions to the existing classes and in relatively minor shifts—for example, 541 QUALITATIVE ANALYSIS and 545 QUANTITATIVE ANALYSIS to 543.061 and 543.062, respectively, as part of 543 ANALYTICAL CHEMISTRY. In fact, UDC, in the area of science that was to be one of its major strengths, retained many of DDC's weaknesses; for example:

523.2 SOLAR SYSTEM 523.3 MOON

523.4 PLANETS 523.5 METEORS 523.6 COMETS

523.7 SUN

523.8 STARS

reflecting a distinctly geocentric view of the universe.

On the whole, however, UDC has successfully retained the century-old framework of this class from DOC because UDC's synthetic approach can restructure a notation to accommodate new topics.

The entry 608 includes an extremely useful area on patents and inventions, derived from DOC but expanded to reflect the scientific and technological orientation of UDC.

Medicine : This includes 618 as a special section on GYNECOLOGY, OBSTETRICS. Also, 619 is VETERINARY MEDICINE, a special class almost abandoned as a discipline by DOC and included with animal husbandry.

Engineering and Technology : In this group of subjects and disciplines UDC departed most radically from DOC. The adoption of UDC by European special libraries demanded the development of the scientific and technological areas, and in particular, the area of technology. Indeed, the UDC schedule for textile technology, developed for the French-language edition of 1928, was translated into English for inclusion in DOC 11 (1927) with the financial support of an American industrialist.

In particular, the dynamic area of telecommunications, especially RADIO AND TELEVISION ENGINEERING, called for expansion and revision. DOC had used 621.384; UDC, following Donker Duyvis's "starvation" policy, moved them to 621.396/ .397 and then later developed 621.38 for ELECTRONICS.

Agriculture : The early DOC had listed the operations and problems of agriculture in 631/632, and the products in 633/638. UDC's colon device has always allowed combination of entity and process, though DOC has recently allowed only limited combination.

65 MANAGEMENT, ORGANIZATION OF INDUSTRY AND COMMERCE, BUSINESS, COMMUNICATION AND TRANSPORT.

The structure of UDC includes a detailed subfacet on management theory that can be applied throughout the class. The rest of the class lists management areas. Unfortunately it still includes transport and communication services (at 654/656), which really belong elsewhere and are not part of management services.

Arts and Recreation : In general UDC accepted (and still accepts) DDC's basis for the organization of this class, but the addition of a special auxiliary for the class allow more detail than does DDC.

For example, 7.025.4 RESTORATION allows

755.025.4 RESTORATION OF RELIGIOUS PAINTINGS.

8 LANGUAGE. LINGUISTICS, LITERATURE

Originally this class contained only LITERATURE; it now also contains LANGUAGE and LINGUISTICS. The entry 801 contains what used to be in 40/41; for example, 415 GRAMMAR has been moved to 801.5 GRAMMAR. The languages that used to be in 42/49 are now it:. 802/809, reflecting the auxiliary table of languages. Detail from 801 may be added to any specific language notation by replacing 801 with the dash that signifies a special auxiliary, so that 809.166 WELSH LANGUAGE may be extended to WELSH GRAMMAR by adding the 5 of 801.5 as a special auxiliary: 809.166-5 WELSH GRAMMAR.

UDC applied its special auxiliaries in 82/89 to improve the DDC model from which it was derived. DDC had subdivided the class hierarchically to produce chains like:

800	LITERATURE
820	ENGLISH LITERATURE
821	ENGLISH POETRY
821.3	English POETRY OF ELIZABETHAN PERIOD

UDC used two special and one common auxiliary to produce an even more sophisticated expression. Languages are left as an integer, and to them are added a special auxiliary to reflect form (e.g.,-1 POETRY) and, if necessary, another special auxiliary to reflect special processes like criticism or translation (e.g., 03 TRANSLATION).

Thus, with 820 ENGLISH LITERATURE we may find:

820"15"	ENGLISH LITERATURE OF THE SIXTEENTH CENTURY

820-1"15"	English POETRY OF THE SIXTEENTH CENTURY
820-1"15	English POETRY 03 TRANSLATIONS OF English POETRY OF THE SIXTEENTH CENTURY
820-1 " 820-1"15" .03=40	TRANSLATIONS INTO French (using the common auxiliary of language) OF English POETRY OF THE SIXTEENTH CENTURY.

GEOGRAPHY, BIOGRAPHY, HISTORY UDC retained the original outline of DDC's Class 900, with the exception of the intoduction of the most useful class 908 – HOMELAND STUDIES. This includes comprehensive studies on the history, geography, economics, and culture of a country. UDC has been used in several projects for the production of indexes or the control of information storage and retrieval systems using data-processing systems. The principal attractions are the synthetic nature of the scheme and its notation, which allows commands or search statements to be directed to selected components in document descriptions, and the hierarchical grouping, inherent in any classification scheme, which allows easy generic searching.

Thirteen

The Helpline

The reference department within a public library has two principal functions. It is firstly a collection of literature maintained wholly, or chiefly, for use on the library premises by people wishing to pursue specific study or research, secure in the knowledge that, as distinct from the home-reading (i.e. lending) library, the material that they require will always be available to them when required. This holds true even when, as in some recently designed libraries, reference and lending library stocks are shelved within the same room. The distinction between the purely reference stock and that which may be borrowed appears to present few problems. Secondly, the reference department is designed as a collection to satisfy the needs of enquiries seeking specific factual items of information.

Sometimes called the 'quick reference service', this function can be effectively exercised in any library. In the largest systems the service may become a separate Current Affairs Information Department embracing all aspects of contemporary life, but in the smaller units, resources will probably confine the potential service to the provision of local directory information, factual data from general encyclopedias and transport time-tables. The telephone may be used to bring in the resources of the central reference library, or perhaps give access to sources of information outside the library system.

The reference library houses such materials as bibliographies, encyclopedias, dictionaries, directories (all both general and specific in coverage), as well as monographs, treatises and textbooks on a variety of subjects. In the larger reference libraries, a considerable proportion of the stock will, indeed, duplicate material provided for home-reading in the lending libraries. The largest public reference libraries are sub-divided into subject-collections – business, science/technology, local history, art and music – looked after by a specialist staff. They are often established as completely separate departments distinct from the 'general reference library'. Large collections may exceed one million volumes in extent, supplemented by several thousand subscriptions to current periodicals and are significant research libraries housing many rare or even unique items and attracting research students from all over the world. This is particularly the case when the library has holdings listed in bibliographies.

Reference libraries with very large stocks – especially long retrospective runs of periodicals – will probably house them in storage stacks which will be located away from the reading areas, or even away from the main library building. The reading room itself may well display only a limited proportion of the more heavily used stock and the principal reference books on open-access, and will have as many as several hundred reader-places available either at open tables in the body of the room or in individual study carrels.

The reference departments of public libraries in the bigger cities often serve a definite, though financially unacknowledged, role as reference centres for the region in which they are situated. In this role they not only draw in 'extra-district' users, but also provide back-up services to smaller, less well-endowed reference libraries and, indeed, other types of library in their area.

Reference Libraries

This wide range of possible activity, and the great variation in quantity as well as quality of the reference library, makes it necessary to decide the extent to which the staff should enter into positive assistance in placing their knowledge of subject-literature and of the contents library at the disposal of the enquirer, or whether that assistance should be restricted to the obvious one of explaining the catalogues, supplying books requested and ensuring that library house keeping is maintained at a proper level.

The trained, qualified librarian has much to offer an education of probably university level plus vocational study at library school in the skills he has gained in training sources of information, be it current or retrospective, but it is reasonable to question how far the quantity of extra work which may be generated can be justified, how far there is an element of responsibility for the facts supplied, how far the reader may welcome staff assistance.

Effective reference librarianship demands a total commitment and wide experience. It is not a job which can be done by staff drafted into it for a short time before being moved on to other things. The more senior posts in a major reference library need to be attractive enough financially to ensure continuity. The most senior staff of this and the various special subject departments must feel encouraged by the rewards, both of salary and job satisfaction, to make a long stay in such work. Junior professional appointments can be a different matter. It is better if these are part of an overall (the-job professional training, so that all junior professionals spend some time in reference library work) learning the thoroughly at the hands of the specialist senior staff before moveing on to other areas of work.

This movement of junior professional staff serves two principal purposes. Reference work is, in some measures, the task of professional librarians in whatever department or type of library they work, and a thorough grasp of the potentialities of the reference department enables them to make more effective use on behalf of their own library users.

As a place intended to be used for extended periods of study great care must be taken over the furnishing and equipment library needs to be both, spacious and comfortable. Natural and artificial lighting must be of very high standards if fatigue and eye strain are to be avoided for staff and users spending many hours in the library. The problems of furnishing reference libraries arise the main, out of the natural desire to keep as much of the stock possible readily accessible on the open shelves, while at the same time to provide as many reading places as possible in the space available. The two factors do not usually mix well, and if an effect overcrowding is thus produced, it is often not conducive to a relaxed atmosphere for study and research. It is better to consider comfort and convenience of the readers by making the provision of reader-places a higher priority, even if this means that only selection of the more heavily used materials can be displayed open-access, with the bulk of the stock being housed in storage, from which the staff must bring it out on request.

The Setup

The receipt and satisfactory handling of enquiries, both simple and complex, is the attractive, rewarding public face of reference library work. It can only be effective, however, when backed than orderly, smooth running routine. Much of reference library behind the scenes is hard and unremitting, by no means interesting and rewarding as the enquiry work at the public service counter, but absolutely essential to it.

The routine work involves the up-dating of loose-leaf reference services by the insertion of amendments as issued, checking receipts of periodicals and other subscription services and following up non-receipt of parts with the suppliers, collecting material before sending to the binders, cataloguing new acquisitions, maintaining current information files and, of course, the acquisition of new stock. Much of this work is little more than simple drudgery, but it is essential to the creation of an efficient library, and it is important that all staff appreciate how crucial it is that such work is carried out properly, and how damaging slip-shod work can be to the reputation of the library in the eyes of its users – if a mis-filed periodical part urgently needed can not be found for example.

Many of the routine tasks of the reference library are monotonous and, if left in the hands of one member of staff for too long, will result in poor-quality of work through sheer boredom and lack of concentration. Thus the accurate shelving of books and clearing of requisition-slips from stack-shelves must be meticulously maintained, despite the uninteresting nature of the work; equally, the supervision of the returned books point in the reading-room must not be allowed to become perfunctory. In the interests of variety of work and full staff training, many of the routine tasks should be regularly rotated amongst staff members. Some tasks should be regularly rotated amongst staff, a judicious mixture of work for each staff member, with everyone having definite responsibility for some function or functions, is essential. Staff members who know they have clear responsibility and are being relied upon, are much more likely to be careful and orderly in their work than staff who feel they have no particular responsibility or importance in the whole scheme.

Even the 'public face' of enquiry work must be backed up by a definite routine to ensure that all enquiries received are dealt with on time and to the limit of the competence of the whole staff. Enquiries are received in a number of ways – by direct application to the staff in person, by telephone, or by letter or telex. Many of the direct person to person enquiries can be dealt with on the spot as received, but for those more complex or time-consuming, and those received by letter, some kind of log or diary should be kept to ensure that all are dealt with properly. The most usual way of doing this is by entering details of all non-routine enquiries received in a desk-diary kept for that purpose, or on specially designed forms. It is necessary to make a regular review of all enquiries in progress at least once a day, with all new staff coming on duty (as meal-time or evening relief for example) being made aware of the nature of the work outstanding in case an enquirer returns to check progress on his enquiry. A staff conference on all enquiries in progress every morning is a good plan.This need not take long and need not be formal, but all staff members will have some experience to contribute to the solution of difficult enquiries, a staff conference has the additional benefit of developing the experience and skills of junior staff through the views of their seniors on the sources and methodology to be adopted.

Many libraries find it useful to keep a supply of specially designed enquiry forms to assist in the orderly development of a routine for dealing with complex enquiries. An enquiry form should contain spaces for the enquirer's name, address and telephone number, a detailed description of the information sought, the initials of the librarian receiving the enquiry, and spaces to note stages in the search—this can take the form of a checklist of major sources and procedures with a place for the librarian carrying out the particular stage to initial it on completion. This enables another member of staff taking up the task of dealing with a particular enquiry to see quickly the progress made. The form enables intelligent and constructive reports to be made to enquirers should they ask about progress, and also provides clues to the library staff about what to do to solve enquiries which are proving difficult. The forms can, of course, also become useful additions to a current information file maintained in the library, and aid in the solution of enquiries of a similar nature in future. A typical search-routine form might contain the following items:

1. Subject of enquiry and approximate library class number of that subject.
2. Name, address and telephone number of the enquirer.
3. Name of staff receiving the enquiry.
4. Mode of receipt of enquiry personal visit/ telephone/ telex/ letter.
5. Nature of information required and time available for search. (Whether detailed research involving recourse to other libraries, inter-libraries loan or photocopy with the payment of any necessary fees, whether a bibliography or list of further readings is required or whether

a collection of items is to be made for the enquirer to return to consult, a note of any constraints of time by which the enquiry must be dealt with).

6. Level of search required advanced/ research/ student/ elementary /For a child aged.

7. Specific resources checked.

   (a) Library catalogue checked and library shelves searched;

   (b) General reference works checked—dictionaries, encyclopedias etc.

   (c) Bibliographies checked; periodicals indexes/ abstracts and specific titles checked; other libraries/ subject contacts checked inter-library loans.

The basic structure of a detailed search for specific information or literature is always the same. Having clarified the enquirer's needs as closely as possible, and determined the constraints of time and elaboration of the search, the first task is to explore the library's own resources to the full. The second is to check other libraries or specialist organisations and employ inter-library loan schemes. In order to obtain material through inter-loan schemes or by photocopying, precise bibliographic information must be supplied. It is for this reason that the smaller reference library should always place a high priority upon the building-up of bibliographic resources. The development of the British Library Lending Division has ensured that even the smaller libraries have access to specialised resources swiftly and cheaply, but accurate and detailed bibliographic information is an essential pre-requisite to a BLLD loan request.

As indicated above, most enquiries received will be solved using the library's own resources. It is also the case that most enquiries are for specific, short answers, using a relatively small proportion of the total reference library stock-directories, dictionaries, bibliographies, encyclopedias and other reference compendia such as Whitaker's almanack, Statesman's yearbook, Keesings contemporary archives and The Guinness book of records. It is usual to group such 'quick reference' material close to the entrance to the library and adjacent to the main enquiry point. This gives the staff quick access to heavily used material—to answer urgent telephone enquiries, for example. It also encourages users to help themselves rather than wait for library staff to attend to them, but at the same time enables the staff to identify enquirers who are obviously floundering and need assistance. The provision of a quick reference collection reduces disturbance of long-stay users in the body of the library through-constant traffic to and from heavily used items shelved in the main sequence.

The Origin : One of the most rewarding and potentially most valuable of special subject collections in reference library work is local history. The challenges in this field is that much of the material must be collected together piece by piece by the library staff through direct requests to individuals, societies and organisations in the area. Very few of the resources for local history will be obtained by the normal and more passive processes of library acquisition, such as purchase from booksellers and library suppliers. Whilst really effective service depends upon a large collection of material built up over a period of years, good work can be done with a new collection which has only just begun. It is, in fact, one of the primary duties of any public library to maintain a local history collection. It is usually the first, sometimes the only, special subject collection in all public libraries.

Many of the outstanding local history collections are based upon, or significantly enriched by, rquests or special purchases of materials gathered together by local antiquaries. Private collections of local materials are still to be found, though in the UK the late eighteenth and nineteenth centuries were the heyday of persons with the means and the leisure to build up scholarly collections. Although the local history librarian must always be vigilant and take any opportunity offered to enrich his collections by the acquisition of private papers, they occur only very infrequently. It is likely, of course, that the local history librarian will know of the existence of most private local collections of any consequence, not least because their owners will usually be regulars in the local history library. The librarian must sometimes undertake the delicate task of persuading the executors of an estate that a collection should not be dispersed or destroyed.

The local history librarian cannot rely upon the normal published schemes of library classification. The schedules of the traditional schemes are not detailed enough to be useful in the local context, and special local schemes must usually be developed, either to amplify the general schemes (which usually leave space for this to be done), or to produce a completely new approach.

Of the various materials of local history, one of the most important is local newspapers. Complete files of all local newspapers should be maintained either in the original or on microfilm. It is best to purchase extra copies of newspapers to be kept specifically for storage, rather than to rely upon the copies bought for public display subsequently being fit for binding. If it is possible, the indexing of each issue of a local newspaper as it appears is a valuable aid, but a time consuming one only to be contemplated if the staff resources are available. A press-cuttings, file built up by using redundant public display copies when their currency expires is an alternative. Press-cuttings, small pamphlets and other small ephemeral items of local interest can be housed in a vertical file in folders arranged alphabetically by subject or in a classified sequence if a scheme has been devised for local use.

Amongst the more significant types of material to be obtained for the local history library copies of any published local histories are obviously important. Many local history libraries make a practice of acquiring copies of any type of published work by authors living locally or born in the vicinity. Files of periodicals of local interest must always be maintained, and the whole library staff, not only the local history library staff, must be vigilant in non-local periodicals and books are passed over to the library for permanent preservation.

The Guildhall Library, London, is especially notable for the compilation of specialised indexes, but that dealing with London itself is of unusual interest in the wide variety of sources which are regularly scanned and for the length of time over which this careful work has been continued.

Materials published by local industrial and commercial companies, societies, clubs, churches, local government units etc., are vital acquisitions, as are playbills, posters, programmes of local dramatic societies, theatres and cinemas. Maps of the area, both current and historical and other photographic and illustrative material, should be obtained and it is often possible to persuade local societies and clubs to deposit their archives in the library on permanent loan.

The most exciting prospect of all in local history work is actually creating archival material. In this context, the commissioning of a local photographic society to undertake a complete photographic record of all of the streets in a town or city, with additional photographs of any especially notable buildings, is often practiced. Tape-recordings of local people talking about their life and work, or about their memories of the town or its folk-lore and local customs, can provide amplification or even correction of printed sources. By putting up displays of old photographs from the local history collection in library entrance halls, or lending departments and branch libraries, and inviting users to recognise them and, where appropriate, offer comments on them, additional useful data can be derived, and also effective publicity for the local history library obtained.

Local history librarianship is one of the most satisfying and time consuming of all library tasks. It has the virtue of being as rewarding and as appreciated in the small library as in the large. Relying, as it does, upon energy, enthusiasm and imagination more than financial power, it brings high-quality, specialised library service within reach of every professional librarian, no matter how small his library.

The Organisation : The growing complexity of society and the manifold regulations legislative measures and social-welfare provisions, both official and voluntary which it spawns pose special problems to the community. In an advanced society there are always more facilities available for the support and succor of members of the community with difficulties—physical, financial, emotional or legal—than is readily appreciated.

A specific form reference service conferring great benefit upon a local community is one in which an attempt is made to gather together and organize all sources of information of this type. It is a natural development of the role of the reference library, as can be demonstrated by the frequency with which citizens advice bureau and consumer affairs centers have been sited on public library premises in the UK. Whether the activities of the library in community affairs should go so far as the active undertaking of specific causes on behalf of enquiries rather than simply providing them with information is an open question. Certainly the attitude displayed by some United States community affairs libraries activities almost akin to 'campaign journalism' may leave the conservative minded British librarian feeling uneasy. Many of these campaigns are directed against local authorities, and there is , paradox where libraries which are supported by local authorities are asked to provide facilities for mounting campaigns, social and political, in effect against themselves.

It is difficult to be specific about the kinds of information provision which fall within the category of community information but a good deal of it is the type which all reference libraries ought to provide and often do. Perhaps the principal factor distinguishing community information from formal reference work is that it usually must be done outside the confines of the reference library itself. The reference library offering a community information service needs to take the service to its potential users in lending libraries and branch libraries and, because many of the most likely beneficiaries of the service will not be members of the public library at all, to place where such 'people meet, for example health centers, community centers, old people's clubs, etc.

The reference library may, indeed, find it worthwhile to hold briefing sessions for those people likely to come into contact with persons requiring advice on social, emotional and other problems-social workers, housing officers, councillors, district nurses, voluntary charitable workers etc.. Among the types of community information provision, which might be attempted under this heading, are problems of consumer protection and advice, details of entitlements under various schemes for the alleviation of financial hardship-free milk, school meals, rate and tax relief, family income supplements – social problems such as the addresses and functions of discharged prisoners-aid societies, and many others.

Community information work is not easy. It requires a great deal more than the largely passive provision of reference service. It needs to be 'pushed', and the approaches and attitudes of the staff must be carefully adjusted. In the nature of things, the type of people most likely to benefit from a good community inforination service are those who are likely also to be suspicious of patronage and with unhappy experiences of officialdom and bureaucracy. There is the additional problem of controlling the amount of assistance to be given, and resisting the temptation to become too involved in individual cases.

Community information work is presently more highly developed in the United States than in the UK, and E.D. Walley's Developments in community information services in public libraries in the United States: a state-of-the-art report and literature guide, BLRD report No. 5276, Leeds Polytechnic Department of Librarianship, 1976, is an account of the progress made and problems encountered there, compiled as a result of an extended tour under the auspices of the British Library in 1975.

Rare Books: *Manuscripts and Archives* : It is a serious temptation to the ambitious reference librarian to accept any valuable, unusual or unique material when offered it, and to seek to build up such collections for their publicity and display value alone. Unless the library is adequately equipped and the library staff suitably qualified, it is a temptation which ought to be resisted, and would-be donors of valuable materials should be referred to libraries which have the necessary facilities for housing and creatively employing the materials. There is a tendency to treat fine bindings, rare books and unique archival material which happens to come in the way of library unused to dealing with them as curiosities. If such materials are to be acquired, then, no less than any other material, a purpose should be served by the acquisition, and should be more than simply providing objects for display. If the smaller library wishes to mount displays of fine books, it would be better to rely upon the loan of special exhibition-collections from the national or other major libraries, from the National Book League, or outside of the UK, from agencies such as the British Council. The situation to be avoided is one in which an individual library with no special facilities or expertise acquires a few rare books, perhaps by donation, and keeps them in inappropriate conditions without any chance of ever building up a genuinely important collection in its own right. It could be that the retention of a few items hampers the chances of rich, specialist, libraries completing set.., or amplifying special collections with additional material in a way which would improve them significantly, whilst ensuring that the books were well looked after.

Government and Official Publications : Public reference libraries often voluntarily accept, or are specifically given, responsibility for acting as depositories and information centers for official publications of various sorts. In some countries the major public reference libraries have the privilege of receiving free copies of all new governmental publications issued. In other government publications are offered to the public libraries for sale at substantial discounts on normal purchase prices. Various international organisations have designated a number of libraries in any given country as depositories for their publications. Other categories of officially inspited government or international organisation publishing which some kind of special terms for library acquisition include patent specifications, or abridgements of patents, standard specifications, and various kinds of map services.

A large reference library receiving all of most of the categories of material mentioned above is faced with severe organisational problems. The quantities of material involved will be enormous and much of it flimsy and unsubstantial in format. It is first necessary to ensure that the library has, indeed, received all items to which it is entitled, and then to effect their arrangement in some form which enables them to be efficiently retrieved for use. The major official series all have a bibliographical apparatus of some sort. It is useful to check the receipt of material against such lists. This is not an easy or especially pleasant task in the case of the more prolific organisations, and may, indeed, be impracticable. In such instances particularly material received free—it may be dispensed with, but wherever possible, careful checking of receipts will avoid later difficulty when trying to trace material, requested. The effective arrangement of material presents many problems. Ideally, full classification and cataloguing of all material received, and its interfiling by subject with the rest of the library stock, would be needed to ensure that official publications were mobilised for effective use. In practice, the magnitude of such a task, given the large number of items involved and their (frequent) complexity, rules such a task out of the bounds of possibility. The usual practice, therefore, is to arrange this material on the shelves in the order in which it is arranged in the relevant bibliographic apparatus, or, in applicable cases, by the serial number of any classification scheme used by the publishers (for example, patents abridgements). The practice often involves filing material into pamphlet boxes. The advantage of this process is that the material is arranged in the order in which may enquirers will solicit it: 'Do you have patent specification number IN 09317', or 'Can you give me a copy of the latest Department of Education and Science Circular?'.

The disadvantages are considerable, however, the material can only be called for effectively if the enquirer and the librarian are aware that the needed document is an official publication separately housed. This is not always obvious, since many official publications are not readily recognisable as such without a full bibliographic citation. Arrangement by form also makes difficult the creative use of library stock for enquiry work and subject searches. Not only is it fatally easy in the stress of a difficult piece of enquiry work to forget the existence of separate sequences, but the subject-indexing of many of the bibliographies of official publications leaves a great deal to be desired. In an attempt to compromise, many librarians regularly review the intake of official publications into their libraries, removing the more significant items for conventional cataloguing into the main library stock-a compromise indeed, but a frequently adopted one of some value.

Priced Service

Only in the largest public libraries are business libraries (or commercial libraries, as they are often rather confusingly called) a separate service. In other libraries, a combined commercial and technical department is often provided. After local history, the business library facilities probably represent the most effective and necessary specialised service a public library can give.

Most industrial and commercial companies can, through their own libraries, and those of local academic institutions and various research and professional associations, provide for much of their own scientific and technical requirements. On matters of management, marketing, distribution, labour relations, or finance, however, the range of business information required will be much more extensive and expensive than the scientific information requirements, and also much less explicit. Given that the individual company would usually find it too expensive to maintain adequate resources of business information, it follows that this area of activity is an important one for the public reference library to supply, relying not only on a multiplicity of published sources, but also on numerous 'home-made' indexes of local information.

Perhaps the most heavily-used materials in the business library are directories of trades, occupational and telephone directories. They are only of real value when they are absolutely up-to-date. Individual items are often very expensive to buy and can only be justified as regular new-edition purchases if they are well used. This is the principal problem an individual industrial company has in the purchase of this type of material. The need for a particular directory may occur once or twice in any particular year. With, as an example, the Kompass directory for Belgium priced at some pound 30 per annual issue, it can be seen that the cost of these consultations is heavy. The economic justification for the purchase of expensive directories by the business library is that the cost of individual consultations will be much lower because of the large number of firms and individuals will access to them. The justification for the public library providing an information service for the business community is that it benefits the local community to encourage the growth of business activity through the provision of effective information services.

Technical Aspects

The first distinct scientific and technical library service in a British public library was opened at Coventry in 1918, though a joint commercial and technical library had been started in Leeds in the previous year.

Scientific and technical information-provision is not to be undertaken lightly by the public librarian. The unequivocal justification for the public library to attempt this service in depth is now less obvious than it once was. As originally envisaged, the provision of scientific and technical information services by the public libraries was designed to promote the improved awareness of the importance of the technical education of both the public at large and the specialists within it. The industrial impetus provided by the 1914-1918 War-the first 'technology based' war in many ways-revealed the lack of technical sophistication and the paucity of formal education machinery for developing it. One response, which had begun to appear in the late nineteenth century but was accelerated after 1914, was the growth of public technical libraries offering facilities for students, process-workers and other employees of local firms to broaden their knowledge of the applications of their daily work.

Technical library provision is expensive. A major part of available funds is devoured by recurring subscriptions to periodicals, abstracting and indexing services, and the upkeep of standing files of standards specifications and patents. The major problem in evolving a philosophy for public library technical provision is to identify the market for it. An attempt to provide a comprehensive technical collection at the level necessary for fundamental research is doomed to failure-the extent and expense of the materials necessary within even a small number of disciplines ensures that, as also the impossibility of employing the necessary subject-specialist librarians. To provide a service related to the industrial background of the firms represented in a particular locality is a more promising possibility on the face of it. Suppose, however, that much of that industry has adequate special library provision of its own covering the particular technologies it uses. What then is the possible role of the public technical library? Technical colleges and universities also generally make their library and research collections readily available to industrial users.

A public library, large enough to offer technical library service, will almost certainly be situated in a town or city possessing a university, a polytechnic, or both. In these circumstances there is high risk of substantial duplication of periodicals, abstracts and indexes. To take one instance, the 1996 subscription price of Chemical abstracts is about $20000; it is difficult to believe that more than one copy of such a work can fully earn its keep in any locality, or that the public library's copy would be the most used. There is a danger that public library technical departments may be maintained as academically-biased collections, especially of periodicals, against any evidence of need for this role.

This does, perhaps, indicate a role for the public library technical department as a subsidiary service supplementing and complementing other available resources. In countries or areas in which technical information provision is poor, the public technical library might, indeed, attempt to take a lead, as it did most effectively in the inter-war years. Where, however, other library services to industry are well developed, the public library might instead offer a clearing-house facility for enquiries, and a coordinating role in cooperative acquisition and stock retention schemes.

Small Ventures

Reference library work is the most exciting and challenging of all library service, and the provision of reference service in the smaller public library with limited resources can, to people of the right temperament, be the ultimate in challenge and excitement. Contemplation of the range of services and the resources necessary to provide them offered by the large reference and academic libraries could be depressing to staff in less well-endowed libraries. It ought not to be so. The fact is that in many ways the ability of the major libraries to provide an intensive service depends upon the effectiveness of the support they are given by the smaller ones; if all enquiries even the most trivial and elementary, were channeled to the major libraries, they would be swamped and, thereby, less effective on all aspects of their work. The establishment of 'quick reference' areas in large libraries is an acknowledgment of this.

The well organized small reference library has a valuable function as an outer defense to the major libraries in dealing with routine enquiries, and, most importantly, in refining difficult enquiries before referring them to the major libraries. There is a great deal of satisfaction to be derived from this work, through the ingenious and economic deployment of limited resources, the key to which lies in the establishment and maintenance of priorities and objectives. A mistake often made is to try to become a large reference library without having the resources to support ambitious attempts at specialised service. It is better for the smaller library to limit its coverage of material but to ensure that which it has kept up-todate. In circumstances like these, the quality of the service which can be given by enthusiastic staff who know that their stock in timely can offset at least some of the disadvantages of limited resources. No library is too small to possess and exploit usefully a reference corner.

Fourteen

Process of Cataloguing

A catalogue is a list of and index to a collection of books and/ or other materials. It enables the user to discover:

What material is present in the collection and where this material may be found.

The 'collection' may relate to one or a number of libraries or information service points. In the fitter case, the catalogue is termed a union catalogue.

The catalogue has much in common with the bibliography, which is also a list of books and/or other material. The same principles are applied to their compilation and they are used interchangeably. For example, the NECRT General catalogue of printed books or the National Book Trust catalogues also act as important bibliographies. The pure bibliography is not an index to a specific collection but simply a list of books and/or other materials within some restricted field, since it would clearly be impossible to list all materials from all countries and all periods on all subjects.

This entry could also be used, without amendment, in a bibliography although there might not be any need to include the classification number and, on the other hand, further detail such as the price of the item might be required. Nevertheless the close relationship between the entry as used in a catalogue and the entry as used in a bibliography is obvious.

The art of cataloguing relates to both catalogues and bibliographies. It is the art of describing and listing material in such a way as to make it as easy as possible to discover the nature and extent of what is available and, if appropriate, where this material may be located or obtained.

Contemporary society has experienced an extraordinary explosion in knowledge; this has resulted in a corresponding increase in the publication of books and other materials which act as information carriers. In general terms, without the aid of technology it is now impractical, if not impossible, to ascertain what material exists and where it may be obtained.

The Two Methods

The cataloguing process basically consists of two operations: first, the creation of the appropriate entry relating to a particular item and, second the subsequent manipulation of this and other entries to form the actual catalogue.

The computer cannot replace the first of these, that intellectual element which only a human being can, at present, supply. The creation of a catalogue entry involves the answering of questions such as: What is the title of the item? Which person or body is responsible for its content? Who published it? When by a machine, which could not, for instance, distinguish between an author, e.g. Charles Dickens, and a title, e.g. David Copperfield.

However, the computer is capable of performing the various clerical functions involved in the manipulation of entries. For example, the computer can quickly sort catalogue entries into any desired order, or search for entries which conform to a particular search profile. And the search facility that can be provided is a much more powerful one than would be possible in a manual index.

Because the computer can rearrange entries into any desired order, it may be used as a means of producing a catalogue or bibliography in 'hard' copy, i.e. 'printed' on to paper or film. However, it is becoming far more common to use 'on-line' access, i.e. the catalogue entries are stored within the machine to use 'on-line' access, i.e. that catalogue entries are stored within the machine and searched for and displayed as necessitated by the requirements of a user.

Definition by Cutter: Cutter defined the functions of a library catalogue more than 100 years ago; he said that it should:

1. Enable a person to find as book of which either: the title is known the subject.

2. Show what the library has, by a given subject in a given kind of literature.

3. Assist in the choice of a book: as to its edition as to its character (literary or topical).

These objectives still hold good today, but the word 'book' should be replaced by 'item' or 'document' and the word 'author' should be replaced by 'responsible person or body'. This is because librarians are now concerned with far more than the printed word, e.g. audio and video recordings, micrograms, computer files, etc.

Various Provisions

Further, it should be noted that today's computerized catalogues and bibliographies can offer a far more flexible search facility than Cutter could ever have envisaged. For example, the user may need to know only part of an author, or part of a title, in order to find a particular entry.

Cataloguing must not be considered a self-contained unit; the relationship with bibliographies has already been stressed for example. There are also obvious links between cataloguing and classification; the same mental process must take place when deciding on the subject of an item, whether this is described in alphabetical terms or by a classification number. In addition, the catalogue can form the basis of an integrated system with ordering, acquisition and circulation control modules. Indeed, when the computerization of the cataloguing process is being planned, it should not be considered an isolation but as part of a larger entity.

Not everyone regards the catalogue as an essential tool. D.J. Urquhart showed, for instance, how effectively the National Lending Library for Science and Technology (now the British Library Document Supply Centre) in its early days could be administered without catalogue. It is seen by some people as a sacred cow and, in the 1960s, Grose and Line referred to it as a white elephant.

Certainly there are many more keys to unlock the doors of knowledge in the form of bibliographies, indexes and databases, and library users can find out very quickly via a computer terminal what is available, in global terms, in any subject field. But what they so often want to know is whether a particular item is available in their particular library, whether it be public, academic or special. Most readers want subject arrangement in the library, so that they can browse and this means that a catalogue is desirable to show not only what is available but also where it is shelved. The descriptive part of the catalogue entry will help the user to decide whether an item not immediately available is likely to be relevant.

There are other reasons for maintaining a library catalogue. It can provide analytical entries for parts of an item and it can record all items in a library's stock, acting as a valuable supplement to published bibliographic tools. At present, bibliographical control of English and American books and periodical article is excellent but this is by no means true of, for instance, report literature, semipublished material and the many forms of non-book media.

Standardization and the road to AACR 2 : The requirement of cooperative and centralized systems make the acceptance of standards of vital importance. Such standardization might relate to the classification scheme used to arrange the stock of a library, to the alphabetical subject indexing methodology, or to the content and arrangement of the catalogue entry. It is the latter with which this chapter is primarily concerned.

The manner in which a catalogue entry is organized with regard to the amount of detail to be included will depend upon the requirements of the particular cataloguing agency.

Despite differences in the amount of detail required, it is clearly advantageous for various cataloguing agencies to agree to work to the one standard, i.e., a set of rules, to be used by all. The standard would prescribe how the content of the entry was to be organized and how the headings, or access points, under which an item was to be entered should be selected and presented. Whilst entries could be simple, because all elements advocated be compatible with those containing more detail because both had been produced using the same standard.

In USA : In the United States, standardization of author-title cataloguing has been a way of life in libraries, especially since 1901 when the Library of Congress took over the printed catalogue card service begun by the Library Bureau in 1893.

In Britain : In Britain, progress towards standardization was much slower perhaps due to the natural independence of British librarians, or perhaps because Britain's National Library did not attempt to take a central role in British librarianship until the 1970s, or possibly simply because no library was willing to accept the Anglo-American code of 1908 without considerable amendment. Even when the British national bibliography began to be published in 1950, using a much amended version of the 1908 code as the basis of its cataloguing, many libraries preferred to continue their own cataloguing practices.

When BNB started to issue printed catalogue cards in 1956 its cataloguing achieved greater acceptance, but there were still libraries which resisted, partly because they had reservation about the BNB's use of the Dewey decimal classification. What such libraries fail to appreciate is that standardization does not mean accepting without question all of the data provided by a central cataloguing agency; rather it means using common practices as far as possible and allowing the agency to do work which cannot be done better locally.

Even though Americans accepted AA 1908 and later the ALA revisions of 1941 and 1949, many of them were not happy with these rules. Their dissatisfaction was voiced by Andrew Osborn on 1941 and, most notably, by Seymour Lubetzky in 1953. Lubetzky's Cataloguing rules and principles of that year came out strongly against the codification of catalogue rules via the elaborate and complex enumeration of innumerable 'cases' and pointed the way towards the possible formulation of a less complex set of rules based encyclopedia, for example, would not be regarded as a particular 'case' or type of publication, but would be treated in a similar manner to all other works, i.e. according to the particular 'conditions' of authorship of responsibility pertaining to it.

Lubetzky's ideas were widely welcomed and helped pave the way for the International Conference on Cataloguing Principles held in Paris in 1961. A draft statement of principles based upon Lubetzky's Code of Cataloguing rules: author and title entry; an unfinished draft (ALA 1960) was submitted to this conference for discussion along with working papers on the various problems of rules prepared by delegates. A final version of the 'Statement of principles' was adopted and participants agreed to work in their separate countries revised rules which would be in agreement with these accepted principles.

The Anglo-American cataloguing rules of 1967 (AACR 1) was one of several codes reflecting the "Paris Principles'; though, unfortunately, it had to be published in two texts (British and North American) because there was not complete unanimity between the two countries' committees, particularly in the areas of description sand corporate headings.

AACR 1 was immediately accepted as a standard by the BNB and by several British libraries, but certainly not by all of them. In the United States its complete acceptance was hampered by the fact that the Library of Congress, one of the bodies responsible for the rules, adopted a superimposition or 'no conflict' policy-headings from AACR 1 were accepted only if they did not conflict with headings already in the catalogue.

Automated Cataloguing

The development of automated cataloguing methods, particularly the MARC (Machine-Readable Cataloguing) Project made the acceptance of an international standard more urgent, but already AACR 1 was being overtaken by events. Apart from the considerable influence of the computer, there were three factors which were of particular significance.

First, there were the rules being produced by a number of different countries throughout the world. Although these were also based upon the Paris Principles, there were some differences of opinion. European libraries, for instance, had never been happy with editors and compilers of collections being given the status of authors, preferring to enter collections under title, and so this rule was revised by the British and American in the interests of international cooperation. Corporate responsibility was another problematic area where unanimity was difficult to achieve.

Second, there were the rules developed specifically for non-book materials, an area which was undergoing rapid expansion and for which AACR 1 was not considered satisfactory. In Britain there was Non-book materials cataloguing rules, produced by the Library Association's Media Cataloguing Rules Committee, published by the National Council for Educational Technology in 1973, and known as LANCET (the initials of its two sponsoring organizations); in Canada there was Non-book materials: the organization of integrated collections by Jean Riddle Welhs, Shirley Lewis, and Janet Macdonald, published by the Canadian Library Association in 1973; and in the United States there was Standards for cataloguing nonprint materials—an interpretation and practical application by Alma Tillin and William J. Quinly, the fourth edition of which was published by the Association for Edicatopma; Communications and Technology (Washington) in 1976.

Third, there was the continuous work being undertaken by the International Federation of Library Associations (now the International Federation of Library Associations and Institutions), a Working Group on the co-ordination of Cataloguing Principles was set up by IFLA as early as 1954 and in 1957 the IFLA General Council adopted a proposal to hold a world-wide conference on basic cataloguing principles. The International Conference on Cataloguing Principles of 1961 was thus IFLA inspired, the necessary financial assistance being forthcoming from the Council on Library Resources in America. The ICCP achieved international agreement on the principles to be adopted for choice of headings but for the international exchange of bibliographic information, whether in written or machine-readable form, it is obviously also necessary to have a generally accepted standard which lists the elements to be included in the descriptive part of an entry the order in which the elements are to be cited the punctuation which is to be used to separate the elements.

An IFLA International Meeting of Cataloguing Experts in Copenhagen in 1969 set up a Working Party to study the possibilities for an International Standard Bibliographic Description for monographs. Such a standard ISBD (M), was subsequently drawn up and was officially adopted by the IFLA Committee on Cataloguing at its meeting in Liverpool in 1971. The publication of this standard necessitated the amendment of the relevant sections AACR 1, in order to achieve conformity. These amendments included the introduction of a new area to accommodate the recently introduced International Standard Book Number (ISBN) as a unique identifier. Later, the International Standard, Serial Number fISSN) also had to be catered for ISBD (M) was to be followed by similar standards for other } media such as ISBD (S) for serials and ISBD (NBM) for non-book materials. Almost inevitably, because a different committee was responsible for each standard, certain discrepancies became apparent and, to counteract this, a 'general' framework for description was produced, ISBD (G).

The above brief historical account clearly illustrates that there was a strong case for revision of AACR 1. There was a need to incorporate the ISBD (G) framework and to take account of other international developments. There was also the very important need for one unified Anglo-American text, which would incorporate all amendments issued since 1967. In addition, there was the need to consider other proposals for changes and the effects of library automation. The latter was particularly difficult because these effects are on-going and have yet to be completely assessed and understood.

The Council on Library Resources agreed to fund the revision, with certain conditions, the major one being that royalties from sale should be placed in a common fund for future activities associated with AACR. A Joint Steering Committee for AACR meeting in 1974 confirmed the participation of five bodies as 'authors' (ALA, LC, LA, BL, and the Canadian Committee on Cataloguing). It was agreed to set up national committees to consider issues and proposals for revision. The new rules, the results of collaboration between the national libraries and professional associations of three countries, were published in 1978. The main objectives were to a great extent achieved and not the least part of this remarkable achievement was the fact that any institution, organization or individual with a point of view was given ample opportunity to express it during the process of revision.

Not Very Popular : The publication of AACR 2 was not welcomed by all librarians but, as Peter Lewis, later Director-General of the British Library Bibliographic Services Division, and former Chairman of the Joint Steering Committee for AACR, stated: 'for every powerful voice speaking against AACR 2, there is an equally powerful one calling for full implementation without delay'.

The major criticisms leveled against AACR 2 are that with the fast developing state of automation it is irrelevant, and its implementation increases library costs without increasing benefits.

Despite objections, four national libraries (the British Library, the Library of Congress, the National Library of Australia and the National Library of Canada) adopted AACR 2 from January 1981. Initially, the Library of Congress decided to retain certain pre-AACR headings for economic reasons but it reconsidered its position and decided to abandon this 'compatible headings' policy from 1982. Thus all of the national libraries were then agreed that the adoption of the rules, as they stood, would bring long-term cost and user benefits.

Whether an, individual library decides to use AACR 2 will depend upon factors such as the use made of centralized services and the staff support available to amend existing catalogues. Cataloguing agencies which have adopted AACR 2 are using what is, in effect, an international standard.

Work on the rules did not cease with the publication of AACR 2 in 1978, indeed, rather was the reverse the case in that a whole series of related activities was generated. These activities included .. the implementation of training programmes, and the production of adoption aids, interpretative manuals, illustrative examples and translations. AACR 2 has spread its influence into a number of Non-English-speaking countries, and translations have been made into languages such as Arabic, Finnish, French, Japan see, Norwegian, Portuguese, and Spanish.

In 1981 the first edition of Gorman's 'The concise AACR 2', a rewritten and simplified version of the rules, was published. This was intended to provide a readily comprehensible summary of AACR 2 practice for librarians and cataloguers in a number of different situations, such as librarianship students, persons working in small libraries, especially 'one-person' libraries, and cataloguers working in a non-English-language environment.

AACR 2 has also encouraged research. For example, cataloguing rules for choice of access points involve conditional decisions; i.e. if a certain condition applies then take a particular decision. A computerized expert system functions in a similar way using a knowledge base expressed as a set of rules. Because of this similarity, several researchers have investigated the feasibility of creating an expert system for cataloguing.

The international Joint Steering Committee for Recession of AACR continued to meet regularly, as did the various national committees, and in 1981 it was agreed to add an Australian representative to JSC. The revision process also continued and three sets of revisions were prepared and published in 1982, 1984 and 1986. Many of these revisions have formed part of a general' tidying-up' and correction process, whilst others have been of a more significant nature.

A major decision was taken by the Joint Steering Committee in 1985, when it was resolved to recommend that a consolidated was to incorporate all rule revisions passed, and topographical errors found, to that date. If possible, it was also intended to include revised rules for computer files, taking note of work that had already been done in this area such as that by Templeton and by Dodd, and for recently introduced media such as compact discs. This consolidation, including a new chapter for computer files and revised rules for recent media was published as Anglo-American cataloguing rules Second edition 1988 revision.

A survey of AACR 2 users taken in 1985 revealed that 98% favoured a loose-leaf format, and the new revision is available in three versions: soft back, hardback and loose-leaf. A new version of the concise AACR 2 has also been published. The period in which AACR 2 has developed has been a time when applications of the computer in cataloguing have also been developing at a tremendous rate. Therefore there are bound to be questions posed by library automation which have not been answered by the rules, even though some new concepts have sprung from, or been precipitated by, advances in automation. Forman, the editor of AACR 2, considers that the fact that AACR 2 has not been able to take I; library automation fully into account is not really the fault of those responsible for AACR but rather is due to the fact that the effect of library automation on catalogues has yet to be completely assessed and understood.

For these reasons, Forman predicts that there will never be an AACR 3 but a new type of code which will deal with the creation of machine-readable records for use in national and international networks. However, in the meantime, revisions to AACR 2 will continue to be made; cataloguing cannot stand still, and the fact that the new revision is available in loose-leaf format reinforce this point.

Committee's Role : An ISBD Review Committee was formed by IFLA in 1981 to implement a five-year review of the ISBDs for monographs, serials, cartographic materials and non-book materials, ISBD (M), ISBD (S), ISBD (CM) and ISBD (NBM), with the intention of publishing revisions in 1987. The Joint Steering Committee for AACR became concerned that ISBD(G), for which, as previously noted, the Joint Steering Committee was jointly responsible, might be effected by this review. Draft texts were circulated for comment in 1983-4; JSC AACR was one of the recipients of these drafts and was therefore given the opportunity to contribute to the review. Special attention has also been given to computer files; a Working Group net for the first time in 1986 and the final version of ISBD (CF) was published in 1990. The influence of AACR can be plainly seen in the latter publication with the ISBD adopting the AACR solution for differentiating between the type of file and physical carrier. A revised draft of the ISBD for rare, antiquarian books, ISBD(A), was circulated for study by appropriate persons in 1988.

The Main-entry Principle: Although rules for standardizing a bibliographic description (as the ISBDs and AACR2) and for selecting and formulating access points (as ARCS 2) may be necessary, one other aspect of AACR 2 is completely redundant in the machine-readable context, namely the concept of main entry. AACR 2 considers 'the concept of main entry to be useful in assigning uniform title and in promoting the standardization of bibliographic citation'. Some cataloguers defend AACR 2 on the ground that, although a number of on-line catalogues have appeared, the majority of present catalogues are still card catalogues. Other cataloguers would take issue with this defense. In Japan, for instance, cataloguers used codes based upon the main entry principle under the influence of AACR 2 and the Paris Principles until 1977, when a new code of Nippon cataloguing rules (NCR) was compiled. These rules abandon main entry not only because of progress in automation but also because of progress in automation but also because, in non-automated systems, it is seen to be less useful than the unit entry, which is now easy to produce and which ensures that each entry in the catalogue has an equal value.

The Japanese rules also differ from AACR 2 in another respect is that an attempt is made to define an item or unit more clearly. It is claimed that this leads to reader consistency where the cataloguing of multivolume sets and multipart items are concerned.

The Suggestions : AACR 2 reverses the pattern of all previous codes of cataloguing rules by placing the rules for description before the rules for choice of headings, because it is believed that this is the pattern followed in most libraries and bibliographic agencies. It also accepts the desirably of integrating bibliographic records of books and other kinds of materials.

Description: ACR 2 Part One-Description-is based upon the framework of ISBD(G). It begins with a general chapter containing rules which apply to all library materials. Each of the succeeding chapters in Part One, except for chapter 13, is concerned with more detailed rules for specific media, e.g. : chapter 2 Printed monographs; chapter 5 Music; chapter 6 Sound recordings; chapter 9 Computer files; chapter 12 serials. More than one chapter, apart from the general chapter, may need to be consulted; a serial, for instance, may also be sound recording. When this sort of situation occurs, AACR 2 states that the description of an item should be based in the first instance on the chapter dealing with the class of materials to which the item belongs. For example, a printed monograph in microform should be described as a microform.

The cataloguer brought up on earlier codes, which were concerned almost exclusively with printed material, must now, therefode, become familiar with some new terminology: public ation, distribution, etc., area' instead of 'imprint', 'Physical description area' instead of 'collation'; and terms such as 'statement of responsibility', other 'title information' and 'statement of extent'. These new terms are largely a reflection of the integrated nature of the rules: 'statement of responsibility' includes the author of a book and the creator of a work of art; statement of responsibility includes the author of a book and the creator of a work of art; 'statement of extent' includes the pagination of a printed monograph or the playing time of a sound recording.

It is not necessary for all of the areas to be present in every case. An item may not, for instance, be influded in a series, or have a standard number. Similarly a note may not always be required. One area, the 'material specific details' are, in fact, used only for maps, music computer files and serials.

The number given on the right is the relevant rule number for that particular area. These numbers are used logically and mnemonically so that rule 1.1 will deal with the recording of the title in general terms, rule 2.1 will deal more specifically with the recording of the title of a printed monograph, rule 6.1 with the recording of the title of a sound recording, and so on.

Each area may be further divided into constituent elements, for example the 'publication, distribution, etc;. area could include such elements as the place of publication, distribution, publisher and date. These elements are separated by a prescribed punctuation.

Cataloguing Management : The quality of good management lies in the application of the principles in such a way as to provide the most effective catalogue for a library and its users. Correct decisions must be made on such matters as the fullness of cataloguing required; whether to use a conventional classified or alphabetical subject catalogue required; whether to use a conventional classified or alphabetical subject catalogue or some other system; the method to be used for establishing subject headings or subject index entries; what filing system to use; policy with regard to analysis and annotation; the physical form of catalogue; and the extent to which CIP (Cataloguing-in-publication) information, centralized services and or the computer are used.

With regard to centralized services, writers such as Foster maintain that to process books efficiently, every library, large and small, must have a good portion of its cataloguing performed by an outside source. If a centralized service is utilized, some decisions may, of course, be taken out of the individual cataloguing agency's hands.

Cataloguing needs may vary, not only in different kinds of library but also within the same library system. In some special libraries the major demands may be for current subject information and more use may be made of a subject-based retrieval system than of an author catalogue constructed according to AACR 2. In others, such as the library of a professional organization sending many items on postal loan, there may be a strong case for detailed cataloguing may vary according to the kind of material, some audio-visual materials may lack 'brows ability' and so be given more detailed cataloguing than books, and books which are on the open shelves may be catalogued less fully than those which are not.

Whatever the kind of library, there are certain management techniques which can be applied to the cataloguing process. There is a bewildering number of techniques, 'more than 250 of them being described in Finch's excellent of guide', but it must be remembered that they are only a means to an end-aids to decision-making or problem-solving. Just as cataloguers should not become so immersed in their cataloguing rules or methods that they overlook the overriding purpose of the catalogue-to help users of the library to find what they want-so managers should avoid becoming so immersed in a particular technique that they forget its purpose-to improve or optimize performance, to measure value or to rectify faults.

Foster, in his Managing the cataloguing department, cites 'management by objectives' (MBO) as 'typical of the most innovative management concepts found in libraries today'. "MBO is so much a part of everyday normal management behaviour that the term is rarely used but it is still very relevant to cataloguing as 'an approach to assessing performance by reference to the achievement of results'. MBO involves formulating objectives (e.g. to ensure that library materials reach the public for whom they have been acquired with a minimum of delay); setting targets to allow these objectives to be met (e.g. cataloguing x number of items per day); and removing any obstacles to the achievement of these targets.

The cataloguing objectives can be defined as 'to ensure the maximum usefulness of the catalogue–

(a) surveying the use of the COM catalogues;

(b) reviewing the information required (i.e. considering the application of MARC and the latest edition of the Dewey Decimal Classification to new stock and old stock); and

(c) considering new applications for the catalogue database (organizing input and retrieving data to provide stock revision information, booklists on a subject and new accessions lists).

The specimen objective on cataloguing in the American Library Association's, 1980 planning manual for public libraries was concerned specifically with automation: 'to automate the acquisitions cataloging, and circulation's functions within the five year period' with a view to lowering the elapsed time from receipt of materials to shelf to 20 days.

At New South Wales Institute of Technology the objectives of the cataloguing department were defined as 'to carry out the cataloguing and classification of all monographs, A/V and serials needed by the staff and students of the Institute, and the method of achieving these objectives reflected the underlying philosophy of the library: 'that the use of technological advances and resources sharing among libraries is the only effective and rational way of operating in these days of economic stringency.,

The Norms **:** In order to set targets it is necessary to have some generally accepted standards. In cataloguing, there are adequate standards of technique or practice but there are no generally accepted standards of timing or performance-inevitably, perhaps, in view of the different kinds of materials to be catalogued, the variation in difficulty of this material, and the differing amounts of information on catalogue entries.

A study at Cornell Lay Library, using the OCLC database, showed that the average cataloguing time was 8-9 minutes per record and, in a survey of members of OCLC network, 91 % of the libraries surveyed reported that the time required to catalogue items had been reduced by on-line cataloguing. A small study at Bath University Library showed that the cataloguing of 160 items took only 293 minutes, or an average of just under two minutes per item, but it must be borne in mind that this involved very brief catalogue entries. The average time taken to classify 148 items was just under five minutes per item, and classification normally forms part of the cataloguing process.

It should be possible for each library to determine its own standards. The Centre for Library and Information Management (CLAIM) at Loughboroughy University, United Kingdom has shown how this can be done using the ' diary' techniques, with each member of staff keeping an accurate record of the time spent on every activity. A study by CLAIM's predecessor, the Library Management Research Unit, of four libraries serving schools, colleges and institutes of a university, showed that one library spent an average of 8 minutes cataloguing each item, two spent an average of 10 minutes per item and one spent an average of 16 minutes per item. The four libraries were commensurate in size and staff involvement.

At La Trobe University, Melbourne, Australia, cataloguers kept detailed monthly statistics of the time spent on each operation. They did not object to the establishment of minimum output figures; rather, they requested such figures because they provided a target and a basis for assessing their performance. It should be borne in mind, however, that all human beings are different; they are not machines, and some people will inevitably perform tasks more quickly and efficiently than others.

The Comparison : A library may well find it helpful to compare its own activities and costs with those of their libraries in the same group, and published comparative statistics are useful from this point of view.

In the UK, for example, the Centre for Interfirm Comparison (CIFC), after its formation in 1959, carried out many comparisons of performance data in industry, showing that such comparisons can be a valuable management tool to help in the establishment of standards and in the evaluation of activities and procedures.

Flow of Work : A smooth workflow will help to streamline the cataloguing process, the various operations being performed in a reasonable chronological sequence and the layout of the cataloguing department being such that no member of staff has to exert himself more than necessary when carrying out his particular tasks. This 'is an example of ergonomics-the relationship between the worker, his environment, and the equipment he uses. Ergonomics is a technique which is sometimes overlooked in librarianship.

The Review : Network analysis can be of value in planning and controlling cataloguing operations, particularly those concerned with recataloguing or retrospective conversion. There are several network planning techniques, the best known being PERT (Program Evaluation and Review Technique) and CPM (Critical Path Method). The time required for the activities and the sequence in which they should be performed are analyzed and represented in the form of a digram known as a 'network'; the activities forming the 'critical path' are then identified to enable the project to be completed in the shortest possible time.

Another management technique applicable to cataloguing is cost-benefit analysis which, as its name implies, involves weighing the cost of an activity against the benefit, accruing from that activity. It may be costly to make a lot of analytical entries, but is the cost justified by the time saved on searching for information and improved service to readers? Conversely, is the cost of full cataloguing justified if few readers use the cataloguing justified if few readers use the catalogue or if the majority simply want to locate an item and are not interested in publication details or physical description?

Item to be considered in costing include the cost of labour and materials, subscriptions to outside services, maintenance and depreciation costs, and overheads such as heating, and lighting. Factors affecting costs include:

The Approach : Cataloguing policy, such as fullness of cataloguing, the rules to be used and the extent of analysis and annotation. The methods employed; for example, computerizing the catalogue. The proper use of staff; for example, it may be cheaper to use clerical staff for routine cataloguing and checking. The extent to which cataloguing is coordinated with other operations.

The benefit part of the cost-benefit equation should not be ignored. Where (d) is concerned, for example, a major advantage of computerization is that it allows on record to be used for many purposes, including ordering, cataloguing, circulation control, interlibrary loans, preparation of reading lists and production of management information. In a survey of OCLC members, 80% of the libraries surveyed reported that their primary objectives had been met. For some libraries the primary objective was reduced costs, whilst for others it was faster cataloguing or improved interlibrary loans. Thus both cost and efficiency benefits had accrued form membership.

A study by the Bath University Programme of Catalogue Research undertaken in 1979 to establish the size and distribution of the market for automated cataloguing services, produced a considerable amount of data relating to the cost of cataloguing. Unfortunately, the report did not relate these figures to the kind of cataloguing or the value of the catalogue to the user, in other words the cost-benefit element was missing.

To change to AACR 2 (or to any other code of cataloguing rules) is major management decision. How many headings in the catalogue will need to be changed? How costly will the change be and, more important, how cost effective? Will it result in a better catalogue or allow more effective use of networks?

A study at La Trobe University Library, Melbourne, indicated that the time spend on cataloguing might rise by 2.3% as a result of introducing AACR 2. Training would be an additional cost, though a one-off cost which need to be absorbed during a brief period of time. All in all, concluded George Sector, 'the adoption AACR 2 . . . is likely to cause financial disaster to libraries with up to date practices'.

Five possible methods of implementing a change to AACR 2 are:

1. Starting a new catalogue for all items acquired after a specified date
2. Starting a new catalogue for all items published after a specified date
3. Superimposition
4. Changing the old headings as required
5. Interfiling the new entries with the old ones and linking as necessary with see also references, e.g :

SMITH (W.H.) & SONS see also W.E. SMITH & SONS W.H. SMITH & SONS see also SMITH (W.H.) & SONS

Very large libraries are likely to opt for closure of the catalogue, but Rosenthal has pointed out that this step has implications for almost every library operation. He has also emphasized the importance of very careful planning of any change and that the public relations aspects should not be ignored. Any system must be properly explained to noncataloguing staff and to the public. If a library opts to automate and to make use of MARC records in some way, e.g. by subscribing to the BLAISE Records Service or by joining a bibliographic utility such as OCLC, the decision to change to AACT 2 becomes implicit.

It is claimed that the 1988 revision of AACR 2 ' is a code supportive of the needs of library automation'. Libraries of all sizes use automated systems and 'there is a greater reliance on, and indeed, a greater expectation of the availability of derived cataloguing copy'. With such 'realities serving as a backdrop, and, with the urgings of ABACUS (Association of Bibliographic Agencies of Britain, Australia, Canada and the United States) to facilitate machine transfer of bibliographic information by further standardizing, in particular, the choice and form of authors, titles, and series. JSCAACR has developed a revision more conducive to automated environments on the evolutionary scale of cataloguing codes, the 1988 revision of the Anglo American cataloguing rules carries us one step closer to the goal of universal bibliographic control'.

For those libraries maintaining non-MARC record-based systems there is more of an option to adopt AACR 2 or not. 'These non-MARC libraries must consider how not changing may effect exchange of information, or may impact on future plans for database or system conversion'.

The claims made for AACR 2 cited above are sweeping claims which some librarians might consider debatable but nevertheless the fact remains that the AACR 2 1988 revision exists; it does form the basis of the MARC record, and therefore the majority of libraries in English-speaking countries and even elsewhere must be prepared to take decisions about its use.

Pre-natal Cataloguing : For many years Ranganathan urged the inclusion of a catalogue entry in each book on publication-'pre-natal cataloguing', as he called it. During 1985-89 the Library of Congress's 'Cataloguing-in source' experiment attempted to establish the feasibility of this, in collaboration with publishers and with the assistance of a grant provided by the Council of Library Resources. At the in-Souse program could not be justified from the viewpoint of financing technical considerations, or utility'. In 1971, 'cataloguing-in-source' was reborn in the United States as 'cataloguing-in-publication', initially for three-year experimental period, but it later became a permanent feature of Library of Congress record supply. For example, catalogue cards are printed from CIP records whenever full MARC cataloguing is not available. CIP entries differ from full MARC cataloguing in that records are shorter and references to pagination and size are omitted.

Brazil implemented a cataloguing-in-publication programme in the same year as the United States (1971). CIP schemes now operate in many countries and they have become an integral part of bibliographic services.

In the United Kingdom, British Library Bibliographic Services began to provide brief catalogue entries on the verso of the title page of some British books in 1976. CIP entries began to appear in the British national bibliography and on MARC tapes in 1977. In January 1985, the first of a new-style CIP entry, conforming generally to AACR 2 Level 2 for description and containing full subject data, appeared in the BNB. Prior to 1985, the CIP entry was not intended to be definitive but the new programme was designed to realize the full potential of CIP as a major input source for the creation of permanent UKMARC records of both high quality and high currency. Thus the CIP record formed the actual basis of the , definitive "national bibliographic" record'. It was a radical move away from the long-accepted principle of using the actual item as the primary source of cataloguing data. An essential requirement for an effective CIP programme is the fullest possible participation of publishers. By 1990 well over 1,0000 British publishers were participating in the scheme. 'It is a mutually advantageous service getting early information to libraries and offering increased marketing potential to participating publishers'.

In 1988 the British Library entered into an agreement with Book Data Ltd. which was intended to lead to improvements in both the quality of data and the coverage of the CIP programme. Book Data's declared objective is to serve publishers, booksellers and institutional buyers-including libraries, with particular emphasis on the acquisitions function-by creating a database of very full descriptive records about titles currently available or about to be published. By 1990 the list of participating publishers include some 900 imprints accounting for more than 25,000 titles a year.

The British Library has stated that from April 1991 it will cease to create CIP records from advance information supplied by publishers. In order to continue providing this service, however, the Library intends, as an interim arrangement, to continue to buy in CIP 1\ records from Book Data Ltd. These records will meet the minimum data requirement of AACR 2 Level 1 with some enhancement. They will include Book Data subject headings and will be classified according to Dewey Decimal Classification abridged edition. CIP records will continue to appear in BNB approximately six weeks before the expected date of publication.

As soon as the book has been published and received by the British Library Copyright Receipt Office a full authoritative record will be created which will then reappear in the main sequence of the BNB.

Whitaker is to supply CIP data to the British Library as from 1992.

Where Book Data is concerned, OCLC is also to mount a Book data file as part of its EPIC Reference Service.

Low Price Cataloguing : If necessary economies are not achieved by a more scientific approach to cataloguing, the library may resort to some form of 'limited cataloguing', an expedient useful also for reducing, cataloguing arrears and speeding up the cataloguing process and for reducing the bulk of the catalogue by eliminating unnecessary entries. The term 'limited cataloguing' is a generic one covering simplified cataloguing and selective cataloguing.

The most usual form of simplified cataloguing is the reduction of the descriptive element of the catalogue, such as the omission of all or part of the publication area or physical description area. Other possibilities include the simplification of author headings and the elimination of certain added entries. These limitations apply to the whole of the library's stock, whereas selective cataloguing involves the use of a variant form of cataloguing" usually a simplified form, for certain items, and/ or the omission of a catalogue entry for some items.

Most libraries can practice some form of selective cataloguing with little inconvenience to their readers. There seems little point in cataloguing standards specifications, especially if a library takes all of them, since they are easily retrievable via published indexes; alternatively they can be given a subject entry but not an author entry. Similarly, libraries which receive all government publications may rely on the official indexes rather than cataloguing each item , though the quality of cataloguing and subject indexing in the official lists may not be satisfactory for the library. Where UK official publications are concerned, a catalogue is also available on CD-ROM (UKOP). This provides over 180,000 bibliographic records for official publications published since 1980. Such materials as town guides, trade catalogues and annual reports need not usually be catalogued as they may be regarded as 'self-indexing'. Some public libraries do not catalogue fiction, though many would consider this to be an undesirable economy.

The Library of Congress adopted a limited cataloguing policy between 1951 and 1963 when, in order to deal with arrears which had accumulated over the years, accessions were divided into four groups of documents considered primarily of interest as groups, and items given entry only. Care should be taken that the costs saved by adopting a limited cataloguing policy are not offset by greater inconvenience to library users because of reference and readers' advisory staff having to consult a large number of different sources for information. It is interesting that L.C. ended its limited cataloguing policy in August 1963 following comments from card subscribers and others. We are back to cost-benefit analysis.

In 1987, the British Library, as part of a plan for future develop-ment, identified certain categories of material to receive 'ARC 2 level I' treatment, i.e. 'minimal level' cataloguing. These categories included modern English fiction (15%). Children's literature (10%), science and technology (25%), material with 32 pages or less (9%) and religion (4%). With overlaps, these categories cover 50% of BIB MACRO annual output and it was estimated that overall savings in record creation of 10% would be made.

The Necessity : Catalogue maintenance is an important part of a cataloguer's responsibility. It is essential that new and revised entries are filed regularly and correctly; superseded entries are withdrawn; worn cards or sheaf slips are replaced; filing errors and other inconsistencies are rectified; obsolete subject headings are replaced; and new subheadings are created when there are a large number of entries under one subject heading. Nowadays, simple instructions to the computer can often deal with these points.

Significant Features

An important aspect of catalogue maintenance is ensuring that library users are:

(a) Aware that a catalogue is available.

(b) Instructed in its use as required given guidance within the catalogue as necessary.

The catalogue is one of the most expensive commodities in the library, so we should surely do all we can to ensure that it is exploited to its full potential.

The first priority is to make the library user aware that a catalogue exists and where it may be found. This can be achieved by a general library plan, publicity leaflets, directional, e.g. hanging, guides, and the positioning of the catalogue in a prominent place. The space-eating card catalogue has, in some large libraries, have, however, rejected the idea of a separate, 'centre' for computer-based catalogues and indexes; the aim being to integrate machine-readable and eye-readable sources. The OPAC is itself a useful means of publicity.

External guides (instructions on how to use the catalogue) may take various forms; for example, a printed sheet or booklet either dealing with the catalogue alone or as part of a general library guide, a printed notice displayed near the catalogue or an introductory section in a book catalogue. The purpose of such guides is not to explain the niceties of cataloguing but to show the user how the catalogue can help him/her to find information. Professional jargon should be avoided and the judicious use of examples can be far more effective than verbose descriptions. The guidelines should be keep it simple made it clear, ensure that it is attractive and has impact.

It is important that the content of microtiches, card catalogue drawers etc.., are clearly indicated and that labels are changed as reorganization of the catalogue takes place.

Internal guides-such as cards, with protruding tabs in a card catalogue and headings at appropriate points in a book catalogue act as 'signposts' within the catalogue. A classified card catalogue is improved if 'feature headings' are used. In a card catalogue, different coloured cards could be used for different kinds of entries, e.g. author, subject, analytics.

In an online public-access catalogue there may be an initial screen containing general instructions on the use of the catalogue and further help screens dealing with specific features may be available as required at the touch of a key or upon typing "Help'. Some online catalogues have more than one mode to provide to both the uninitiated and the more experienced user. The interactive nature of the online catalogue can be utilized to provide clear guidance to the user and thus make it easier for required material to be located. Online tutorials are also a possibility.

The Administration

Communication is an essential feature of good staff management; staff must be kept informed of what is happening and why. Wherever possible some form of participative management is desirable, staff being involved in the decision-making process. One useful technique to employ is management by excepection, whereby matters are dealt with according to precise instructions or well defined objectives and only exceptional issues are referred to senior management.

The setting of objectives is an integral part of MBO techniques and there continues to be interest in MBO in British libraries, although the number of published references to its application has been on the decline. In the United States, however, academic libraries appear to have abandoned MBO in favour of Management Review and Analysis Program (MRAP), an approach which relies very heavily on staff participation. MRAP was initially designed for use in large research libraries in the US in response to a perceived need to respond positively to the new economic, personal and external pressures of the 1970s. The focus is placed firmly on management functions: planning, budgeting, management information, policies, organization, staff development, supervision and leadership, personnel and communication for example.

MRAP is not concerned with appraising or even developing a plan but with improving the procedures for planning. In more general terms, MRAP can be seen as a method of introducing participatory management into a library, for analysing the library's functions and for providing a new framework for decision-making. MRAP has been used in a considerable number of American libraries with, it must be said, very mixed results and , does not seem to have caught on outside the United States.

Staff participation becomes absolutely essential when a library is implementing an automated system. In Norway, for example, the relevant trade union became interested in finding out what effect computerization had on personnel. After interviewing staff who had recently experienced automation in their libraries, one of the major findings was that adequate training is a very important requisite and this training should include staff participation at all stages as the system develops.

Lovecy tells us that 'the most damaging element for staff morale is run our and speculation'. From the initial consideration of possible automation, it is important to involve members of staff in discussions. ' This makes sense from all points of view, since no librarian really wants to make a decision on whether or not to computerize without someone to discuss it with the more staff that can be drawn in to the discussion at this early stage the better.' Good staff management is helped by the use of a procedure manual, which should ensure consistency without endless repetition of verbal instructions.

Role of Computer

The quality of good management lies in the application of the principles in such a way as to provide the most effective catalogue for a library and its users. Correct decisions must be made on such matters as the fullness of cataloguing required; whether to use a conventional classified or alphabetical subject catalogue required; whether to use a conventional classified or alphabetical subject catalogue or some other system; the method to be used for establishing subject headings or subject index entries; what filing system to use; policy with regard to analysis and annotation; the physical form of catalogue; and the extent to which CIP (Cataloguing-in-publication) information, centralized services and the computer are used.

Increasing use of the computer; and of networks such as BLCMP and OCLC, is bound to have an effect on the management of cataloguing. The benefits of a computerized cataloguing system are indisputable but a decision to automate or not to automate the catalogue will depend upon a great many factors, including:

Size and type of library

Staffing levels

Financial support

Computer availability

Computerizing the Catalogue: It might be difficult, for example, in a small one-person library with very restricted financial provision and no access to any sort of computer. It is appreciated that some small libraries, unfortunately, cannot afford even an adequate book, stock, let alone consider automation. On the other hand, a large academic library with considerable resources and, in all probability, access to a large mainframe computer might find it difficult to resist automation. It is not unknown, however, in the case of the small library, for things to change overnight and if, for instance, a chance were suddenly offered to purchase a microcomputer system, as might happen in a school or college library, then the possibility of automation would have to be reviewed.

This is not, of course, to imply that the larger library will always find it easy to automate. A number of sizable libraries, such as Liverpool City Libraries, continue to have to manage with manual catalogues. Before adopting an automated system it is necessary to carry out a process of systems analysis, which means that the existing method of operation must be examined in order to ascertain whether computerization might lead to an improvement. Initially, objectives must be defined and a feasibility study undertaken.

The feasibility study will examine the various ways that the defined objectives might be achieved and it will look at the costs that might be incurred in relation to the benefit accrued (cost-benefit analysis). It will also investigate cost effectiveness in terms of manpower.

There are several options which a library planning to automate its catalogue might choose from:

to develop a completely independent in-house system; to purchase a turnkey package ; to join a bibliographic utility or cooperative network.

Whichever of the above is selected, it may be possible to make use of a centralized cataloguing service such as MARC in someway. Indeed, it may be obligatory to do so as in the case of the bibliographic utilities. Turnkey packages may not cater for the MARC format and for the importing of MARC records but many do and, in some instances, two approaches to the creation of the cataloguing database are offered-MARC and non-MARC. It should also be rioted that the bibliographic utilities usually offer some form of standalone turnkey system. This may also permit remote access to, and interaction with, the central database. There may well be, therefore, some overlap between options.

The 'go-in-one', completely independent in-house system can vary from a single microcomputer configuration to a sophisticated set-up with large mainframe-computer support. If in-house development is chosen, care should be taken to ensure that on-going back-up and maintenance are available and that enhancement will be possible as and when necessary. It is not unknown for an in-house system to grind to a halt as it grows and develops, owing to the lack of such facilities.

One library which preferred to use its own independent automated system was Derbyshire, UK, because it provided control over what to accept or reject, control over standards, and priority of access.

The prime example of an in-house development is probably that of the University of California's MELVYL catalogue system, which is recognized as one of the most sophisticated and advanced public online cataloguing systems in existence.

Follow-up studies have tended to confirm the above findings. For example, the University of Wyoming conducted a survey of online catalogue users in 1986. This was an adaptation of the Council on Library Resources study and the results were consistent with national findings, with very few exceptions.

Liverpool Polytechnic has undertaken two surveys relating to PRECIS—a survey of reactions of indexers in all kinds of libraries , and a study of user reactions.

Of the 377 organizations respondings to the first survey, 255 (67%) had given no thought to its adoption, and of the remaining 122, only 25 were actually using the system for indexing. The reasons quoted most often for rejecting PRECIS were its complexity and labour-intensiveness and it is interesting to note that the British Library is now simplifying the methodology. Some indexes regarded the document-specificity of PRECIS and the open-endedness of its vocabulary as advantages, and others say them as disadvantages.

The small number of organizations using PRECIS in their own systems is not, of course, an indication of the total number of users. Anyone who makes use of the British National Bibliography or of UKMARC (1971-90) for subject access (including those he access British Library files online) can be considered a PRECIS user.

In the PRECIS user study, the main conclusion was that users generally reacted favourably, the document specificity was considered very useful. Users found the full subject statements more helpful than a string of terms, as in chain indexing, or broaded subject headings, as in the Library of Congress subject headings. Some non-librarian users found this aspect of PRECIS particularly Impressive. The ability of PRECIS to show relationships between terms was also appreciated.

By removing the human intellectual element from indexing and allowing a machine, that is a computer, to select terms for index entries, a form of automatic indexing is obtained. Computerized 'keyword from title' indexes are automatic to a degree, but is there any way in which a computer can be programmed to identify appropriate terms from the text of an item? Initial attempts at automatic indexing were based upon determining, by statistical methods, the words which occur most frequently in a document. This method can be improved by comparing the number of times a particular word appears with the number of items it might be expected to appear. The advantage gained is immediately obvious; with the earlier technique a word occurring only a few times would be ignored but, using the latter method, the word might be proved to be very significant. Other experiments have concentrated upon the discovery that if words are 'paired' together in a document upon a number of occasions then this has an added significance.

In addition to the simple descriptors which are normally used in automatic indexing systems, it has also been shown that it may be possible to improve the quality of such systems by the addition of more complex descriptors, for example phrases, and other techniques evolve around the selection of sentences. Sentences can be weighed according to predetermined measure of significance. Sentences with the highest weights are likely to be those which best summarize the subject-content of an item. Examples of 'measures' are 'word frequency', as described above, and the position of a sentence-for example, the first sentence of a paragraph might be an important indication of the paragraph's subject-content.

An automatic indexing system can be linked with a machine-based thesaurus to provide controlled language indexing.

Research into techniques such as those described above has continued over many years and operational systems have been devised. Some of these systems have been shown to possess a number of defects and inadequacies; others have been put to practical use and are claimed to be successful. For example,

Thonssen describes an automatic indexing system (PRIMUS-IDX) which interfaces with an automatic thesaurus management program (INDEX) to enable large quantities of texts to be indexed quickly, consistently and cheaply. The recent application of expert system technology should also be noted.

The overall objectives of research into automatic indexing can be said to be rather more than simply to represent the subject-content of a document by index terms; it is possible to produce an automatic extract ('autoextract') which compares reasonably well with an abstract prepared by a skilled abstractor.

The SMART project, which was developed in the United States by Saltine, and which is sometimes referred to as Saltine's Magical Automatic Retrieval of Text, is concerned with the effectiveness of computer-based retrieval systems relying entirely or almost entirely on machine processing of text. Out of the early experiments evolved new techniques for the construction of computer-generated thesauri. The system could be used online and a comparison with MEDLARS proved that the SMART procedures worked well. A detailed discussion is outside the scope of this work but it is, perhaps, worth recording that Salton came to the sweeping conclusion that there is little jurisdiction for maintaining controlled many indexes.

Allied to automatic indexing, although somewhat outside the scope of this present work, is automatic classification. At the Cambridge Language Research Unit, for instance, investigations panning a number of years from the early 1960s were involved with the machine analysis of documents for the discovery of 'keywords' for indexing purposes. Attempts were made to construct automatically a classification of key words based upon the way in which terms 'co-occur' in documents. Terms thus related are grouped together into 'clumps', terms 'outside'. Using clumps alone did not lead to very satisfactory results and later experiments utilized four different kinds of group, the original' clumps', together with 'strings', 'stars' and 'cliques'. A 'string', for example is a set of terms in which each term is found to be most strongly associated with the one next to it.

This is 'clearly and indisputably a newer form of classification' which may have far-reaching effects in the future. At present such work is still mainly at a theoretical level but there is a possibility that it could well improve the search capability in computerized databases to a marked degree.

Spark Jones considers that the immediate prospects for operational automatic classification are "not bright", because of the failure to fully establish appropriate methods and applications, and the high cost of experiments. Yet she believes that large files need more sophisticated tools, such as classification, and since automatic classification has not been conclusively shown to be unhelpful compared with human classification, its longer prospects should be interesting to all concerned with information systems.

It is certainly possible that some form of classification, whether 'automatic' or not, 'built-in' to computerized databases could improve the search capability to a marked degree. It might, for instance, be feasible that a search on one term could be translated automatically into a search for other related coordinate or subordinate terms indicated by the classification. This could greatly improve the efficiency of the system. If, to take a simple example, an item dealing with the 'use of parachutes to stop ocean-going tankers' was searched for under 'parachutes' and 'slips', the automatic classification facility would reveal that 'tankers' was closely related to 'ships' and the relevant document would be retrieved.

Other Features : Part of the British Computer Society's approved definition states that an expert system is regarded as the embodiment within a computer of a knowledge-based component from an expert skill in such a form that the system can offer intelligent advice or take an intelligent decision about a processing decision. In other words, an expert system is a computer program which can take the place of a human expert in some particular area of knowledge. As such, clearly there are possible applications within the cataloguing and indexing field.

For example, expert system techniques might be successfully applied to the task of selecting index terms. On such system is that operated by the Central Abstracting and Indexing Service of the American Petroleum Institute (API-CAUSE), which selects index terms from abstracts of articles appearing in the technical literature. A rule-based system has been created, using the API thesaurus as a base, which has been operational since 1985. The index terms selected by the computer are reviewed by a human index editor (as are the terms selected by CAIS's human indexers). After editing, the terms are used for printed indexes and for online computer searching.

Other examples include L-IDIA (L-Intelligent Document Information Analyser), which is the central part of an expert system designed to analyse automatically the content of documents in natural languages (relevant to well defined domains of knowledge) and an expert system described by Gauch and Smith for searching in full-text. Where the later is concerned, an intelligent search intermediary helps end-users to locate relevant passages.

An obvious possibility is automatic cataloguing based upon a set of rules as embodied in a code such as AACR 2, and there have been several pieces of research aimed at achieving this. One example of the research carried out by Hames at the University of Exeter, another is the work of Hjerppe at Linkoping University, and an investigation into automated title-page cataloguing has been carried out under the direction of Weibel at OCLC. However, 'for an expert system to generate the required conditions for a specifically designed goal, the logic in the knowledge base must be consistent. There have been problems in every attempt to convert AACR 2 into the highly structured rules necessary to run an expert system'. Meador and Whiting conclude that this may well lead to further changes in the rules because the impact of technology will demand greater consistency. Apart from this, Weibel cites other unsolved problems as the incorporation of the cataloguer's general knowledge into the system, the complexity of the rules, and a lack of reliable data capture techniques.

One of the problems that has exercised the minds of librarians over the years has been that of switching from one indexing language to another. Apart from direct one-to-one translation, there is the possibility of the use of having an intermediate neutral languages designed to switch indexing decisions recorded in one indexing language into equivalent decisions in other languages.

The intermediary should have the same coverage and specificity as the languages with which it is to be used and should be hospitable to index languages with different structure; that is, faceted or enumerative classification, thesauri or alphabetical word lists. Horsnell investigated the feasibility of a switching language in the field of information science. She reported that switching is possible and that overall recall and precision values far normal indexes and indexing obtained by switching are similar.

Other developments in this area include work conducted under the auspices of UNISSIST to provide an international switching language which could be applied to all publications to indicate the subject fields covered. The original intention was that this would be an intermediate language between two established languages, for example:

German natural language-switching language-French natural language, but the eventual product was the Broad system of ordering. This is a general classification scheme, with a fairly low level of specificity (as the title suggests). Although the scheme, which was the work of an FID (International Federation for Documentation) /BSO Panel, is intended for information exchange and switching, it is not a true switching language in the context of the criteria explained above. It can be concluded that we should investigate and attempt to evaluate indexing systems rather than take their performance for granted, but we should not be too surprised if the results of these investigations are sometimes inconclusive. Cleverdon wrote, when reporting on the second Cornfield investigations: 'As with Cranfield I, the outcome of this test is to raise more questions than it answers. It would be absurd for any organization to abandon conventional indexing and controlled index languages, whether thesauri or classification, on the basis of these test results.

Fifteen

Regulation Framework

Laws and Rules

The laws of library science were evolved by Dr. Ranganathan. These are also called as fundamental laws. These are five in number. The laws of library science have a sway over the entire discipline, i.e., library science. They help in resolving any conflict that may arise during the functioning of libraries. They guide the library staff in deciding what is right and what is wrong in given situation.

The laws of library science were evolved in the year 1928 and a detailed account of these laws and their implications were given in the form of a book by Ranganathan in 1931. These laws are :

Ist Law	Books are for use;
2nd Law	Every reader his/her book;
3rd Law	Every book its reader;
4th Law	Save the time of the reader/staff
5th Law	Library is a growing organism.

First Law : Books are for Use : The elementary truth of a library is 'Books are for Use'. During 15th and 16th centuries books were chained to the shelves. Books are filled in brass frames and rings and were chained to selves. In those days libraries were regarded as organisations for preservation, but not for furthering their use.

In olden days books were lent to a favoured few. Later they were made available at a fee. The modern concept is 'free book service for all'.

Location of the Library: In the earlier days libraries were located at the outskirts of the towns in order to keep them free from dust and away from 'all sorts of people'. For some time library is regarded as an ornament to the city. They tried to keep the library away from inhabitants. Those who have a living faith in the first law located the library in the heart of the city.

In some of the colleges, library was located in the room which is regarded as unfit for any thing else so as to put them to use. Of course, today in many colleges the chief building of the college which took pride is the library.

Library Hours : So long as preservation had the upper hand, libraries were more closed than open. Open mostly to dust books and chase out book-worms. In the middle of the 19th century the Oxford Library was kept open for two hours, on two days of a week. Now, it is almost kept open for the whole of the day, on all days of the year.

Library Furniture: In the earlier days books were stacked upto the roof as books were meant for preservation. Now-a-days, the height of the shelves are kept in such a way that a reader can lay his hand on any book he wants. Now the libraries have adopted open access system where any reader can move freely among the stacks of the library. Big reading rooms with cosy furniture; sound-proof floor; good ventilation and light; drinking water; toilets, retiring rooms; canteen facility are the characteristics of a modern library.

Library Staff **:** Earlier, librarian was regarded as a caretaker against the four enemies-fire, water, vermin and man. In the past matriculates were appointed as librarians. It took a long time to realise that one who deals with learning, help scholars as well, should possess scholarship. These days, the status of a librarian in a college is that of a teacher and of an university is that of a professor.

Responsibilities: The library staff should not forget the noble cause which secured them their scholarship, training, emoluments and status. They should see that the books are put to maximum use by the readers. They should keep the library up-to-date in all respects. They must welcome the readers cheerfully and see that the readers come to the library not only to use the books, but also, to meet the librarian and his staff.

Second Law: Every Reader His/Her Book **:** While the first law replaced the concept of 'books are for preservation'; the second law replaced the concept of 'books are for a chosen few'. This law is from the side of the users of books.

Implications

Occupational and Income Lines **:** In the good olden days, education and privilege of learning rarely crossed occupational and income lines. Some said, "too much knowledge is dangerous and libraries may become the political centres". When a library school was started in Moscow, they asked as to "how the government tolerates library courses which pave the way for revolution"

The concept of democracy made education and libraries open for all.

The Men and the Women **:** It is not merely the income line that has divided the humanity, sex is another example that restricted the enforcement of the second law. In India also there is still this, barrier. Girl child is deprived of education. In Europe, it is said that "no respectable girl should be educated". St. Paul said

"Women are inferior dependent class". Chesterfield was of the opinion that "Women are children of a larger growth". Experiments now revealed that women are as competent intellectually as to men to undertake any and all human vocations. All books have a perfect right of going to the hands of women.

City Folk and Country Folk: Right of the country folk to book came to be respected in most of the countries these days. It is said that "India lives in villages" and rural libraries have to play an important role in bringing changes in agricultural practices; cottage industries; rural hygiene, health and family welfare. Village library has to be the nerve centre of social activities like musical concerts, lectures, dramas, exhibitions, audio-visual shows, etc.

The village librarian has to play an important role in dissemination of information to the villagers. He should use local fairs and festivals in popularising the library.

Normal and Abnormal : Special libraries are to be established to cater to the information needs of patients in hospitals, prisoners, blind and other physically handicapped.

Adult and Child : It has been held for long by all that "child has no right to any book other than the textbook." As education does not end in the class room, they should be given widest opportunity in the school library and local public library to form the correct reading habit.

Third Law : Every Book its Reader : Third law urges that an appropriate reader should be found for every book.

Implications

Open Access: The reader should have free access to the books in the library. He should feel free to move in the stack-room and lay hand on any book at his will and pleasure. Open access provides opportunities to readers to discover books which he never expected to have. Less used books are that way put to use. Library staff should display all new books in a proper manner, so that readers could discover and use. Most readers have no definite approach, which will take a shape only on seeing and handling a book.

Shelf Arrangement **:** This plays an equal role in an open access library in canvassing for books. Subject arrangement on selves; a special shelf for displaying recent arrivals; and novelty in arrangement and display will attract the attention of the users.

Catalogue **:** It is the catalogue that provides useful information about books and helps in selection. Added entries, analyticals and cross references help the readers in location and selection.

Reference Work **:** With all the classified arrangement, shelf arrangement and catalogue entries, there is the need for 'human factor'. The Reference Librarian should act as a canvassing agent for books. Books are mute and inert. They cannot select a match. It is the duty of a Reference Librarian to act like a marriage match maker. He should find a suitable reader for each and every book. He should identify books which are in less use or no use. He should try to find out a suitable reader for each such book.

Publicity **:** Reference Librarian should try to tell the public the value of books; role of the library as a social institution; library services etc.

He should make use of mass media like press, radio, television, public lectures, demonstration tours, exhibitions, library weeks, brochures and leaflets, special library publications, etc. for publicizing the library.

He should play an important role in book-selection. Proper, timely, local demand, local history, local needs as well as individual needs are to be considered while selecting books. This also plays an important role in satisfying the third law of library science.

Fourth Law of Library Science : Save the Time of the Reader : This law demands saving the time of the reader as well as staff. 'Save the Time of the Staff' is regarded as a corollary to this law.

Implications

Open Access vs. Closed Access : In a closed access system there will be a good loss of time in going through the catalogue. It is even a greater difficulty, in the cause of a sheaf or book catalogue.

In big libraries, waiting at the counter to get a book may take a longer time-some times stretching into a few hours. This may be on account of many causes-the slip may be returned with the comment 'entry incorrect', 'on-loan', 'engaged', etc.

Open access saves all these problems. It also saves the time of the staff.

Shelf-Arrangement : The more useful method of shelf arrangement saves much time of the reader. Arrangement by subject has been found to be useful and easy to locate a book. The subject represented in an artificial language of ordinal numbers is proved to save the time in locating the books.

It has been the practice in libraries to arrange books in great demand at the entrance. This type of broken order is found to save the time of the users.

Subjects with less number of books be given broad classification. This will help in locating books on the same subject at one place in the catalogue. Such class numbers will be brief and easy to remember.

Stack Room Guides : Proper guides in the stack room will save the time of the users.

At the entrance there should be a large, broad plan of the library to help the readers in locating the section in which they are interested. These should be a 'Signal Guide' on each rack. Inclusive class numbers be provided on the shelf plank. The tags on the books should be in a line (above the bottom) so that it will be convenient for the eye to look-at.

Catalogue : Catalogue should have necessary and sufficient number of analytical entries and cross-references. Complete set of added entries be provided. Cooperative and centralised cataloguing also saves the time of the readers.

Bibliography: Topical bibliographies, cumulative indexes to journals; national and regional bibliographies, union catalogues, computerised databases; national networks; etc., also saves the time of the readers.

Reference Service : Assistance to users by way of' invitation of freshman, guidance to the users; ready and long range reference assistance; help in selection books: documentation services like indexing, abstracting, translation, reprography; information services like Current Awareness Services, Selective Dissemination of Information, Referral Service, Information Consolidation and Repackaging, etc. will definitely help in the dissipation of research potential of the nation.

Circular System : 'Two Card' system is found to save the time of the readers over 'Daybook and Ledger' system. Computerised circulation system will further save the time of the users.

Other Services: Centralised and cooperative cataloguing, location of the library; mobile libraries; library service for special classes are other means that saves the time of the users.

Fifth Law : Library is a Growing Organism : The fifth law enunciates a fundamental principle that should govern the planning and organisation of libraries. It is an accepted fact that growing organism alone will survive. Library as an institution has all the attributes of a growing organism.

Implications

The main parts of the organism are-books, readers and staff. A modern library is a trinity of these factors. There should be a harmonious growth among the basic components of the organism, i.e., the books, readers and the staff. The consequence of growth on different aspects of library organization is discussed below :

Books: The number of books in a live library must and does grow. It is also impracticable to adopt the 'quincy plan' which advocates to the equalization of the rate of weeding out and the rate of accessioning once the collection reaches an arbitrary norm.

Stack Room and Fittings: The part of the building which is much effected by the growth is the stack-room-its size, book racks and relative position. Looking to the exponential growth of the stack, while planning the library building, we have to take into account the needs of the present as well as the needs of the next 20 to 25 years atleast.

'Compack Shelving' (packing racks just as in a godown is of no use) is against the third law, constant shifting is against the fourth law. Thus, there should be enough room in the library building for future expansion.

Periodical Room: The number of volumes of periodicals increase from year to year. Arrangement of back volumes and display of current numbers should be properly done.

The current numbers should be arranged in a classified manner. To economies space, current numbers be arranged in four rows.

Catalogue Room : A standard unit catalogue cabinet occupies a floor space of 50 cm x 70 cm and can hold 48,000 catalogue cards. There should be enough space to accommodate present and future cabinets. It is advisable to go in for computerised cataloguing which saves the problem of space.

Classification Scheme : Classification scheme selected should be comprehensive, having accommodated all the subjects of the past and present and can accommodate new subjects that could crop-up in the future. The notation of the scheme should be simple, flexible, less complicated, hospitable, and easy to read, write and remember. The scheme should give brief class numbers. It is advantageous if the class number is broken into different blocks which facilitate ease in writing, reading and remembering. A faceted classification is thus more suitable.

Reading Room: A reading room should be sufficient to accommodate readers of the present as well as the increase in the number in the future. It is suggested to have separate reading room for undergraduates, postgraduates and teachers.

Other Sections : There should be room for accommodating periodicals, audio-visual material, computer server, OPAC, CD-ROM server and terminals, etc.

Safeguards: Proper counter facility, wire-meshing, fire fighting equipment, protection from white ants, silver fish, rodents and other enemies are essential.

Staff : There should be minimum staff required. However, every effort should be made to provide professional growth among staff members. Proper organisation and management is key to the success of a library. Apart from proper planning to meet the growth in collection and readers, there should be planning for increase in the number of staff and staff training. Periodical transfer of the staff, proper selection policy, staff council, proper interaction among the staff holds key for success of a library in the present as well as for the future.

Administrative Rules

Management is an activity that converts disorganised human and physical resources into useful and effective results. Management is a distinct process consisting of activities of planning, organising, actuating and controlling, performed to determine and accomplish stated objectives with the use of human beings and other resources. There are six basic resources: Men, materials, machines, methods, money and market. These resources are utilised by four fundamental functions, viz., planning, organising, actuating and controlling to achieve the objectives.

Management exists in every of human organisation. We all are affected by good or bad management practices, and we should therefore learn to recognise and influence the quality of management that affects our lives.

Management makes human efforts more productive. It brings better equipments, plants, offices, products, services and human relatio s to our society.

Management brings order to endeavors by combing isolated events and disjoint information into meaningful relationships. These relationship then work to solve problems and accomplish goals.

During the present century, certain schools of management thought have developed. Each school reflects the problems of the period during which they were popular. Those schools which have survived today are influencing management thought.

Various Theories

We may recognize the following three groups of schools of management thought:

(i) *Scientific Schools:* Scientific schools include scientific mana-gement school, classical school and system school.

(ii) *Human Relation Schools:* Human relations schools include human behaviour school and social system school.

(iii) *Decision Theory Schools.*

Scientific Management School

This school uses the scientific method to obtain desired objectives in the workplace. The scientific method uses the following steps to achieve an objective:

1. Identify the objective
2. Acquire information about the objective through observation
3. Formulate an hypothesis about the objective
4. Investigate the objective thoroughly by controlled experiments

5. Set priority and clarify the data obtained

6. State the tentative solution to the objective

7. Adjust and implement the answer to the objective.

Frederick W. Taylor has been called the father of scientific management. He believed that management, not labour, was the cause of and potential solution to problems in an organisation. Taylor called for a mental revolution to fuse the interests of labour and management into a mutually rewarding whole. This mental revolution was based on four vital principles:

1. the development of the best work method,

2. the scientific selection and development of workers,

3. the relating and bringing together of the best work method and

4. the close cooperation of managers and non-managers, which include the division of work and manager's responsibility for planning the work.

Taylor had many disciples that spread the gospel of efficiency. Carl Barth, Hanry gantt, Frank Gilberth, Harington Emerson, and Morris Cooke all made valuable written and practicing contributions to the growth of management as a sceintific discipline.

Classical School : This school developed in France. This school is referred to as the traditional" or "universalist" school. It regards management as a universal process. The management process is analyzed, conceptual framework is established, principles are identified and a theory of management is built from it. Henri Fayol, a Frenchman is considered as the father of the classical school. He applied scientific approach but looked at administration from the top to down.

The principles of administration by Fayol are as follows:

Division of Work. As an organization grows, there should be an early division of duties. Activities concerning management should also be separated out and made distinct. As division of work takes place, it leads to development of specialization.

Authority and Responsibility. Responsibility is a corollary of authority.

Discipline. Discipline is essential in an efficient organization.

Unity of Command. This principle implies that a subordinate should receive orders from one senior only.

Unity of Direction. There should be one head and one plan for a group of activities having the same objective.

Subordination of individual interest to general Interest. Growth of the organization should be the primary concern.

Remuneration of Personnel. Remuneration and methods of payment should be fair.

Centralization. There should be centralization of authority.

Scalar chain. There should be unbroken line of authority and command from highest to the lowest level in the organization.

Order. There must be place for everyone and everyone must be in its place. A right person must be given a right job most suitable to him.

Equity. In dealing with subordinates, justice and human approach is essential.

Stability of Tenure of Personnel. Management should aim at minimizing employee turnover. Unnecessary turnover is both the cause as well as effect of bad management.

Initiative. The principle of initiative refers to the ability and quality of a manager to think and execute a plan. Every manager should encourage subordinates to develop quality of taking initiative.

Esprit de Corps. This principle emphasizes teamwork and the importance of effective communication in achieving the same.

System School : Max Weber emphasized specialization within an organization and considered hierarchy of the decision making process of great importance. He analyzed the authority and responsibility of the office rather than the individual. He made monumental contribution to authority structures in a complex organization.

Luther Gulick, an American, has described the functions of an executive in terms of an acronym POSDCORB, representing Planning, Organizing, Staffing, Directing, Coordinating, Reporting and Budgeting.

Human Relation Schools : The Human Relation Schools consider that as managing involves getting things done through people, therefore management studies should be evolved around interpersonal relations. Thus the main emphasis is on the individual and the informal group in the formal organization. The basic concern is to study people as human beings rather than as mere work units. Sociologists and psychologists have been very active in developing these schools of thought.

Human Behaviour School: The focus of the Human Behaviour School is on behaviour of the individual, the group, and the organization. This theory looks at the human factor as the central theme. It lays greater emphasis on interpersonal relations, leadership, group dynamics and motivation of personnel. The basic assumption is that in case the management can keep the employees happy, then this will result in the maximum performance.

Mary Follett emphasized the psychological and sociological aspects of management. She looked at management as a social process and felt that coordination was the most important principle.

In 1930s, Elton Mayo and a group of industrial psychologists conducted experiments at the Western Electric Hawthrone Plant in Chicago. They came to the conclusion that social interaction and psychological factors are important in determining the level of productivity and satisfaction.

Social System School: The Social System School encourages employees to develop social groups on the job, to participate in management and allows democratic functioning in the enterprise.

Chester Barnard has written about contribution-satisfaction equilibrium. He has identified four specific inducements. He regarded communication as the first function of a manager.

In 1950s Peter Drucker introduced Management by Objectives. He has been supported by Douglas Mc Gregor in his "Theory" Abraham Maslow has further built up his "Need Theory" According to it, man has a hierarchy of needs starting with low needs (physiological needs-food, shelter, and clothing), ultimate proceeding to highest needs (intangible needs—self-actualizing and fulfilment). He concluded that when one set of needs was satisfied then that kind of needs ceased to be a motivator. His identification of basic needs has been fairly popular but hierarchical aspects of theory has been questioned.

Decision Theory School: These schools perceive management in terms of decision-making. These are primarily concerned with the study of rational decision procedures and also the way managers actually reach decision. The inbuilt assumption being that mathematical models and quantitative processes can serve as a basis of all management.

Different schools of management thought have provide different versions regarding management creating confusion. Classical school regards management as a universal process. The behaviourists consider human factor as the central theme, which simply involves inter-spersonal relations. Some consider management simply as decision-making. However, the different schools management thought are interrelated. All the schools are concern with management process.

The Administration

Principles of management are generalizations based experience and careful analysis of case studies. These are universally applicable. These are not rigid. Change in circumstances would require adoption of these. Intelligence, judgment, experience and understanding of human relations are necessary for adaptation principles.

Principles of management is a powerful tool in the hands of administrator/ manager but these must be used rather carefully after analysis of the problem and its diagnosis.

Henri Fayol was the first to put forward a list of administrative principles. On the whole, his observations are valid even today. Lyndall Urwick examined the principles formulated by different authorities and succeeded in coordinating them into a unified system.

Henri Fayol is regarded as the father of classical school, sometimes, this schools is referred to as the "traditional" or "universalist" school. Fayol used scientific approach. His principles are:

Division of Work: In a small one-man library, one person would be carrying out all the functions such as ordering, classification, cataloguing, preparation, shelving, servicing of documents etc., there would be no division of work. But in a large library if all the professional assistants carry out all these functions, then this would lead to inefficiency and confusion. As the library grows, there should be a division of duties, and the activities. As division of work takes place, it will lead to specialization. This is desirable in a large set up. Division of work should be carried out up to a point.

Authority: Authority can be either statutory or personal. Statutory authority belongs to a person due to his position. Personal authority is achieved due to qualities of leadership. Possession of authority means responsibility for actions. Actual work in the library may be done by different persons but the ultimate responsibilities lie with the chief librarian for all that goes on. He can delegate authority for a certain job. If the same is misused, then it can be withdrawn. An individual should be given authority equal to his responsibility. In case a person is given responsibility for a given job/task, then he should also be delegated authority to take necessary action to make it possible to fulfil the job/task successfully.

Discipline: In the best interest of the organization, there should be complete obedience, diligence, energy and outward marks of respect. This is equally applicable to every body. The best way to establish and maintain discipline is to provide good leadership to staff, dissolve disputes with justice and enforce penalties without prejudice.

Unity of Command: An employee should be responsible to, and also receive orders from only one superior. Any orders by the chief librarian to a professional assistant should be transmitted through an assistant librarian, who is incharge of the section. Thus an organizational structure should be such that each employee is supervised by only one supervisor. He should be responsible for giving assignment to him and also assess his work. This principle protects an employee from awkward situations if he is supervised by two or more supervisors.

Unity of Direction: According to Fayol, there should be "one manager and one plan for all the operations which have the same objective in view". Unitys of command depends on working of staff togethcr properly but Unity of direction is provided by means of properly arranging organization so that there is one head and one plan to make it sure that coordinated effort would be achieved.

Subordination of Individual Interest to General Interest: According to this principle individual interests must be subordinated for the same of common good. Thus primary concern of an employee should be the growth and development of the organization. Head of the order section should not be permitted take long leave during the last days of the financial year, if fund remain to be spent and bills have to be passed before the end of t financial year.

Remuneration: Salaries to employees and method of payment should be fair enough, comparable to other staff of the parent body with equivalent qualifications. Employees should be given incentives for successful efforts.

Centralization: Centralization of administration may be carried out in varying degrees, depending upon the local situation. Anything that increase the importance of the role of a subordinate should be decentralized. On the other hand any thing that decreases the importance of the role of a subordinate should, be centralized. In a university library system book selection should be highly decentralized because head of departmental libraries know more about their fields of specialization than other librarians of the central library. But ordering should be centralized so that there is no duplication of bibliographical tools, records and books. Managerial function should be decentralized to a limited extent. As a result, the operation would improve and it would be possible to take advantage of the special knowledge acquired by the members of the staff working in departmental libraries.

Scalar Chain: This principle implies that authority and responsibility should flow in a clear unbroken line from the highest executive to the lowest rank. This refers to hierarchy. A hierarchy consists of a series of steps, extending in an unbroken line from chief librarian to the lowest employee an attendant. This line serves as a means of communication. Authority flows from superior to subordinates throughout the entire organization. Orders go down along the line traveling from top to bottom. However information and appeal travel in the reverse direction.

Order: Order refers to the best possible arrangement to achieve the most efficient operation of the organization.As regards movement of materials, it would be economical if order section and cataloguing section are located side by side.

As regards employees, a right person must be given a right job most suitable to him. It would be a wrong decision to put an expert classifier in the maintenance section. A right place or job must be identified for everything and every individual.

Equity: In dealing with employees treatment of equality must be put into practice. Justice must be combined with friendliness and kindness by those in executive towards staff. Salary scales must be based on education, ability, experience and level of responsibility. Preferential treatment should be based on the question of superiority of a person in terms of the factors mentioned above.

Esprit De Corps: This principle refers to 'strength in unity' being an extension of principle of unity of command. Library administration should create environment which leads to harmony and unity. Equity, initiative, unity of command and leadership qualities of the senior staff can do much to promote esprit de corps. It requires team work. Communication is considered as the key to the satisfaction of a working group, resulting in team work.

Besides principles put forward by Fayol, other principles often included are span of control, coordination; line and staff, and accountability .

Span of Control : This refers to the number of persons with whom a manager deals directly. There is no established criteria to determine how many individuals one manager can supervise efficiently. In practice the number of supervisors assigned to one manager vary usually five to nine.

However, in certain situations more supervisors can be attached to one manager. This depends upon the kind of assignment allotted to different supervisors. In case nature of activities allocated to different units being supervised supervisor are similar in nature then the number of persons supervised by him can be increased. However, if the activities varies a great deal then he would be able to supervice fewer persons efficiently.

Coordination: Coordination is very important in running an organization may be regarded as the essence of managership. If work periodical section and documentation section is not coordinated then this will lead to problems. Aim of coordination being to achieve harmony of individual efforts towards accomplishment of group goals. The manager reconciles differences of interest, efforts to accomplish goals.

Line and Staff : Persons belonging to line positions are decision makers, possess authority and command. Staff positions are those which do not carry authority. These are advisory positions meant providing information, advise and counsel. Such persons delegated authority and decision makers are not obliged to accept the advice given by them. A chief librarian can ask head of a section, for information and advice because of his special knowledge but the chief may accept his advice or not. Now a days a staff unit may have systems analyst, a research unit, a public relations office, etc.

Accountability: In case a library has to be run efficiently, then emphasis should be on measurement of quality and quantity of performance measurement of performance can be used towards the accountability of an employee. Accountability means liable to account. The principles of management are universally applicable. These are flexible and not absolute. These are applicable regardless of changing conditions. These form basis of scientific management.

The principle of management listed above have been recognized by librarians. The application of scientific management based on these is beginning to be used in libraries. Librarians seem to be showing more interest in this area of study and application. However, it is true that libratians have been slow to accept these ideas.

Sixteen

Policy on Libraries

Policy is a statement of general principle of intent that helps translate programme objectives into accomplishments. An objective is a desirable future condition. To achieve an objective, we have to draw a course of action. The course of action we may describe as a plan. The plan has to be implemented. The process of impelmentation needs a programme. A programme warrants several procedures.

The Shortcomings

For the most part, information agencies have not developed or used policies. They are guided by rules of thumb or were following trial and error method. Scientific management brought in the concept of policies, planning, implementation, evaluation, etc.

Basic Policy Questions : Policies can be formulated at different levels, say, at local, regional, state, national and international. At the local level, different institutions may have different policies. Thus, the policies of different institutions may differ. However, there will be some basic policy questions in general which even evolved separately may come out to be common.

Policy Statement : Policy statements provide the basis for orderly, smooth and thoughtful change. They further assist and enable longer range management planning. There can be policies to cover every decision or to meet every contingency.

The following basic premises are likely to be useful:

1. Programmes and activities must operate within one framework and be directed towards a common set of objectives.

2. The establishment of performance goals and the determination of priorities is contingent upon a clear understanding of general policies.

3. Consistency and efficiency of operations are ultimately dependent upon the existence of a sound body of policies.

4. Clear policy statement reinforce and protect the information service in matters where its position is questioned or challenged.

Value of Policies : Policies are of value in a number of ways. To name a few:

(i) They standardise activities;

(ii) Facilitate decision making;

(iii) Minimise confusion;

(iv) Coordinate the activities of various units; and

(v) Conserve time in training personnel.

Policy Questions : Information organisations must address themselves to the following basic policy questions:

1. What is the major role of the information service?

2. What are the components of the information system? And how are they related?

3. What information services are provided? And how?

4. What are the different categories of users served?

5. Which levels of services are to be provided?

6. What role is to be played by the Information Unit in relation to the services available from outside agencies?

7. What are the roles, responsibilities and relationship of the users vis-a-vis the information services administration and staff.

8. What are the lines of authority and process of decision making?

Issues for a Policy Statement **:** As mentioned earlier, policy statements are to be formulated at the institutional level, regional, state, national and international level. Whatever may be the level at which the policy has to be formulated, it should comprehend a set of basic issues. Some of these are illustrated below:

1. Identification of the objectives and thrust areas of the institution.
2. Requirement of the users.
3. Existing infrastructure and new infrastructure to be developed.
4. Manpower, material and monetary requirements.
5. Increased control of locally generated information.
6. Access to databases and databanks.
7. Information dissemination methods.
8. Information analysis and consolidation.
9. User studies and identification of user needs.
10. Improving access to new technologies.
11. Guidance for utilisation of the new technologies.
12. New services with new technologies.
13. Sharing of resources and services.
14. Increasing training of manpower.

15. Initiation into new technological developments.
16. Organising continuing education programmes.
17. Training in user training.
18. Training of trainers.
19. Guidelines for policy formulation.
20. Study and evaluation of systems and services.
21. Reviewing of the policy and its effectiveness.
22. Preparation of policy manual.
23. Cooperation and coordination with organisations at different levels and in different fields.

Process of Policy Formulation : The following framework for policy formation may be adopted:

Initiation of Policy Development : Involves preparation of a plan of action.

Review of Existing Policies : Covers identification of existing formal and informal policies.

Analysis of Existing Policies : A staff group may take up this task and identify the areas of the existing policy which may need to be rewritten or modified; as well as, new areas to be comprehended in the revision. Such decisions should primarily be based on the judgement of the effectiveness of each item of the present policy statement.

Recommendation of the New and Revised Policies : Areas in the policy that need to be rewritten or modified are to be drafted. Policy has to be formulated.

Process of Formulating Policies : A priority list of written policies that need to be drafted and outline of areas that need policy statements should be formulated.

Preparing a Policy Manual : This will form an ideal tool for management. Such a manual should comprehend objectives, planning, implementation, evaluation and revision of the policy; areas like institutional framework and linkages, services, systems and networks: personnel and management.

Dissemination of the Policy : Once the manual has been published the same need to be circulated widely for review and expert opinion.

Finalisation of the Policy : Valuable suggestions extended by reviewers and peers should be incorporated and the policy statement should be implemented.

Periodic Review of the Policy : The policy implemented has to be closely monitored for its performance. A policy review and revision programme has to be worked out.

It is increasingly being realised that information is vital for national development as like energy and manpower. Most of the nations started evolving national policies for information generation, organisation and dissemination. Inspite of restrictions trans-border data flow has become imperative and common.

Essential Needs

By and large nations have realised that the progress (if a nation depends upon the information it generates, disseminates to the users, and puts it to work. Lack of information is going to adversely affect the development.

Secondly, the cost of information is directly related to its use or application. Generation of new information needs lot of inputs by way of research, gathering, processing and storage. Information dissemination is governed by the factor of recovery of investments in research, gathering, processing and storage costs. The cost of information make it imperative to share the information in a planned manner and coordination of information activities within a nation.

In almost all countries national governments are the major investors and disseminators of information. As such, each country should evolve a national policy of its own taking into consideration the developments at national and international level.

The Guidelines

Guidelines for the National Information Policy : A national information policy should comprehend the following:

1. Identification of the information needs of different socio-professional groups.
2. Establish priorities in regard to these needs.
3. Visualise a 'National Information System' with various sub-systems, sectoral systems, etc.
4. Services to be offered and methods to provide the services.
5. Keep a watch on the capacity of the national information infrastructure (manpower, material, money etc.)
6. Decide the measures needed to enable the national information system to perform its role and ensure compatibility among the various information systems in the country.
7. Decide as to how the national information system should be further developed.
8. Development and improvement of primary publications and ensure generally of the availability of information and data.
9. Strengthening the collections and improve the accessibility.
10. Policy regarding access to foreign collections of documents and databases.
11. Development of translation services; databases; networks; preservation, dissemination and conservation of documents.
12. Bibliographical control of documents generated in the country.
13. Coordination between various information units and sub-systems.

14. Establishment of standards for information processing and communication of information.
15. Manpower planning.
16. Financing of information systems and pricing of the services.
17. Enacting appropriate legislation for regulation of information activities.
18. Promotion of user education and services.
19. Encouragement of education and research in library and information science.
20. Cooperation with other national and international organisations and institutions.

National Policy Initiative : The Department of Culture, Government of India sets up a Committee on National Policy on Library and Information Systems (Conpolis) on 7th October 1985 under the Chairmanship of Prof. D.P. Chattopadhyaya, Chairman RRRLF.

During the period between December 1985 and February 1986, the Committee toured different parts of the country and discussed with cross-sections of people. Suggestions were also received from several individuals and institutions.

An interim report was submitted in March and the final Report on 30th May 1986.

Salient Features of the Report

1. The most important task before the Government is to establish, maintain and strengthen the free public libraries in the country and enable them to work as a system.
2. The main thrust in this area should go to the rural public library. A village or a village cluster with an adequate population should have a community library which will also serve as an information centre. Resources

of different agencies engaged in the work of public health, adult education, local self-government and such others may be pooled to build up this composite centre.

3. An important link should be established between the community library of the village and the village primary school. If the school does not have a library of its own, the community library should provide the children with an adequate book-corner.

4. The community library should also importantly cater for adult education and make-adequate audiovisual aids available to attract the illiterate villages.

5. The district library should serve as an apex library for each district with public libraries at city, town and village levels constituting important components in the district library system. In addition to the usual services to be rendered by it, it should also provide for learning facilities and recreation for the handicapped, wherever possible, district libraries and comparable city public libraries should provide literature in Braille. The district library and branch libraries serve within its area wherever it is necessary and feasible. Special services should be rendered to hospitals, prisons and the infirm in their homes.

6. Libraries for special groups should be built in areas of tribal concentration or of minority communities to develop their distinctive cultures. Government will provide all encouragement for such communities to develop their own libraries through voluntary effort.

7. Each public library should have a section for children and, in addition, separate libraries for children with attractive books and audio-visual supporting material should be established wherever possible.

8. The district library will take the leadership in establishing linkages between all other public libraries of the district and work towards resource sharing within the area.

9. The key role of public libraries as chief sustaining agencies of distance education should be recognised and they should be adequately equipped with the relevant resources for this purpose.
10. All the libraries within a state should form part of a network extending from the community library of the village through intermediary levels to the district and to the State Central Library. This state network should eventually be connected with the national level network.
11. The role of the State Central Library is crucial in networking and the establishment of uniform library procedures within the State. The State Central Library or Directorate of Public Libraries has to perform as the co-ordinating agency for public libraries in the state.
12. To bring about the development of the public libraries in a state it is vital that each enacts its own library legislation. The Central Government should revise the Model Public Library Bill, which it has already prepared, in the light of experience gained in recent years and urge upon the states the importance of enacting such legislation. Finances for library development should be funded by each state either from its general revenues or from local taxation.
13. The Central Government should assist the state in the development of public libraries in a larger way than it has done so far. The Raja Rammohan Roy Library Foundation as the national agency for co-ordinating and assisting the development of public libraries be suitably strengthened enabling it to discharge its responsibilities effectively.

Empowered Committee

The Department of Culture, GOI appointed an Empowered Committee in November 1986 again under the Chairmanship of Prof D.P. Chattopadhyaya to lay down the programme of action for the implementation of the recommendations made in policy statement. The Empowered Committee submitted its Report in April 1988.

Working Group

On examination of the Empowered Committee's decisions, the Department of Culture felt that certain decision would be difficult to implement in the form envisaged by the Empowered Committee. It was accordingly decided to constitute a Working Group to go through carefully each decision of the Empowered Committee and indicate how best to implement them. This Working Group was chaired by Ms Komal Anand (Jt. Secretary to the Govt. of India, Department of Culture). The President ILA was a Member of the Group.

The Working Group discussed the whole matter in four sittings between July-September 1992 and submitted its suggestions in December 1992. These have since been accepted by the Government for implementation.

Salient features of the Empowered Committee Report as accepted by the Working Group are given below:

1. Declaring Director, National Library as the Head of the Central Reference Library.
2. Initiating action for creation of National Commission on Library Documentation and Informatics within the Government set-up.
3. Establish, maintain and strengthen public libraries in the country and enable them to work as a system.
4. Making rural library service available in each village under the "Minimum Needs Programme" by 2001 AD by Central and State Government agencies.
5. Every rural public library should have a children's section.
6. Community Centre Libraries should have AV material and equipment. Such libraries should have an important role in Adult Education Programme.

7. District Libraries should provide more facilities for the handicapped and under-privileged classes.

8. Public libraries should act as chief sustaining agencies for distance education and should be adequately equipped.

9. State Central Library should play an important role in networking, establishment of uniform library procedures and standards within the state.

10. RRRLF may establish 100 model rural libraries in collaboration with state agencies.

11. The Central Government may revise Model Public Library Bill in the light of the experience gained in the recent years.

12. The Central Government in collaboration with State Governments may establish at least one multilingual library in each state.

13. Every school and college must have a library and a qualified librarian.

14. Association of Indian Universities may take up a project evolving academic library norms on priority basis.

15. To begin with, a few selected University Library Science Departments may be provided with adequate resources as part of manpower development programme.

16. The National Library, INSDOC, DST and ICSSR may take suitable steps to create national databases.

17. There should be a National Library System (NLS) consisting of the National Library, National Depository Libraries in Delhi, Mumbai and Chennai; National subject libraries and other libraries of national importance.

18. There is a strong need of having a national R & D Centre for Library and Information Science. National

Commission on Libraries once established may consider this proposal.

19. A national 'Grid' of public libraries be developed linking village community centre library with national grid.

20. The Department of Culture may take suitable steps in preparing the Draft Bill on National Commission on Libraries (NCL) giving the detailed provision under powers and function of the NCL; Bodies of NCL; Finances of NCL, etc.

21. Department of Culture has been requested to constitute a "Library Unit" which will be entrusted with the implementation of Empowered Committee's decisions.

Most of the recommendations of the Empowered Committee are of general nature. It seems no action has been initiated either in creating the envisaged "Library Unit" or in the establishment of NCL.

The Department of Culture was vested with the responsibility of preparing the Draft Bill on NCL. The Department of Culture should appoint a 'Committee of Experts" to draft the Bill.

The proposed NCL should have more of ex-officio members rather than ad-hoc nominations. Professional associations and senior professionals should have place in the NCL.

In fact, the Department of Culture should appoint yet another committee to draft a National Library Plan giving long-term and short-term programmes, spelling out details of a "National Library System' networking: norms for cooperation and coordination of services; etc.

Seventeen

Social Role

Libraries are service centres. Libraries help the users to get the information they want. For this purpose the library staff has developed a number of tools and techniques. The classified arrangement of books on the shelves helps the users to locate easily the books they want. The library catalogue helps the users to know whether a book is available in the library or not; it is the call number in the catalogue entry helps to locate the book on the shelf. The various maps, plans, guides, etc. provided in the library helps the users to find their way in the complex library mechanism. In addition, the Reference Library Staff provides personalised service whenever the user is in difficulty. The lending, reference, bibliographic, inter-library loan, translation, reprography etc. are the general services provided by the library. Services other than these normal services, we can call as extension services.

Basic Requirements

Extension services are employed for the following purpose

1. To help the users to better utilise the library services;
2. To attract and see that more and more people make use of the library.

For achieving the first objective mentioned above, the libraries have to employ what some call as the "International Extension Services". For achieving the second objective, one has to apply what we call "External Extension Services".

Internal Services : Apart from providing assistance to users, the reference librarians or reference assistance are expected to orient the users in the library mechanism. Because libraries are these days mechanised things. Mechanised things are dependent ones. One needs orientation to exploit the resources to the fullest extent. The activities to be carried out by the Reference staff within the library to orient or educate the users are called 'Internal Extension Activities'. Some address these activities as 'User Education Programme'. Such as lower education or 'orientation' programme not only help the users in exploiting the resources of a library, but also, help the library staff in better organisation and management of the libraries. Some of these Internal Extension Services are detailed below:

Orientation into the Library Mechanism : The Reference staff may orient the users either formally or informally into the library systems. In an informal way, the user may be taken to the Library Map/Plan and explain the various sections, special collections and services. The Reference Staff may take the user personally to various sections and explain the type of material available, kind of information one can get, etc. It will be more effective if it is demonstrated to the user as to how to locate the information from various types of source material. In the formal system of orientation, the structured orientation programme may be planned wherein one can combine lectures supported by audio-visual aids; tour around the library demonstration; etc., can be used effectively.

In a formal programme, the following areas may be comprehended:

Introduction to the Library : Concept and role of the library; types of libraries; kinds of documents; sections of a library; services provided etc.

Documents : Sources-Primary, Secondary and Tertiary, Kinds-Books, Periodicals, Audio-Visual, etc.

Parts of a Book : Preliminaries-Half title page, Title page, Back of the title page, table of contents, preface, introduction; Body of the book Parts, Chapters, Paragraphs, Sectional headings, references, notes, etc., End matter-Notes, references, index etc.

Care of Books : How to pick-up a book from the shelf, opening of the book for consultation, protecting books from its enemies, improper ways of handling, etc.

Arrangement of Material: Books-textbooks, reference books-pamphlets; pictures; clippings; periodicals; films and film strips; slides; wire, tape; phono; cassettes-audio, visual; floppies; CDs, DVDs; etc.

Location of Documents : Use of catalogues-Kinds of entries; arrangement of entries; location in the catalogue; Call Number-Parts and role of each part; Arrangement of books on the shelves-Bay guides, shelf guides, inclusive numbers on the tier, arrangement are spine labels; identification of the book; etc.

Reference Books: Characteristics, Kinds-Encyclopedias; Dictionaries, atlases, almanac, guide books, gazetteers, gazettes, biographical dictionaries, indexes, etc.

Bibliography : Selection of items, arrangement; preparation of index cards; etc.

Technical Writing and Editing : Planning a study; ordering of the subject; chapterization; paragraphing; providing feature headings; hints on punctuation and capitalization; citing references; arrangement of references; editions; proof reading; etc.

Other Activities

Other extension activities that a library may take-up to bring books and users together are :

Organisation of Exhibitions- Which will help in bringing to the notice of the users the richness of the collection of the library:

topical exhibitions will attract large number of users; provide an opportunity to discover books which were not expected of.

Display of New Additions : Many libraries display the jackets of the new additions at the entrance of the library so that they can draw the attention of the users and thus tempted to read. Nagpur University Library has started a 'Monthly Book Exhibition' wherein, books added in the previous month are displayed from 3-11 of every month. This provides an opportunity for users to have a look at books on all subjects at one place. Inter-disciplinary nature of the research support such displays.

Lectures : Libraries should arrange topical lectures; lectures suitable to different sections of the users-men, women, children, students, etc. This opportunity should also be utilised for arranging suitable exhibitions/display of books and other reading material which help the users to select the right book for extended reading. Dr. Ranganathan used to bring out topical bibliographies also on such occasions and distribute them among the listeners so that they can easily select literature on their choicest subject.

Other Extension Activities: Many public libraries are also organising dramas, musical concerts, film shows, quiz programmes, elocution and essay competitions, etc. to attract the public to the library and finally become beneficiaries of its resources.

External Services : External Extension Services are those provided outside the library. These services are aimed at :

1. Creating awareness among the general public about the role of libraries, library services, etc.

2. Use of external sources like mass media, mass contact programmes, etc. for the spread of the message of the libraries as sources of enlightenment and education;

3. Organising community services, group oriented programmes, etc., as supportive to library service; and

4. Plan an integrated, coordinated and well modulated library and information services at various levels.

Reader Friendly Service : Regular users of the library know the role and resourcefulness of the libraries. There may be many who are not aware of the role of the libraries and how to exploit the resources of the library. The creation of awareness among the public may be taken up either by library staff or by voluntary organizations (NGOs).

Staff at Work

The library staff may attract the people to the library and appraise them about the role and services of the library. In fact, the library staff can serve the public at large and make them willing beneficiaries of the library-literates, neo-literates as well as illiterates. The ways and means by means of which the library staff can achieve this objective will be detailed in the next section.

Service Centres

In India, voluntary organizations (NGOs) have been playing an important role in the establishment, maintenance and execution of innovative services. The Library Movement in Andhra Desa was described as 'peoples movement' because the enlightened public took initiative in spreading the library movement to the nook and corners of the region. The Andhra Desa Library Association (established in 1914) organised 'Library Pilgrimages' for spreading the message of library movement. They used to go from place to place convince the local public the need for establishing a library, as well as, advice the existing libraries in organizing libraries on technical lines and organise various extension services to enhance their utility.

Publicity : Publicity is the art of influencing public opinion and demand. The publicity target may be general or individual. General, here we mean, those programmes which are aimed at making the public aware of the need of libraries; value of books and other reading material; educative role of libraries; services offered by the libraries; etc.

Mass Media : In this context, mass media can be exploited in spreading the message by writing articles in newspapers and magazines; radio and television talks; organising public lectures; demonstration tours; attractive sign boards; organising exhibitions: observing library weeks; publishing brochures; leaflets; bulletins; etc.

Library Bulletin : Publication of library bulletin would be a valuable medium which can be used to provide general information about library services, particularly new initiatives; routine programme of the library; topical issues: book reviews; literature survey articles; rules and regulations; special announcements; etc.

Meant for People

Use of Fairs and Festivals : India is said to live in villages. Villages have the tradition of holding fairs and festivals. These provide greater opportunity to have mass contact programmes. Programmes like lectures, exhibitions, etc. on libraries and books can be organised which will enable the public to realise the importance of libraries and the social change that the books can bring.

Wall magazines, posters, charts giving useful information about libraries, literacy, education, etc. be displayed at the venue.

Exhibition of manuscripts, maps, microforms, phonorecords, use of internet, CD-ROMs, etc. will prove to be useful.

Cultural events like dramas, film or video shows, musical concerts, etc. can be arranged at the venue of the lecture or exhibition which will attract more and more people to the event.

Social Orientation

Adult Education Programmes : As a part of the extension programmes, library enthusiasts were organising adult education classes to make the public literate so that they could make use of the libraries. Even today many of the public libraries are conducting adult education programme.

Local Broadcasting **:** Village libraries have been organising film shows, audio and video broadcasts, lecture programmes, etc. In order to enlighten the illiterate public in terms of health, hygiene, family welfare, agriculture, culture and heritage, contemporary politics and economics, etc.

Reading Newspapers, Display of Wall-newspapers **:** Libraries in the villages, in localities where there is a considerable number of illiterate population have been reading newspapers and magazine articles of interest to the illiterate public at specific hours in the morning and evening, during those hours where majority of them have a free time.

For the benefit of neo-literates, libraries do prepare wall newspapers and display in the library as well as at places where majority of the public congregates.

Collective Efforts

Reading Circles **:** Many public libraries are organising 'Reading Circles' for various groups, like, 'Women Circles'; 'Children's Circle'; 'Student's Circle'; 'Special Reading Circles' on the basis of subject, profession, etc.

Such circles are found to be always effective. These groups provide an opportunity to come together discuss, common issues, problems and get the information from the library at their disposal.

Libraries should provide suitable time, space and reading material for these groups. In the United States of America some of the public libraries are providing free accommodation for NGOs to locate their offices and offer services.

Special 'Summer Reading Programmes' for pre-schoolers; special awards or incentives to children who visit the library often and for those who read more books; special programmes like story-telling; film showing; library tours; reading lists for different age groups; different standards; lists of books giving fairly fables; poems; etc., guides to parents giving information as to how they can help their children succeed in schools.

To Young Adults : College bound students should have access to material that help develop skills for college entrance examinations (like PMT, GATE, etc.); complete set of college prospectuses; computer and internet facility: job information; career planning literature etc.

To Adults : Health guides and medical tips; events lists; reference and referral service; bibliographical service; book lists; workshops and seminars; etc. integrated services.

Extension service also implies providing library service by way or cooperation and coordination among libraries at different levels in the state.

In order to reach every person in a country, planning and service of nationwide integrated library service is essential. This implies the establishment of a National Central Library, State Central Library for each State, Regional Libraries for each of the regions within a State, Local Library Service Units in city and rural areas. The library service at the national, state, city and district levels can be provided by establishing stationary libraries, but in the suburban and rural areas below a district an independent library would not generally be a viable unit.

Promotion activities should be planned at official as well as non-official levels. Officially, the National or State libraries departments should make available financial and other assistance on a permanent basis. Besides, special National/State Commissions or Committees should be set up to report on the needs of various types of libraries. At the unofficial level, the National/State Library Associations have to play a vital role in extending extension library services. Internally, the associations should arrange various seminars and conferences so that exchange and dissemination of views and experience of the library personnel, library administrators and the readers are made possible. Externally, the associations should draw the various publicity and propaganda programmes against apathy and lack of understanding on the part of readers and other educational administrators.

SECTION TWO

OBJECTIVE QUESTIONS (SOLVED)

First Set

1. How many levels of description AACR-II provides?
   (a) Two (b) One
   (c) Three (d) Five
2. Which form of filing is also called "Nothing before something" method ?
   (a) Word by word arrangement
   (b) Letter by letter arrangement
   (c) Dictionary
   (d) Alphabetical
3. Who suggests arrangement of entries in a strict alphabetical order as in a dictionary and prefers avoiding the rule "Nothing before something" ?
   (a) Cutter (b) S.R. Ranganathan
   (c) BLA (d) ALA
4. What is the standard size of the catalogue card:
   (a) 14 cm. x 7 cm. (b) 12.5 cm. x 7.5 cm.
   (c) 10.5 cm. x 5.5 cm. (d) 12.7 cm. x 7.6 cm.
5. Rules prepared by Anthony Panizzi under the title "Rules for compiling the catalogues in the Department of Printed Books" are popularly known as .... code.
   (a) British Museum (b) Anglo-American
   (c) Dictionary Catalogue (d) Vatican
6. Ranganathan published his classified catalogue code in:
   (a) 1932 (b) 1934
   (c) 1967 (d) 1933
7. The different elements that provide information about the document in the catalogue entry are the:

(a) Data elements
(b) Access points
(c) Descriptors
(d) None of the above

8. AACR-II provides for .... areas of descriptions, however it is not necessary that every document catalogued should be provided with all the areas of description.
(a) 10
(b) 8
(c) 12
(d) 13

9. In AACR-II under "Choice of Names" there are .... rules of which four are about Pseudonyms.
(a) 16
(b) 19
(c) 10
(d) 20

10. Match the following cataloguing codes with the years given below and tick the correct answer:

A. AACR-I	(1) 1978
B. AACR-II	(2) 1967
C. ALA Code	(3) 1934
D. CCC	(4) 1949

(a) A-1 B-2, C-3, D4
(b) A- 1, B-2, C-3, D4
(c) A- 1, B-2, C-3, D4
(d) A-2, 13- 1, C-4, D-3

11. McGraw-Hill International Editions 1988 and Oriental Longman College catalogue 1987 are the examples of:
(a) Trade Catalogue
(b) Library Catalogue
(c) Union Catalogue
(d) Dictionary Catalogue

12. The catalogue which represents the collection of a number of libraries, that catalogue is termed as :
(a) Subject Catalogue
(b) Author Catalogue
(c) Joint Catalogue
(d) Union Catalogue

13. According to AACR-II Physical description about a document in a catalogue entry is called .... :
(a) Collation
(b) Imprint
(c) Physical description
(d) Additional useful information

14. In CCC the subject analytical entry is called
(a) Cross Reference Index Entry
(b) Explanatory Reference Entry
(c) Cross Reference Entry
(d) Specific Subject Entry

15. Two or more than two notes for a document are to be written separately as a separate paragraph as per:
(a) CCC (b) AACR-I
(c) AACR-2 and CCC (d) ALA

16. When a work is shared by two or more corporate bodies, AACR-II advocates entry under:
(a) The first name
(b) The first and second name
(c) The second and first name
(d) The first name with the word etc.

17. According to CCC, Ministry of Finance is an example of:
(a) Judicial body
(b) Inter governmental body
(c) Legislature body
(d) Executive body

18. The equipments such as chaindex and stripdex are associated with:
(a) Microform catalogue
(b) Machine readable catalogue
(c) Visible index form of catalogue
(d) Physical form catalogue

19. Ranganathan designed .... method of deriving subject headings for documents.
(a) Book Index Entry (b) List of Subject Entry
(c) Chain Procedure (d) Subject Index Entry

20. PRECIS adopts .... entry format for all the entries.
(a) Four line (b) Three line
(c) Five line (d) Two line

21. POPSI was designed by:
(a) Ranganathan (b) P. B. Mangala
(c) G. Bhattacharya (d) M.A. Gopinath

22. Ranganathan's Chain Procedure is based on:
(a) Canons of Classification
(b) Postulational approach
(c) Class Number
(d) Principles of Facet Sequence

23. The elementary categories of POPSI are:
(a) DEAPM (b) DEAPMP
(c) PAEDM (d) PMEST

24. Sears list of subject headings was compiled by .... and published in the year :
(a) Ranganathan, 1929 (b) Eric J. Coats, 1923
(c) Library of Congress, 1925 (d) Minnie Earl Sears, 1923

25. TCSH uses four types of cross references viz. see, see also, General and:
(a) Subject to name (b) Specific see
(c) Specific see also (d) See and see also

26. Which punctuation mark is used before the place of publication in AARC-II:
(a) Comma and space
(b) Full stop space and dash
(c) Colon and space
(d) Full stop only

27. In the collation area the size of the book is preceded by a ....:
(a) Semicolon (b) Full stop
(c) Colon (d) Full stop and dash

28. The area where the information about the place of publication, publisher and date of publication is written, is known as:
(a) Collation (b) Note section
(c) Publication (d) Imprint

29. In the main entry for a catalogue the standard ISBN or ISSN are written:
(a) In the publication area
(b) After the note area
(c) After the collation area
(d) Along with the descriptive elements

30. The primary purpose of a library catalogue is to serve as a .... to the collection of materials.
(a) Locator (b) Source
(c) Descriptor (d) None of the above

31. The National Union Catalogue of the library of Congress is an outstanding example of category of .... catalogues.

(a) Bound register (b) Printed book
(c) Card (d) Machine readable

32. Name catalogue is a variation and extension of an catalogue:
(a) Title (b) Alphabetical
(c) Author (d) None of the above

33. Stripdex, Chaindex, Kardex etc. come under the category of .... form of catalogue.
(a) Visible index (b) Card
(c) Alphabetical index (d) Machine readable

34. A .... catalogue is "a catalogue in which all entries author, title, subjects, series etc. and their relative references are arranged together in one general alphabet.
(a) Dictionary (b) Classified
(c) Alphabetical (d) Alphabetico-classed

35. In a title entry, the titles of the document are given in the .... section.
(a) Leading section (b) Author section
(c) Series section (d) None of the above

36. .... form of catalogue is one in which slips of paper are fit into a loose leaf binder and bound by some mechanical device into a volume.
(a) None of the below (b) Bound Register
(c) Card (d) Sheaf

37. It is sometimes stated that in a computerised catalogue, cataloguing rules and classification codes serve no purpose. Do you agree that in a computrised catalogue:
(a) Cataloguing rules are not necessary
(b) Classification serves no purpose
(c) Both are required
(d) None of the above

38. Cataloguing is a process and catalogue is a ....
(a) Service (b) Machine
(c) Stationary (d) Tool

39. In AACR-II uniform titles are used for:
(a) Ordinary Composite Book
(b) Artificial Composite Book
(c) Serial Publications
(d) Sacred Scriptures

40. In AACR-II periodical publication are entered under the:
(a) Publisher Name (b) Series
(c) Title (d) Name of Author

41. According to CCC, a periodical publication which has sponsoring body name as part of the ....
(a) Title section (b) Note section
(c) Heading section (d) Holding section.

42. In case of books having two series, the series name is recorded in the CCC:
(a) In the same circular brackets
(b) In separate square brackets
(c) In separate circular brackets
(d) Square brackets

43. The alphabetical part of the classified catalogue consists of:
(a) Main entry
(b) Cross reference entry
(c) All Main entry and added entry
(d) All added word entry

44. In the case of Institution as corporate author, if two or more institutions or organizations have the same name, according to CCC they are to be individualised by:
(a) Year of estabishment
(b) Name of the head of the institution
(c) Name of the organization
(d) Place name

45. According to CCC, when the different volumes of a set are published in different years, the volume that is published .... should be used for constructing book number.
(a) Second (b) First and last
(c) First (d) None of the above

46. In CCC for the editor of the series is prepared.
(a) Cross Reference Index Entry (b) Added Entry
(c) Cross Reference Entry (d) Series book Index Entry

47. The proceedings of conference which are held at regular intervals, are treated as .... by CCC.
(a) None of the Below (b) Periodical Publication
(c) Multi-volumed Publications (d) Corporate Bodies

48. CCC recommends that the name of the series for series book index entry will be rendered in the:
(a) Heading section (b) Title section
(c) Note section (d) Leading section

49. In the main entry prepared as per rules of CCC, the accession number is written on the:
(a) Fifth line of the card (b) Fourth line of the card
(c) Second last line of the card (d) First line of the card

50. Which code provides that circular brackets are to enclose each individualising and secondary elements ?
(a) AACR (b) AACR-I
(c) AACR-II (d) CCC

51. How many editions of classified Catalogue Code was published upto 1994 ?
(a) 7 (b) 8
(c) 9 (d) 5

52. The Canon of Recall value was devised by:
(a) P.B. Mangla (b) P.N. Kuala
(c) M. A. Gopinath (d) S. R. Ranganathan

53. The different organs of government in multiple corporate heading are separated in CCC by a:
(a) Full stop dash (b) Colon
(c) Comma (d) Semicolon

54. In chain procedure, class index entries is derived from
(a) Call Number (b) Book Number
(c) Collection Number (d) Class Number

55. The two indexing models viz. LCSH and SLSH are of .... type
(a) Classified (b) Alphabetical
(c) Descriptive (d) Enumerative

56. SLSH is widely used in which types of libraries ?
(a) College
(b) University
(c) Small
(d) Academic and large library

57. Free text indexing language is commonly used in which system ?

(a) Abstracting
(b) Indexing
(c) Computer based
(d) Post co-ordinate indexing

58. Subject Headings and Thesauri are two types of .... indexing language:
(a) Free
(b) Controlled
(c) Natural
(d) Conventional

59. In CCC for a periodical publication, three kinds of Class Index Entries are prepared :
(a) Specific, Generic, Optional
(b) Special, General, Optional
(c) Specific, General, Optional
(d) Optional, Generic, Special

60. If a book is having Author as well as collaborator then the name of the collaborator is .... in case of CCC.
(a) Written in the title section of the main entry
(b) Written in the heading section of the main entry
(c) Written in note section
(d) Written in the tracing

61. According to CCC, for a publication of Supreme Court of India the Entry Element will be :
(a) INDIA, SUPREME COURT
(b) Supreme Court of India
(c) SUPREMECOURT, INDIA
(d) Government of India, Supreme Court

62. Festschrift is an example of
(a) Artificial composite book
(b) Ordinary composite book
(c) Corporate composite book
(d) Multivolume and serial publication

63. The proceedings of conferences which are held at regular intervals, are treated as .... by CCC.
(a) Serial publication
(b) Multivolumed publication
(c) Government publication
(d) Corporate bodies publication

64. CCC recommends that the name of the Authors in Book Index Entry will be rendered in the:
(a) Leading Section
(b) Heading Section
(c) Title Section
(d) Note Section

65. In CCC, for the editor or editors of the series is prepared
(a) Cross Reference Index Entry
(b) Series Book Index Entry
(c) Collaborator Book Index Entry
(d) Cross Reference Entry

66. If there are two or more than two parts of Class Index Entry in CCC, they are separated by a :
(a) Full stop and dash
(b) Semicolon
(c) Comma
(d) Dot

67. Class Index Entry and Book Index Entry is a:
(a) Class No. Entry
(b) Number Entry
(c) Number and Word Entry
(d) Word Entry

68. The Tracing Section of the main entry card is a helpful aid for the :
(a) Readers
(b) Readers and Stafves
(c) Reference Librarian
(d) Library Stafves

69. According to CCC, in the main entry, the leading section is made up of:
(a) Accession Number
(b) Book Number
(c) Collection Number and Class Number
(d) Call Number

70. In case of periodical publication the information about the library holdings is entered in .... in CCC.
(a) Tracing section
(b) At the end of the card
(c) Note section
(d) Holding section

71. In case of multivolumed books having a common running title and each volume having individual titles, the information about the individual title is to be given
(a) Heading Area
(b) Tracing Area
(c) Physical Description Area
(d) Note Area

72. Union catalogue is a form of:
(a) Centralised catalogue
(b) Limited catalogue
(c) Cooperative catalogue
(d) Descriptive catalogue

73. According to CCC, the safest course to determine the choice of heading is to rely on the canon of:
(a) Prepotence and Context (b) Individualization
(c) Recall value (d) Ascertainability

74. British Museum general catalogue of printed book is a catalogue
(a) Series (b) Author
(c) Title (d) Name of Collaborator

75. Subject analytical entry in AACR-2 is known as .... analytical entry.
(a) Reference (b) Author
(c) Subject (d) Title

76. .... link in chain procedure is usually a part of class number, which has no meaning in a verbal heading.
(a) False (b) Sought and Unsought
(c) Missing (d) False and Missing

77. CCC puts societies, associations and religious bodies under:
(a) Personal name (b) Agencies
(c) Institution (d) Government

78. In CCC, societies are entered directly under:
(a) Name of societies
(b) Their official names only
(c) The best known name
(d) The subordinate body

79. In PRECIS, the index entries and references are brought together and merged according to:
(a) Alphabetical and classified sequence
(b) Word by word arragement
(c) Letter by letter arrangement
(d) Single alphabetical sequence

80. In LCSH, complex headings display .... concepts.
(a) Array and Facet (b) Facet
(c) Phase and Facet (d) General

81. LCSH can serve as Index to .... documents.
(a) Micro and macro
(b) Graphic
(c) Non-documentary and documentary
(d) All the above

82. LCSH originated at the Library of Congress in the year
(a) 1897
(b) 1896
(c) 1884
(d) 1823

83. The area of the Main Entry where the name of a person, a corporate body, pseudonym or the title of the book is written is known as :
(a) Call No. section
(b) Descriptive element area
(c) Heading area
(d) Collation area

84. Data comprising author, publisher, title, place and year of publication, number of pages and illustrations etc. is called:
(a) Annotations
(b) Imprint
(c) Standard format
(d) Bibliographical data

85. For cataloguing of document the .... is the main source of information.
(a) Half Title
(b) Title page and back of title page
(c) Title Page and half title page
(d) Overflow Page

86. A subject approach in a library, a library catalogue fulfills two functions : to show library holdings on a particular subject and on:
(a) Compound subject
(b) Complex subject
(c) Related subject
(d) Other subject

87. Chain Procedure, PRECIS and POPSI are the systems based on:
(a) Alphabetical method
(b) Classificatory principles
(c) Descriptive method
(d) Enumerative method

88. While helps shelf order by Subject arrangement of the documents .... represents them in card files.
(a) Classification, catalogue
(b) Shelf list, documentation list
(c) Shelf list, classification
(d) Shelf list, catalogue

89. .... form refers to the preparation of bibliographical entries of documents of the library and their arrangement to fall into specified sequence to retrieve information about documents in the library.
(a) Physical (b) Outer
(c) Inner (d) Modern

90. In DDC, the Class Number of Dictionary of Philosophy is :
(a) 100.3 (b) 100.003
(c) 103 (d) 100.03

91. In DDC, Table-3 is mainly meant for the main class :
(a) 100 (b) 800
(c) 500 (d) 300

92. In DDC, Table-4 is exclusively meant for the main class :
(a) 600 (b) 900
(c) 400 (d) 200

93. The standard subdivisions always consist of atleast two digits of which the first one is :
(a) 024 (b) 09
(c) 0 (d) 089

94. The use of abbrevations r.e.n. in the relative index of DDC stands for the notation in:
(a) Table-4 (b) Table-3
(c) Table-1 (d) Table-5

95. The use of abbrevations s.s. in the relative index of DDC stands for the notation in :
(a) Table-2 (b) Table-6
(c) Table-7 (d) Table-1

96. Which of the following denotes the relative position of a document in a library and the position of its entry in the catalogue :
(a) Class Number (b) Call Number
(c) Accession Number (d) Book Number

97. The call number 2: 55 N6 N88 indicates that it is the call number of a :
(a) Undersized Book (b) Oversized Book
(c) Abnormal Book (d) Wornout Book

98. Tell-Tale the means :
    (a) Story telling book
    (b) Short title of the book
    (c) Fanciful title
    (d) Title that discusses the subject of the work
99. According to AACR-II, in Main Entry, Statement like Bound Together with or Published Earliest as or Merged with, are recorded in the :
    (a) Tracing Area (b) Material area
    (c) Note Area (d) Heading Area
100. The formation of subject heading in PRECIS is done by Human Indexer and :
    (a) Computer (b) Photocopy
    (c) MARC (d) Duplicator

Answers

1. c	2. a	3. b	4. b	5. a
6. b	7. a	8. b	9. b	10. d
11. a	12. d	13. a	14. c	15. c
16. a	17. d	18. c	19. c	20. d
21. c	22. c	23. a	24. d	25. a
26. b	27. a	28. d	29. b	30. a
31. b	32. c	33. a	34. a	35. a
36. d	37. c	38. d	39. d	40. c
41. a	42. c	43. d	44. d	45. c
46. a	47. b	48. d	49. c	50. d
51. d	52. d	53. c	54. d	55. d
56. c	57. c	58. b	59. a	60. a
61. a	62. b	63. a	64. b	65. a
66. c	67. d	68. d	69. d	70. d
71. d	72. c	73. d	74. b	75. c
76. a	77. c	78. a	79. d	80. b
81. d	82. a	83. b	84. d	85. b
86. c	87. b	88. a	89. c	90. c
91. b	92. c	93. c	94. d	95. d
96. b	97. c	98. d	99. c	100. a

Second Set

1. The unit card principle that came up with the .... has enabled the growth of centralised and co-operative cataloguing.
   (a) Register Catalogue (b) Sheaf Catalogue
   (c) Printed Catalogue (d) Card Catalogue
2. According to AACR-II, political parties, firms and associations come under the category of:
   (a) Governmental body (b) Institution and societies
   (c) Societies (d) Conference
3. The word catalogue has been derived from the .... expression katalogus
   (a) French (b) Greek
   (c) Latin (d) Spanish
4. "Cataloguing in publication" was termed as Prenatal cataloguing by .... :
   (a) S. R. Ranganathan (b) M.A. Gopinath
   (c) H.E. Bliss (d) Anthony Panizzi's
5. "The Library of Congress Filing Rules" was published in:
   (a) 1971 (b) 1968
   (c) 1956 (d) 1957
6. Machine Readable Catalogue (MARC) finally came into existence in :
   (a) 1966 (b) 1967
   (c) 1968 (d) 1969
7. The Revised 2nd Edition of Anglo-American Cataloguing Rules was published in:

(a) 1941 (b) 1978
(c) 1968 (d) 1988

8. Work of unknown authorship is called:
(a) Corporate author work (b) Periodical publication
(c) Fictitious work (d) Anonymous work

9. Most of the sacred books and many old and medieval texts are .... works:
(a) Artificial Compositive (b) Ordinary composite
(c) Anonymous (d) Pseudonymous

10. Sacred Scriptures are to be rendered under:
(a) Published Title of the Scripture
(b) Edition name
(c) Commonly known name
(d) Uniform title

11. In case of English Names, ... is the entry element.
(a) Title of honour (b) Fore name
(c) Surname (d) None of the above

12. According to CCC .... is a name assumed by an author to conceal, is identity:
(a) Pseudonym (b) Pen name
(c) Private name (d) corporate bodies

13. According to CCC, political parties, firms and associa-tionscomes under the category of:
(a) Institution (b) Subordinate bodies
(c) Adhoc bodies (d) Government

14. .... reflects the arrangement of document in the library:
(a) Shelf list (b) Kardex
(c) Bibliographic list (d) Cataloguing list

15. Catalogue consists of strips mounted on a frame or cards held flat, hinged and with edge of each card protruding so as to make the heading visible:
(a) Visible index (b) Micro form
(c) Loose leaf form (d) Machine readable

16. When a book is written by two authors, then according to AACR-II, the heading is made under ?

(a) First Author (b) Title
(c) Editor (d) Both the Authors

17. When a book is written by 4 Authors then according to AACR-II, the heading is made under ?
(a) All Authors (b) Title
(c) Sub Title (d) None of the above

18. When a book is written under editorial direction of two persons, the entry in AACR-2 would be made under ?
(a) First Editor (b) Well known editor
(c) Title (d) None of the above

19. Apart from the author, if there are two or more persons like editors, translators etc., responsible for the publication of the book they are called :
(a) Collaborators (b) Compilers
(c) Editorial (d) Corporate bodies

20. According to AACR-II, periodical publications are entered under:
(a) Name of sponsoring bodies (b) Name of editor
(c) Title (d) Name of publisher

21. According to AACR-II, Bible comes under the category of
(a) Heavenly work (b) Uniform title
(c) Anonymous work (d) Corporate authorship

22. In case of Publication by the Department of Higher Education, Ministry of Education, Government of India, the entry according to AACR II would be:
(a) India, Ministry of Education, Department of Higher Education
(b) Ministry of Education. India
(c) India Department of Higher Education
(d) Department of Higher Education (India)

23. In case of proceeding of 11th International Management Congress, held in Madras in 1984, the entry would be made under:
(a) 11 th International Management Congress (Madras)
(b) International Management Congress (11 th : 1984 : Madras)

(c) Proceeding of 11th International Management Congress. (1984 Madras: 11th)

(d) None of the above

24. The rendering of the "Festival of United States held in India in 1980" would be:
(a) India, Festival of United States
(b) Festival of United States (1980 : India)
(c) Festival of United States, India 1980
(d) United States, America, Festival of United States

25. The name of the authors in the heading section of the Main Entry card will be joined with the word .... according to CCC.
(a) and (b) or
(c) comma (d) hyphen

26. .... are the translation of the class numbers of documents into their verbal equivalents, representing the different hierarchical levels of the subject.
(a) Feature headings
(b) Title and subject heading
(c) Descriptors
(d) None of the above

27. Subject heading and Thesauri come under the category of .... indexing languages.
(a) Controlled (b) Free
(c) Natural (d) None of the above

28. According to CCC book written by three authors, the entry is to be made under:
(a) Title (b) All the authors
(c) First author (d) First two authors

29. According to AACR II, book written by four authors entry is to be made under:
(a) Title (b) Under first
(c) All authors (d) None of the above

30. According to AACR-II, in case of a publication by the Lok Sabha, the entry would be made under:
(a) India, Lok Sabha

(b) India, Parliament, Lok Sabha
(c) India, Parliament. Lok Sabha
(d) Lok Sabha (India)

31. According to CCC, in case of a publication by the Lok Sabha, the heading would be made under:
(a) INDIA, LOK SABHA
(b) INDIA, PARLIAMENT, LOK SABHA
(c) LOK SABHA (India)
(d) India, Parliament, Lok Sabha

32. In case of publication by the Planning Commission of India, CCC advocates entry under:
(a) INDIA, PLANNING COMMISSION
(b) PLANNING COMMISSION (India)
(c) PLANNING COMMISSION (New Delhi)
(d) None of the above

33. If a book is having author as well as collaborator then the name of the collaborator is .... in case of CCC.
(a) Written in title section of the main entry
(b) Note section of the main entry
(c) Heading Section of the main entry
(d) None of the above

34. According to AACR II, for a publication of Supreme Court of India, the entry element will be:
(a) India Supreme Court
(b) Supreme Court of India
(c) INDIA, JUDGE OF THE COURT
(d) Judiciary, India Supreme Court

35. .... is generally used in big Indian libraries for maintaining records pertaining to current periodicals.
(a) Kardex (b) Card catalogue
(c) Register form (d) Magnetic form

36. In the main entry .... gives information about the additional entries that are provided for the document.
(a) Heading area (b) Note area
(c) Physical description area (d) Tracing

37. In .... system, the main entry and the added entries carry the same description about the document.
    (a) Unit Card
    (b) Multicard System
    (c) Alphabetical
    (d) Dictionary and Alphabetical

38. Arrangement of entries in the .... catalogue will be according to the alphabetical order of the surname of the authors, if any, title, subject, collaborator etc.
    (a) Dictionary (b) Classified
    (c) Alphabetico-classed (d) Card

39. Which entry is known as reference entry in CCC ?
    (a) Optional index entry (b) Cross reference entry
    (c) Cross reference index entry (d) Book index entry

40. .... entry in CCC is known as subject analytical.
    (a) Main (b) Cross reference
    (c) Cross reference index (d) Class index

41. According to AACR-II, a work which is the result of the responsibility shared by two corporate bodies should be entered under :
    (a) First name of the corporate body
    (b) All the names of the corporate bodies
    (c) Title of the documents
    d) First and second name of the corporate body

42. Classification and Cataloguing are two distinct but interrelated techniques for organising a library collection while classification helps in subject arrangement of documents, catalogues represent them in:
    (a) Shelf order, Card file form
    (b) Cataloguing, alphabetical order
    (c) Indexing and retrieval
    (d) Abstracting

43. .... of documents in the library is reflected by shelf list:
    (a) Grouping (b) Class number
    (c) Arrangement (d) Alphabetical Filing

44. Some of the catalogue codes like Vatican code and the .... have included filing rules also in their cataloguing rules.
(a) CCC
(b) AACR-I
(c) British Museum Code
(d) Cutter's Rules for a Dictionary Catalogue

45. International Communication format for the exchange of catalogue data:
(a) MARC (b) SGML
(c) CIP (d) HTTP

46. CCC states that the safest course to determine the choice of the heading is to rely on the:
(a) Canon of Prepotence
(b) Canon of Currency
(c) Canon of Parsimony
(d) Canon of Ascertainability

47. A library catalogue is a time saving device, this statement helps us in realizing the objectives of the .... law of library science.
(a) Fourth (b) First and Second
(c) Third (d) Fourth and Fifth

48. Library of Congress subject heading list, SLSH, Chain procedure, POPSI and PRECIS are the examples of the:
(a) Alphabetical Indexing System
(b) Abstracting Systems
(c) Alphabetical System
(d) Conventional Systems

49. In AACR-II, standard numbers ISBN or ISSN are written:
(a) Physical description area (b) Note area
(c) After the note area (d) Tracing Area

50. According to .... in the main entry, the leading section is made up of call no.
(a) CCC (b) ALA Code
(c) AACR-I (d) AACR-II

51. In the directing section of the Class Index Entry in CCC, the last is followed by the

(a) Class number
(b) Book number
(c) One part of the Class number and one part of Book number.
(d) Call no.

52. As per CCC, the headings in the Class Index Entry are to be written in.................form the .... vertical.
(a) Small letters, first (b) Small letters, second
(c) Capitals, first (d) Capitals, Second

53. International Conference on cataloguing principles held at in year ....
(a) Paris, 1962 (b) America, 1961
(c) Paris, 1961 (d) Spain, 1961

54. The rendering of the name James Aryhor John as per AACR-II would be :
(a) Arthor John, James (b) James Arthor John
(c) John, James Arthor (d) John, (James Arthor)

55. The rendering of the name Joaquim Pedro Ferreira and John Suckling as per AACR-II would be:
(a) Ferreira, Joaquim Pedro
(b) Ferreira, Joaquim Pedro and Suckling, John
(c) Ferreira (Joaquim Pedro) and Suckling (John)
(d) None of the above

56. As per AACR II, when relevant information is taken from outside the main source, it is written in
(a) Square brackets (b) Small letters
(c) Capital letters (d) Circular brackets

57. In the .... level of description all elements set out in the rules of AACR-2 which are applicable to the particular item that is being catalogued are to be included:
(a) First (b) Second
(c) Fourth (d) Third

58. The three types of analytical entries in CCC are Author Analytical, Subject Analytical and
(a) Name Analytical
(b) Title Analytical
(c) Series Analytical
(d) Joint Collaborator Analytical

59. The two prominent inner forms of cataglogues are:
(a) Classified Catalogue and Dictionary Catalogue
(b) Alphabetical and Alphabetico-Classed Catalogue
(c) Alphabetical Catalogue
(d) Subject Catalogue and Title Catalogue

60. The classified catalogue is a :
(a) Subject Catalogue (b) Title Catalogue
(c) Author Catalogue (d) Collaborator Catalogue

61. The concept which enables libraries to use the bibliographical data available on the verso of the title page of the book for the preparation of their catalogues is called
(a) Prenatal Cataloguing
(b) Cataloguing in Publication
(c) Cataloguing in Source
(d) Both (a) and (b)

62. Name catalogue is a variation of .... catalogue :
(a) Author Catalogue
(b) Title Catalogue
(c) Person Catalogue
(d) Joint Author and Collaborator

63. When a publisher provides the catalogue entry in the book itself, it is known as:
(a) Cataloguing in source (b) Subject catalogue
(c) Book trade catalogue (d) Book catalogue

64. In a classified catalogue, the Main Entry, cross reference Entry and Class Index Entry are .... entries.
(a) Subject Entry
(b) Title Entry
(c) Author and Collaborator Entry
(d) None of the above

65 . Indexing systems are a systems :
(a) post coordinate (b) Alphabetical
(c) POPSI (d) Pre-coordinate

66. In AACR-II when the book is entered under title. The title information begins from the first indention and continues from second indention, this type of transcribing is known as:

(a) Analytical Indention (b) False Indention
(c) Imaginary Indention (d) Hanging Indention

67. In AACR-II the entry element for Government is the:
(a) Geographical area of the Country
(b) Head of the Government
(c) Name of the Head of the particular department
(d) None of the above

68. Indian Council of Medical Research is a Government agency. According to AACR-II in such cases, the main entry is made under
(a) The name of the Organization
(b) Name of the Director
(c) Name of the Registrar
(d) Name of the Geographical Area

69. According to AACR-II Bhagvada Gita, Ved and Upanishad are the example of:
(a) Artificial Composite Book (b) personal Authorship
(c) Corporate Body (d) None of the above

70. In the main entry of CCC, the leading section is made up of the .... of the document.
(a) Author (b) Call Number
(c) Class Number (d) None of the above

71. In CCC, the Class Index Entries are prepared for the .... only.
(a) Unsought links (b) False links
(c) Missing links (d) Sought links

72. In CCC, tracing gives information about the:
(a) Word entries only
(b) Additional entries of the document
(c) Book index entries of the document only
(d) Class index entries only

73. Pseudo series is the creation of:
(a) AACR-I (b) AACR-2
(c) CCC (d) Publisher

74. In CCC, the name of the series in the book index entry is rendered in capitals in :
(a) Heading Section (b) Note Section
(c) Leading Section (d) Title Section

75. In AACR-2 when relevant information is taken from outside of the main source, it is written :
(a) In bold (b) In Italics
(c) In square brackets (d) In circular brackets

76. The book Anglo-American Cataloguing Rules, Edition 2 has two parts namely:
(a) Description, Determination of heading
(b) Alphabetical, Classified
(c) Rule part, Practical part
(d) Rule part, Description part

77. A person who collects matter from the books of various person, a :
(a) Collaborator (b) Reviser
(c) Author (d) Compiler

78. The classified part of the Catalogue consists of main entry and:
(a) Cross Reference entry (b) Reference entry
(c) Class Index entry (d) Main entry

79. In CCC, tracing is done on the .... of the main entry cards.
(a) Below portion of main card
(b) Back side
(c) Right portion of the front side
(d) Left Portion of the front side

80. If all the volumes of the book, which have been published are not possessed by the library is called
(a) Half set (b) Broken set
(c) Complete set (d) Incomplete set

81. If the book is not having any author but contains the name of the collaborator, the heading section contains .... in .... CCC.
(a) Title information (b) Publisher's name
(c) Collaborator's name (d) Series information

82. In CCC if the head of the government is the author, then the heading would be:
(a) The Name of the geographical area
(b) The designation of the head
(c) The name of the head
(d) The name of the office of the head

83. In CCC, the rendering of the Author Dr. S.M. Tripathi will be:
(a) Tripathi, (SM) (b) TRIPATHI (SM)
(c) Tripathi, S.M. (d) S.M. TRIPATHI

84. In AACR-II if all the works by one person appear under his pseudonymous name, the entry element should be, under:
(a) The Title
(b) The Real Name
(c) Both the Real and the Pseudonym
(d) The Pseudonym

85. In CCC, the title page contains two names of the authors, the heading section contains
(a) Both the names (b) First author only
(c) Second author only (d) Title only

86. Cross Reference Entry may also be called .... Entry in CCC.
(a) Book Index Entry (b) Class Index Entry
(c) Subject Analytical (d) Title Analytical

87. A .... is inserted between the name of the sponsor and the title proper of the periodical in CCC.
(a) Comma (b) Colon
(c) Semicolon (d) Dash

88. The document, Annual Report of the Reserve Bank of India is an Example of:
(a) Government as Author (b) Institution as Author
(c) Conference as Author (d) Committee as Author

89. The Main Entry of Simple periodical publication consists of leading, heading, series, holding, tracing and
(a) Periodicity Section (b) Note Section
(c) Second Section (d) Index Number Section

90. KWIC Indexing was devised by:
(a) Derek Austin (b) C.W. Cleverdon
(c) Mark Taylor (d) H.P. Luhn

91. In AACR-2, the series are in Main Entry comes after the:
(a) Edition Area
(b) Material Detail Area

(c) Publication Distribution Area
(d) Physical Description Area

92. According to CCC, in a Class Index Entry of a periodical publication, the directing words are omitted for:
(a) Optional Class Index Entry
(b) Specific Class Index Entry
(c) Generic Class Index Entry
(d) All of the above

93. In AACR-2, individual title of different volumes are to be recorded in the :
(a) Heading area
(b) Physical Description Area
(c) Note area
(d) Tracing Area

94. In AACR-2, in case of sacred scriptures, the heading part of the Main Entry is the:
(a) Parallel title (b) Uniform title
(c) Collective titles (d) Sub title

95. In the case of Commission and committees, the name of the Commission or Committee is written in the .... area of AACR-2.
(a) Heading (b) Note
(c) Publication Distribution (d) Physical Description

96. In CCC, in case of Pseudonymous works if the title page contains Pseudonym and the real name is subordinate manner than the heading section contains the pseudonymous of the author and the real name of the author added thereafter and enclosed
(a) In a square bracket (b) In a circular bracket
(c) In a single inverted comma (d) In the next line

97. When articles by different authors are published under the one title, that book is known as .... in .... CCC.
(a) Ordinary Composite Book
(b) Anonymous work
(c) Composite Book
(d) Artificial Composite Work

98. Common usage, uniformity in headings, and .... are the principles involved in determining subjects heading
    (a) Special Reference entry (b) Direct entry
    (c) Specific Reference (d) Scatter References

99. In the case of three or more than three authors responsible for the work, the heading section contains .... in CCC.
    (a) The name of the first author
    (b) Title
    (c) The names of all the authors
    (d) The names of the first mentioned author with the word 'and others'

100. In CCC, the Class Index Entry is derived from the:
    (a) Book Number (b) Class Number
    (c) Call Number (d) Accession Number

Answers

1. d	2. c	3. b	4. a	5. c
6. a	7. d	8. d	9. d	10. d
11. c	12. a	13. a	14. a	15. a
16. a	17. b	18. c	19. a	20. c
21. b	22. a	23. b	24. b	25. a
26. a	27. a	28. c	29. a	30. c
31. a	32. a	33. c	34. a	35. a
36. d	37. a	38. a	39. b	40. b
41. a	42. c	43. b	44. d	45. a
46. d	47. a	48. a	49. c	50. a
51. a	52. c	53. c	54. c	55. b
56. a	57. a	58. b	59. a	60. a
61. d	62. a	63. a	64. a	65. a
66. d	67. a	68. a	69. d	70. b
71. d	72. b	73. c	74. c	75. c
76. a	77. d	78. a	79. b	80. d
81. c	82. a	83. b	84. d	85. a
86. c	87. a	88. b	89. a	90. d
91. d	92. d	93. c	94. b	95. b
96. b	97. a	98. b	99. d	100. b

Third Set

1. Which kind of notations are used in DDC ?
   (a) General (b) Mixed
   (c) Pure (d) More than three
2. In DDC, when not instructed in schedule, -089 is used for...........table:
   (a) Second (b) Third
   (c) Fifth (d) Seventh
3. .... can ensure subject approach to library material and strengthen other services in library.
   (a) Cataloguing (b) Abstracting
   (c) Reference service (d) Classification
4. When the number of table 5th and 2nd are used together, then is used between them:
   (a) 09 (b) 088
   (c) 089 (d) 0
5. The ...... lay down the process of work in the idea plane.
   (a) Canons (b) Common Isolate
   (c) Postulates (d) Laws
6. Subject arrangement of documents is also known as:
   (a) Facet sequence (b) Sequence
   (c) Filiatory sequence (d) Chronological device
7. Who was the chief architect of the dynamic theory of library classification ?
   (a) Fremont Rider (b) P.N. Kaula
   (c) S.R. Ranganathan (d) E.C. Richardson

8. Who was the first classification is to use simple Indo Arabic Numerals (0-9) as ordinal numbers for the systematic listing of subjects in his classification scheme.
   (a) S. R. Ranganathan (b) W.T. Harris
   (c) Melvil Dewey (d) J. D. Brown

9. Placing closely related subjects in close proximity in a scheme of classification is called
   (a) Reduction (b) Collocation
   (c) Literary Warrant (d) Facet Sequence

10. What is "Law of local variation" formulated by Dr. Ranganathan ?
   (a) Common Isolate (b) Basic Laws
   (c) Principles (d) Five Laws

11. Canons for ...... plane have been grouped into basic canons, mnemonic, growing universe and book classification.
   (a) Verbal (b) Idea
   (c) Notational (d) All the above

12. The concept of facet analysis and fundamental categories deals with:
   (a) Devices (b) Connective symbols
   (c) Principles (d) Laws

13. Brown's subject classification is based upon two basic principles of:
   (a) Dynamic theory and Descriptive theory
   (b) General and Special theory
   (c) Pure and Applied theory
   (d) One place theory, Science and application theory

14. Terms like classification, cataloguing, circulation, accession, documentation denote which isolate idea ?
   (a) Material (b) Property
   (c) Energy (d) Space type of

15. In CC7, the Physiology and diseases are which type of isolates?
   (a) Energy (b) Personality
   (c) Matter Property (d) All the above

16. DDC is an .... classification.
(a) Analytico-synthetic (b) Almost enumerative
(c) Faceted (d) Freely faceted

17. UDC is a/an .... classification scheme:
(a) Freely faceted (b) Almost Faceted
(c) Enumerative (d) Faceted

18. The mapping of subjects, in DDC proceeds from ...... and end up with hierarchical chains :
(a) Main headings to sub-headings
(b) Sub-heading to main headings
(c) General to particular
(d) All the above

19. In CC, the class numbers for specials are derived by which device ?
(a) Enumerative (b) Chronological
(c) Subject (d) Alphabetical

20. What kind of notations are used in UDC.
(a) Pure (b) Faceted
(c) Rigid (d) Mixed

21. In DDC 20th ed. tables .... can be used as required with any appropriate number from the schedules.
(a) 3, 4 and 5 (b) 1, 2 and 6
(c) 1, 2, 5 and 7 (d) 3 and 7

22. Ranganathan found out away to recognise .... by the method of residue.
(a) Time and space (b) Matter
(c) Energy (d) Personality

23. According to CC, in book number, the volumes of the set are to be individualised by putting a
(a) Colon (b) Colon and semicolon
(c) Comma (d) Dot

24. Dr. Ranganathan has identified four kinds of Mnemonics as Alphabetical, Scheduled, Systematic and:
(a) Unscheduled (b) Verbal
(c) Seminal (d) None of these

25. Which notation contain two or more kinds of sets of symbols, e.g., numerals or letters?
    (a) Pure (b) Mixed
    (c) Facted (d) Hierarchical
26. The collection number scheme must be formulated and maintained by which section of the library ?
    (a) Reference (b) Periodical
    (c) Computer (d) Technical
27. Which device is used for increasing the capacity of an array with the aid of an empty digit:
    (a) Subject (b) Geographical
    (c) Gap (d) Sectorising
28. Which canon out of the following states that the sequence of the classes in an array of classes, and of the ranked isolates, should be helpful to those for whom it is intended?
    (a) Helpful Sequence (b) Consistent Sequence
    (c) Exclusiveness (d) Exhaustiveness
29. In 6th edition of CC common isolates are of two types namely:
    (a) Common subdivision and ACI
    (b) ACI and PCI
    (c) Energy and PCI
    (d) None of these
30. In UDC, the common auxiliaries of form are put in parenthesis with a connecting symbol
    (a) Dash (b) Naught
    (c) Colon (d) Hyphen
31. In DDC Common Isolates are called
    (a) Common Subdivision (b) Standard Subdivisions
    (c) Other Auxiliaries (d) Form Divisions
32. In DDC 19, table-3 is meant for
    (a) Literature
    (b) Language of Literature
    (c) Subdivision of Language
    (d) Subdivisions of Individual Literature

33. The concept of Common Isolates was first introduced by:
(a) Ranganathan (b) Brown
(c) Melvil Dewey (d) Paul Otlet

34. Colon (:) was first used in which classification scheme
(a) CC (b) UDC
(c) DDC (d) LC

35. An interaction between two subjects is called
(a) Intra Facet Relation (b) Phase Relation
(c) Intra Array Relation (d) All the above

36. Practical classification becomes methodical with the help of:
(a) Facet analysis (b) Postulational approach
(c) Canons (d) Principles

37. In UDC, which one of the facet relation signs is used when a reverse of two facets is not required ?
(a) Colon (b) Semicolon
(c) Double colon (d) Hyphen

38. "Cataloguing of periodicals in University Library of Rajasthan in 1996" , in this title the following elements can be identified:
(a) PM,E,S,T (b) BS.PE,STMT
(c) BS. E,PM,S,T (d) BS., PM,E,S,T

39. In CC 6th revised edition, which indicators are used to combine the facets (PMEST) ?
(a) (;) (:), (.),(,) (::) (b) (,), (;), (:), (.), (')
(c) Only (d) (:) and

40. The single idea that can go with any basic subject is called
(a) Main class (b) Facet
(c) Common Isolate (d) Isolate

41. According to S. R. Ranganathan, which category is the central core of a subject
(a) Space (b) Time
(c) Personality (d) Energy

42. In CC 6th revised edition, single inverted comma(') is used for:
(a) Space (b) Space and time both
(c) Only time (d) Energy

43. For the title "Basmati Rice" the class number according to CC is J381 B. In this class number which device is used ?
(a) Alphabetical device (b) Schedule device
(c) Chronological device (d) Geographical device

44. In DDC, wherein the synonymous terms are listed?
(a) Schedule (b) Table-4
(c) Introduction table (d) Relative index

45. Library Classification yields subject-wise arrangement of library material in which each subject is followed by another subject related to it, is known as
(a) Broken Arrangement
(b) Author Arrangement
(c) Classified Arrangement
(d) Alphabetical Arrangement

46. What is the means of bringing the related documents of same subject at one place on the shelves, or in form to their entries in a catalogue :
(a) Abstracting (b) Thesaurus
(c) Documentation (d) Classification

47. Match the following:

A. Richardson	1. Principles of Book Classification
B. Hulme	2. Canons of Classification
C. Sayers	3. Prolegomena to Library Classification
D. Ranganathan	4. Classification : Theoretical and Practical

(a) A-4, B-1, C-2, D-3 (b) A-3, B-2, C-4, D-1
(c) A-4, B- 1, C-3, D-2 (d) A-4, B-2, C-3, D-1

48. Dr. Ranganathan has recognised three manifestations of the matter fundamental category. What are they
(a) Energy, Time and Material
(b) Matter material, Matter property, Matter method
(c) Matter material, Matter Method, Matter energy
(d) Matter process, space, Matter energy

49. In UDC, which symbol is used to indicate all types and kind of phase and facet relations:
(a) Dot (b) Double Colon
(c) Colon (d) Semicolon

50. In CC "p" means:
(a) Periodical (b) Publication
(c) Conference (d) History

51. The method of analysis of subject contents of a document into their facets is known as :
(a) Analysis (b) Contents analysis
(c) Categorical analysis (d) Facet analysis

52. Second edition of DDC was published in:
(a) 1876 (b) 1895
(c) 1989 (d) 1885

53. In a specific subject if the extension .... then the intension:
(a) Decrease, increase (b) Increase, decrease
(c) Decrease, static (d) Static, decrease

54. RIC stands for:
(a) Round in classification
(b) Round increasing code
(c) Riders International Classification
(d) None of these

55. S.C. stands for:
(a) Schedule Caste (b) Subject Classification
(c) Subject Cataloguing (d) Sub class

56. Relation between the same facets in the basic class is known as:
(a) Intra subject phase relation
(b) Intra array phase relation
(c) Intra facet phase relation
(d) All the above

57. Which connecting symbol is used in CC6 for time ?
(a) ' Single inverted comma (b) : Colon
(c) . Dot (d) ; Semicolon

58. In Book No. 'P means:
(a) Facet (b) Fundamental
(c) Form (d) None of these

59. Phoenix Schedule means:
    (a) Rigidly faceted
    (b) Freely faceted
    (c) Special scheme of classification
    (d) A completely new development of the schedule for a specific discipline

60. Melvil Dewey first worked as a library assistant, when he was student in which college
    (a) Columbia College (b) Amherst College
    (c) Columbia University (d) California

61. Who is well known for his principles of Scientific and Educational Consensus ?
    (a) Ranganathan (b) H.E. Bliss
    (c) J.D. Brown (d) Phillips

62. How many volumes are in full edition of BBK:
    (a) 4 (b) 32
    (c) 28 (d) 30

63. The concept of mnemonic is not used in which scheme of classification?
    (a) CC (b) DDC
    (c) Library of Congress (d) UDC

64. Dichotomy Classification is also known as :
    (a) Faceted classification
    (b) Binary classification
    (c) Colon classification
    (d) Enumerative classification

65. C.A. Cutter used dot (.) in Expansive Classification for:
    (a) Main class (b) Space
    (c) Time (d) Common Isolates

66. Retroactive ordinal notation invented by:
    (a) H.E. Phillips (b) H.E. Bliss
    (c) A. Neelamegham (d) Erec de Groiler

67. Fourth International Study Conference was held in June-July 1982 on:

(a) Classification (b) Cataloguing
(c) Documentation (d) Bibliography

68. What do Biscoe time Numbers indicate in book numbers ?
(a) Date of birth of author
(b) Time facet
(c) Second level of time facet
(d) Year of publication of the document

69. In which scheme of classification zero (0) is used for time isolates ?
(a) Colon classification (b) UDC
(c) DDC (d) None of these

70. What was colon(:) known as when it was used as indicator digit in CC (edition 4) ?
(a) Indicator digit (b) Connecting symbol
(c) Joint symbol (d) Connecting apparatus

71. How many steps are taken informing the class number of a subject?
(a) 20 (b) 09
(c) 05 (d) 10

72. Who recognised the concepts of Public& Private Times?
(a) Kempt (b) Dewey
(c) Sayers (d) Ranganathan

73. Which of the canons promulgates that each subject should be represented by one and only one class number ?
(a) Ascertainability (b) Chain of classes
(c) Expressiveness (d) Synonym

74. Common Isolates are not provided in:
(a) UDC and LC (b) RIC and DDC
(c) LC and RIC (d) BC and EC

75. UDC is:
(a) Advanced form of DDC (b) Infunctional Version of Dewey
(c) Based on DDC (d) None of these

76. Paul Otlet, Henry La forntaine and Donker Duyvis worked for the development of:

(a) UDC (b) Reference Documents
(c) Lib. Sc. (Cataloguing) (d) DDC

77. UDC under the title of 'Classification Bibliographic' was published between the years 1899 and:
(a) 1900 (b) 1910
(c) 1905 (d) 1904

78. In which scheme of classification, the circular brackets are used for space :
(a) DDC (b) CC
(c) EC (d) UDC

79. Evelyn May Seymour edited DDC for:
(a) One time (b) Five times
(c) Always (d) Seven times

80. In DDC 20,07 (T1) means:
(a) Education, Research, Related topics
(b) Study and Teaching
(c) Research and Education
(d) Teaching , Study

81. Who is the editor of DDC (edition 20) ?
(a) Melvil Dewey (b) John P. Comaromi
(c) Benjamin Custer (d) Evelyn May Seymour

82. In DDC 20, elimination of many unlikely and unwanted entries and the removal of see references make to index :
(a) Useless (b) Complex in use
(c) Big size (d) Small size

83. In DDC-20 manual is given in which volume?
(a) 1 (b) 3
(c) 4 (d) 2 and 3

84. Schedule of Music (780) and British Columbia (T2-711) completely revised in which edition of DDC ?
(a) DDC- 18 (b) DDC-2
(c) DDC- 16 (d) DDC-20

85. Library Classification : Fundamentals and Procedure (1944) was written by.:
(a) A.P. Srivastava (b) S.R. Ranganathan
(c) P.N. Kaula (d) G. Bhattacharya

86. Classes belonging to the same array are called :
(a) Co-ordinate Classes (b) Subordinate Classes
(c) Main Class (d) Non Basic Classes

87. What are the three empty-emptying digits postulated in 7th edition of CC ?
(a) X, Y and Z (b) V, W and X
(c) U, W and Y (d) All the above

88. Which main class in CC has facet formula providing four levels of personality facet ?
(a) History (b) Library Science
(c) Mathematics (d) Literature

89. E.W. Hulme was the librarian of :
(a) Patent Office Library, Paris
(b) Patent Office Library, London
(c) Imperial Library, India
(d) Library of Congress Library

90. First depth schedule on the topic "Devaluation" was published in the year:
(a) 1956 (b) 1987
(c) 1950 (d) 1960

91. Which indicator digit is used for Phase Relation in BC-I
(a) Colon (b) Hyphen (-)
(c) Zero (d) Ampersand

92. Space Isolates in CC-6 are arranged according to .... population clusters, orientation divisions and physical features.
(a) Sociological division (b) Geographical division
(c) Political division (d) None of these

93. In the seventh edition of colon classification, the connecting symbol for phase relation is :
(a) Semicolon (;) (b) Zero (0)
(c) Ampersand (&) (d) Plus (+)

94. Complex subject is formed by a combination of :
(a) Two or more basic or compound subjects
(b) One basic subject and two isolate idea

(c) One isolate idea on two basic subjects
(d) Only two isolate ideas

95. In UDC, the facet indicators which combine facets are :
(a) Comma, colon, dot
(b) Double colon, semicolon, dot
(c) Colon, double colon, square bracket
(d) Colon and ampersand

96. E.C. stands for :
(a) Empty imaginary column (b) Emergency contents
(c) Empty column (d) Expansive classification

97. The add to instructions appearing throughout the DDC schedule is an example of mnemonics :
(a) Schedule (b) Parallels
(c) Seminal (d) Alphabetical

98. There are two kinds of tables in UDC, namely :
(a) Main and auxiliary
(b) ACI and PCI
(c) Form division and S.S. Division
(d) General and Special

99. In DDC form divisions were included in :
(a) 19th edition (b) 21st edition
(c) 1st edition (d) 2nd edition

100. Kardex is used for receipt of :
(a) Newspaper (b) Books
(c) Periodical (d) Text book

Answers

1. c	2. c	3. d	4. d	5. c
6. c	7. c	8. c	9. b	10. b
11. b	12. c	13. d	14. c	15. c
16. b	17. b	18. c	19. d	20. d
21. c	22. d	23. d	24. c	25. b
26. d	27. d	28. a	29. b	30. b
31. b	32. d	33. c	34. b	35. b
36. b	37. c	38. d	39. b	40. d

41. c	42. c	43. a	44. d	45. c
46. d	47. a	48. b	49. c	50. c
51. d	52. d	53. a	54. c	55. b
56. c	57. a	58. c	59. d	60. b
61. b	62. d	63. c	64. b	65. d
66. b	67. a	68. d	69. c	70. a
71. b	72. d	73. d	74. c	75. c
76. a	77. c	78. d	79. d	80. a
81. b	82. d	83. c	84. d	85. b
86. a	87. c	88. d	89. b	90. c
91. b	92. c	93. c	94. a	95. c
96. d	97. a	98. a	99. d	100. c

Fourth Set

1. Job description may serve as tool for :
   (a) Job Analyser (b) Performance evaluation
   (c) General staff management (d) None of the above
2. A formal document in the library describing duties and responsibilities of the library personnel :
   (a) Job Description (b) Job Evaluation
   (c) Job Analysis (d) Job Title
3. POSDCORB is given by:
   (a) Luther Gullick & Lyndall Urwick
   (b) F.W. Taylor & Gullick
   (c) L. Gullick & Wilson Kiplector
   (d) F. Taylor & M. Johnson
4. Who was regarded as father of classical school of management:
   (a) F.W. Taylor (b) Luther Gullick
   (c) Henry Fayol (d) McGregor
5. MBO is developed by:
   (a) Peter F. Drucker (b) Henry Fayol
   (c) Max Weber (d) Allen Prost
6. The book "Motivation Factor : A theory of personnel management" is published in:
   (a) 1989 (b) 1986
   (c) 1981 (d) 1979
7. The book "Motivation factor: A theory of personnel management" is authored by:

(a) Martin and Larry A. Bruskemp
(b) McGreger & A-Hezeberg
(c) Martin L. Machr and Peter Drucker
(d) None of the above

8. The Human side of enterprise is written by:
(a) D. Mc Gregor (b) Micheal Douglas
(c) Peter Drucker (d) F. Herzberg

9. The theory X and Y appeared in:
(a) 1967 (b) 1960
(c) 1965 (d) 1969

10. Motivation and Personality" is a work of:
(a) D. McGregor (b) F. Herzberg
(c) Peter Drucker (d) Abraham Maslow

11. Motivation Hygiene theory appeared in:
(a) 1968 (b) 1969
(c) 1970 (d) 1965

12. "The fifth discipline" is written by:
(a) Peter Drucker (b) Peter Martin
(c) Peter Senge (d) Peter Rafter

13. "The Good Society" is written by
(a) R. Bellah (b) R. Burdock
(c) R. Phyor (d) P. Mayor

14. "General and Industrial Administration" is written by:
(a) F. W. Taylor (b) Henry Fayol
(c) Luther Gullick (d) Lyndwall Unwick

15. "Principle of Scientific Management" were given by
(a) F. W. Taylor (b) Peter Drucker
(c) Henry Fayol (d) R. Ballah

16. Administration is generally concerned with
(a) Seven Function (b) Eight Function
(c) Sex Function (d) Nine Function

17. The Marketing mix contain of:
(a) 4 Ps (b) 7 Ps
(c) 6 Ps (d) 8 Ps

18. Match the following:

List-A	List-B
a. F. W. Taylor	1. Need theory
b. Douglas McGregor	2. Scientific Management
c. Henry Fayol	3. Theory of X and Theory of Y
d. Abraham Maslow	4. Human Behaviour

(a) a(2), b(3), c(4), d(1) (b) a(2), b(3), c(1), d(4)
(c) a(4), b(1), c(2), d(3) (d) a(4), b(c), c(2), d(1)

19. Motion & Fatique studied under:
(a) Classical School of Thought
(b) Human Relation School
(c) Scientific School of Thought
(d) Human Behaviour School

20. General system theory is proposed by :
(a) Ludwing Von Bertlanffy (b) Lynwall Urwick
(c) Luther Gullic (d) Lany Allisan

21. Likert name is associated with
(a) Theory of motivation (b) Style of leadership
(c) Discussion making theory (d) Scientific management

22. The five element of marketing mix are Product, Place, Price, Promotion and:
(a) Staff (b) Salary
(c) Advertisement (d) Finance

23. MIS stands in place of:
(a) Mass Information System
(b) Management of Information Society
(c) Management Information System
(d) Master Information System

24. Path Goal Theory of Leadership is developed by
(a) Robert House (b) R. Likert
(c) J. Thomson (d) H. Fayol

25. PERT stands for
(a) Programme Evaluation Review Technique
(b) Programme Explaining Review Technique
(c) Programme Evaluation and Revision Technique
(d) Programme Expert and Reviewing Technique

26. "Critical Path Method" is developed by
(a) G.E. Evans (b) Du Pont
(c) U.S. Navy (d) V.K. Navy

27. The concept of "Quality Circle" was developed in:
(a) Japan (b) U.S. A.
(c) UK (d) India

28. Peter Phayor developed which of the following system:
(a) Program Budgeting
(b) Zero Based Budgeting System
(c) Performance Budgeting
(d) Formula Budgeting

29. Staff Formula for University & College in India have been developed by :
(a) M.A. Gopinath
(b) S.R. Ranganathan
(c) ILA and Yashpal
(d) IASLIC and Deshmukh, C.D

30. Zero Based Budgeting System developed in
(a) 1949 (b) 1970
(c) 1965 (d) 1971

31. While planning the library budgeting, following should be consulted ?
(a) Librarian (b) Architect
(c) Library Authority (d) All of the above

32. Delphy method is used for
(a) Planning (b) Budgeting
(c) Forecasting (d) Evaluation

33. Study circle are exclusive area created for:
(a) Students
(b) Librarian
(c) Researchers and Academic Staff
(d) General Reader

34. The top authority for prescribing standard in India is
(a) Institute of Indian Standard

(b) University Grants Commission
(c) Indian Standard Information Centre
(d) Bureau of Indian Standards

35. He described Henry Fayol as the "Father of Modern Operational Management". Who is he ?
(a) Koontz and O'Donnel (b) F.W. Taylor
(c) Elton Mayo (d) Abraham Maslow

36. "Theory of Bureaucracy" was given by:
(a) Henry Fayol (b) Max Weber
(c) Koontz (d) O. Donnel

37. The author of the book entitled "The principles of scientific management" is
(a) Henry Fayol (b) Max Weber
(c) Koontz (d) Miner

38. The "principles of management" given by Fayol in year:
(a) 1911 (b) 1949
(c) 1924 (d) 1919

39. How many type of needs were described by Maslow in his "Hierarchy of need theory"
(a) 4 (b) 7
(c) 5 (d) 3

40. "Affiliation need" is also known as :
(a) Belonging Need (b) Safety Need
(c) Esteem Need (d) Living Wage

41. Herzberg's Motivation-Hygiene Theory was first developed in
(a) Early 1970 (b) Late 1960
(c) Late 1950 (d) Early 1950

42. Theory X and Theory Y appears in:
(a) 1955 (b) 1960
(c) 1966 (d) 1959

43. "Managerial Grid" is also called
(a) Primary Grid (b) Authority Grid
(c) Leadership Grid (d) Classical Grid

44. The author of the book "New patterns of management" is:
(a) Rensis Likert (b) Henry Fayol
(c) Black and Mouton (d) Kinlow

45. Leadership Grid was developed by
(a) Renies Likert
(b) Robert Black and Jane Mouton
(c) Trevino
(d) Peter Drucker

46. The term BASIC stands for:
(a) Basic All-purpose Scientific Instruction Code
(b) Basic All-purpose symbolic Instruction Code
(c) Beginners All-purpose Symbolic Instruction Code
(d) Beginners All-purpose Scientific Instruction Code

47. RAM means:
(a) Road and Machine
(b) Read and Memory
(c) Random Access Memory
(d) Rate Announcement Method

48. The fifth generation of computers is characterised by
(a) VLSI (b) Integrated Circuits
(c) KIPS (d) LSI

49. Who invented Microchip ?
(a) Intel (b) IBM
(c) BARC (d) Macintosh

50. Where vacuum tube technology is used ?
(a) First generation of computers
(b) Second generation of computers
(c) Second and third generation of computers
(d) Fifth generation of computers

51. A byte is a string of:
(a) 4 bits (b) 6 bits
(c) 8 bits (d) 24 bits

52. Chip technology is used in which type of computers ?
(a) Main frames (b) Super computers
(c) Micro computers (d) Mini computers

53. Gopher is a internet based :
    (a) Document Retrieval System
    (b) Document Presentation System
    (c) Document Supply System
    (d) Document Procuring System
54. Which of the following is a search engine
    (a) Google (b) Excite
    (c) Infoseek (d) All of the above
55. URL stands for:
    (a) Universal Resource Locator
    (b) Uniform Resource Locator
    (c) Uniform Record Locator
    (d) Universal Record Locator
56. FAQ stand for:
    (a) Frequently asked question
    (b) Frequently answered question
    (c) Frequently added question
    (d) Frequently advised question
57. Internet Explorer is a ....
    (a) Server Software (b) Client Software
    (c) Translator Software (d) All of the above
58. Which of the following is Web Browser:
    (a) Netscape Navigator (b) NCSA Mosaic
    (c) Microsoft-Internet Explorer (d) All of the above
59. JPEG stands for:
    (a) Joint Photographic Experts Group
    (b) Joint Photogroup Explaining Group
    (c) Joint Photostate Extending Group
    (d) Joint Picture Expert Group
60. WAIS stands for:
    (a) Wide Area Information System
    (b) Wide Area Information Source
    (c) Wide Area Internet System
    (d) Wide Area Internal Source

61. WAIS is an Internal Tool which helps in locating:
(a) Graphic Document (b) Text Document
(c Meta Document (d) All of the above

62. ISOC stands for:
(a) Internet Society
(b) International Society of Companies
(c) International Society on Computer
(d) Information Society

63. Empty Element is an element which does not have :
(a) An opening tag (b) An ending tag
(c) Both of the above (d) None of the above

64. The Major components of information technology are:
(a) Communication Technology and Reprography
(b) Computer Technology and Micrography
(c) Reprographic & Micrographic Technology
(d) All of the above

65. The reference model of OSI have:
(a) Seven Layers (b) Five Layers
(c) Six Layers (d) Eight Layers

66. The word computer has been derived from:
(a) Latin (b) Greek
(c) French (d) Spanish

67. Microchip was invented by:
(a) BARC (b) IBM
(c) Intel (d) Microsoft

68. The first electronic computer called ABC was developed by
(a) J. P. Eckert (b) Howard Read
(c) M. Taube (d) J.V. Atonsoft & C. Berry

69. CHECKMATE software package is used for:
(a) Acquisition (b) Information storage
(c) Serial Control (d) Circulation

70. Sanjay Software for libraries is devised by:
(a) INSDOC (b) NASSDOC
(c) UNESCO (d) DESIDOC

71. Videotext and teletext are ... information services.
    (a) Static
    (b) Interactive
    (c) Direct
    (d) Both (a) and (b)

72. Computer memory is measured in
    (a) Byte
    (b) Kilobyte
    (c) Megabyte
    (d) All of the above

73. Java Originally known as:
    (a) Java
    (b) Oak
    (c) Palm
    (d) Mosaic

74. Linux is a Unix clone
    (a) True
    (b) False

75. Unix was developed by Thompson & Ritche in:
    (a) 1973
    (b) 1969
    (c) 1971
    (d) 1970

76. GUI version of Linux is:
    (a) X Window
    (b) Y Window
    (c) G Window
    (d) Linux for window

77. CORBA stands for .....
    (a) Common open Request Booker Architecture
    (b) Common object Request Broker Architecture
    (c) Common Object Reprint Broker Architecture
    (d) Common Object Read Broker Architecture

78. 'C' Language is categorised as:
    (a) Second Generation Computer
    (b) Third Generation Computer
    (c) Both (a) & (b)
    (d) Only (a)

79. C++ developed by:
    (a) Bjarre stroustrip
    (b) Denis Ritche
    (c) Martin Pychaned
    (d) James Gosling

80. HTML developed by:
    (a) Lee Hua
    (b) Denis Ritche
    (c) Tim Bener Lee
    (d) Karen Olson

81. RMI stands for:
(a) Remote Method Invocation
(b) Remote Machine Invention
(c) Remote Method Invention
(d) Remote Machine Invocation

82. Which of the following is an operating system
(a) DOS (b) LINUX
(c) UNIX (d) All of the above

83. The concept of 'Technological Gatekeeper' was first proposed by:
(a) Diana Crane (b) Allen
(c) De Sola Price (d) Gosling

84. In computer terminology, an error in program is known as ....
(a) BUG (b) BUS
(c) VIRUS (d) Error

85. Which of the following language has OOPS concept:
(a) C++ (b) C
(c) BASIC (d) PASCAL

86. ASCII stands for
(a) American Standard Code II
(b) American Standard Code for Information Interchange
(c) American Standard Coding for Information Integration
(d) American Standarised Coding II

87. Linux was developed by:
(a) Linus Torvalds (b) Linux Grolier
(c) Linus Gosling (d) Peter Deslema

88. Two factor theory of motivation is enunciated by :
(a) Peter Drucker (b) H. Fayol
(c) F. Hezberg (d) McColvin

89. The book "Guideline for Handling Library Order for Microforms" published by .... in ....
(a) LA, 197 (b) ALA, 1977
(c) ASLIB, 1967 (d) ILA, 1967

90. The united serial and book exchange is a :
(a) Exchange Organisation
(b) Book Delivery Organisation
(c) Purchase Organisation
(d) None of the above

91. The united serial & book exchange is formerly known as :
(a) United State Book exchange
(b) United Kingdom Book exchange
(c) United Nation Book exchange
(d) United Arab Book exchange

92. The united serial & book exchange was established in year :
(a) 1948 (b) 1947
(c) 1958 (d) 1957

93. The United Serial Book Exchange is situated in :
(a) Washington, D.C. (b) New York
(c) London (d) Brussels

94. Parry Report comes in :
(a) 1965 (b) 1967
(c) 1966 (d) 1970

95. Kardex is used for receipt of :
(a) Newspaper (b) Books
(c) Periodical (d) Textbook

96. Some of the catalogue codes like Cutter's Rules for A dictionary catalogue and the .... have included filling rules also in their cataloguing rules.
(a) Classified Catalogue Code (b) Vatican Code
(c) Anglo-American Code (d) British Museum Code

97. In KWIC Indexes, the keyword appears :
(a) At the beginning of each entry
(b) As a highlighted word
(c) At the centre of the line
(d) At the end of the entry

98. In CCC, tracing is done on the backside of the ....
(a) Cross reference entry (b) All added entry
(c) Main entry (d) None of the above

99. According to AACR-2, in tracing section of the Main Entry card we record :
(a) Collaborator entries (b) Series entry
(c) Added entries (d) Author entry

100. When the records representing the different document in a given library are organized systematically to form a retrievable files, it becomes the :
(a) Bibliography (b) Abstract
(c) Classification scheme (d) Library catalogue

Answers

1. b	2. a	3. a	4. c	5. a
6. b	7. a	8. a	9. b	10. d
11. a	12. c	13. a	14. b	15. c
16. a	17. b	18. a	19. c	20. a
21. b	22. a	23. c	24. a	25. a
26. b	27. a	28. b	29. b	30. b
31. d	32. c	33. c	34. d	35. a
36. b	37. c	38. b	39. c	40. a
41. c	42. b	43. c	44. a	45. b
46. c	47. c	48. c	49. a	50. a
51. c	52. c	53. a	54. d	55. b
56. a	57. b	58. d	59. a	60. a
61. b	62. a	63. b	64. d	65. a
66. a	67. c	68. d	69. c	70. d
71. b	72. d	73. b	74. a	75. a
76. a	77. b	78. c	79. a	80. c
81. a	82. d	83. b	84. a	85. a
86. b	87. a	88. c	89. d	90. d
91. a	92. c	93. d	94. c	95. b
96. b	97. c	98. c	99. c	100. d

Fifth Set

1. Simple observations is as:
   (a) Controlled (b) Uncontrolled
   (c) Good (d) Systematic
2. The first Indian candidate who obtained his Ph. D. Degree in Library & Information Science in Year 1957 was :
   (a) Dr. S.R. Ranganathan (b) Prof. P.N. Kaula
   (c) A. K. Rao (d) D. B. Krishna Rao
3. The second Indian Ph.D. in LIS was awarded in 1977 by the:
   (a) Delhi University
   (b) Banaras Hindu University
   (c) Punjab University, Chandigarh
   (d) University of Rajasthan, Jaipur
4. Research as a movement, which starts from the .... to ....
   (a) Data analysis to Interview
   (b) Known situation to unknown situations
   (c) Unknown to known situations
   (d) Experimental to Hypothesis
5. On the basis of purpose, research can be classified into categories
   (a) Four (b) Five
   (c) Two (d) None
6. In Research, word 'C' refers to:
   (a) Coding of data (b) Critical observation
   (c) Classification (d) Current

7. One of the following is not a technique of data collection
   (a) Sampling (b) Scheduled
   (c) Interview (d) Review of literature
8. Role of hypothesis is very important before:
   (a) Selection of problem (b) Data collection
   (c) Preparing research report (d) Drawn conclusion
9. Historical method of research is based on:
   (a) Historical places (b) History subjects
   (c) Documentary sources (d) Survey
10. The term "Bibliometrics" was first coined by .... in year..
   (a) Ranganathan, 1969 (b) Sayers, 1922
   (c) Pritchard, 1969 (d) Dewey, 1964
11. Earlier, the bibliometrics was also known as:
   (a) Research bibliometrics (b) Statistics
   (c) Sociometry (d) Statistical Bibliography
12. Content Analysis was introduced in year ....
   (a) 1926 (b) 1933
   (c) 1940 (d) 1876
13. Diagrams and graphs were used in statistics first by William Play fair in :
   (a) 1930 (b) 1954
   (c) 1762 (d) 1786
14. Result of 30 items out of 60 is a .... statistics.
   (a) Inferential (b) Sampling
   (c) Descriptive (d) Time series
15. Zipf's law is relates to
   (a) Productivity of scientists
   (b) Word frequency ranking
   (c) Distribution of publications
   (d) Core literature
16. Ibid, p means for:
   (a) as previous reference
   (b) as previous page reference
   (c) that reference which have used any chapter of report
   (d) none

17. Who introduced the speculative mode of thinking ?
    (a) Aristotle (b) Kant
    (c) Weber (d) None
18. Research design gives the
    (a) Procedure for designing tools
    (b) Technique of research
    (c) Blue print of the research activity
    (d) Procedure of research
19. Select the correct options
    (a) Knowledge-Subject-Data-Information
    (b) Data-Information-Knowledge-Subject
    (c) Information-Subject-Data-Knowledge
    (d) Data-Information-Subject-Knowledge
20. A systematic organisation of data in column and rows is called
    (a) Data Collection (b) Coding
    (c) Tabulation (d) Graphs
21. .... research is concerned with search for ways of using scientific knowledge to solve practical problems.
    (a) Pure (b) Basic
    (c) Quantitative (d) Applied
22. Pure research is also called .... research.
    (a) Explanatory (b) Causal
    (c) Basic (d) None
23. .... is studying the phenomena event, situation or development through a thorough and detailed analysis:
    (a) Case study method (b) Statistical Method
    (c) Historical Method (d) Survey Method
24. Any research is valid, when its conclusions are
    (a) Attractive (b) Good
    (c) Simple (d) True
25. .... is a planning a strategy for conducting research.
    (a) Research design (b) Survey
    (c) Sampling (d) None
26. Main function of research design is:
    (a) It is helpful (b) It provides blue print
    (c) Drawn conclusion (d) Collection of Data

27. Questionnaire, is a tool of:
(a) Hypothesis (b) Research report
(c) Data collection (d) Tabulation

28. Interview is .... questioning.
(a) Written (b) List of
(c) Verbal (d) None

29. The concept of content analysis was introduced in
(a) 1928 (b) 1932
(c) 1924 (d) None

30. .... observation is a method in which the investigator becomes a part of situation he is studying.
(a) Non-participant (b) Participant
(c) Quasi-participant (d) None

31. Case study is not a method of:
(a) Research (b) Data collection
(c) Data Analysis (d) Hypothesis

32. Father of Positivistic Mode of Thinking is
(a) Aristotle (b) August Comte
(c) Kautilya (d) None

33. Authority mode of thinking is derived by
(a) S.R. Ranganathan (b) W.C.B. Sayers
(c) Max Weber (d) Hume

34. Positivistic mode of thinking is also called
(a) Past thinking
(b) Real thinking
(c) Actual thinking
(d) Scientific mode of thinking

35. Speculative mode of thinking is also called
(a) Imaginative
(b) Speculating
(c) De Jure thinking
(d) Metaphysical mode of thinking

36. The word "Speculative" is derived from the latin word:
(a) Specul (b) Speceare
(c) Specere (d) Spesear

37. The word "Positivism" is derived from the latin word "..................." which means sure, certain etc.
    a) Posit (b) Pocitivism
    (c) Positives (d) None
38. "Guru Granth Sahib" is the .... for Sikhs.
    (a) Speculative (b) Authority
    (c) Positivistics (d) None
39. Historical research deals with experience of
    (a) Present (b) Future
    (c) Past (d) Future and Past
40. The preparations of .... is an important step in research methodology.
    (a) Research report (b) Research Proposal
    (c) Direction (d) None
41. In .... method of research, neither facts or events may be re-examined nor they may be revised again.
    (a) Scientific (b) Descriptive
    (c) Survey (d) Historical
42. Historical method is a method of studying .... development of events.
    (a) Necessary (b) Good
    (c) Research (d) Chronological
43. Scientific method of research is a strong path, for reaching up to the door of:
    (a) Action (b) Truth
    (c) Imaginary concept (d) None
44. The highest limit of one class becomes the lowest limit of another class like 5-10, 10-15 is called :
    (a) Inclusive method (b) Exclusive method
    (c) Statistics (d) Descriptive
45. The highest limit of one class becomes is one digit less than the lowest limit of next class as 0-4, 5-9 is called :
    (a) Inclusive Method (b) Statistical Method
    (c) Descriptive Method (d) Exclusive Method

46. ... . is necessary for describing an event or for knowing cause and effect relationship of an event.
(a) Action (b) Methodology
(c) Data Collection (d) Data Analysis

47. .... is a temporary result.
(a) Research (b) Hypothesis
(c) Action research (d) Data collection

48. In .... sampling, the universe is divided into different categories.
(a) Grid method of (b) Quata
(c) Purposive (d) Stratified

49. .... of a distribution is the value of the variable which divides it into equal parts.
(a) Median (b) Mean
(c) Mode (d) None

50. The first learned scientific periodical "Journal of Royal Asiatic Society of Bengal" was published in India in year:
(a) 1832 (b) 1842
(c) 1942 (d) 1949

51. Geological Survey of India was established in year:
(a) 1924 (b) 1851
(c) 1876 (d) 1933

52. Botanical Survey of India was established in 1889 in
(a) Calcutta (b) Madras
(c) Lucknow (d) Delhi

53. The Zoological Society of India was established in .... with an object to promote zoological studies.
(a) 1862 (b) 1872
(c) 1974 (d) 1939

54. In 1958, Indian society for Plant Physiology was established at
(a) Calcutta (b) Bombay
(c) Delhi (d) Kharagpur

55. National council of applied economic research was established in New Delhi in

(a) 1956 (b) 1929
(c) 1931 (d) 1894

56. Indian council of social science research was established in year
(a) 1972 (b) 1969
(c) 1952 (d) 1955

57. 'Filler question' are those question which moved from
(a) General to specific question
(b) Specific to general question
(c) Contingency to general question
(d) None of the above

58. Research report is an account of
(a) Research work with conclusion and suggestion
(b) Only conclusion
(c) Data analysis
(d) Suggestion only

59. Nadir, Ascendant, Zenith and Descendant are the four cardinal points of
(a) Library Cataloguing
(b) Documentation
(c) Survey Research
(d) Spiral of Scientific Method

60. Spiral means:
(a) A research tool (b) An unending circle
(c) Research process (d) None

61. Fourcell design methods are used in
(a) Observation (b) Experiment
(c) Hypothesis (d) Research Design

62. Hypothesis is a
(a) Tentative Statement (b) Derived Statement
(c) Real Statement (d) None

63. To study "Poverty in State of U.P." , the most suitable sampling method would be
(a) Random (b) Stratified
(c) Mixed (d) Census

64. The research proceeds from General to Particular is
    (a) Deductive Logic (b) Inductive logic
    (c) Both (a) & (b) (d) None of the above
65. The research proceeds from Particular to General is
    (a) Deductive Logic (b) Inductive Logic
    (c) Both (a) & (b) (d) None of the above
66. Which of the following is a tool for research
    (a) Questionnaire (b) Graph
    (c) Diagram (d) Charts
67. "Cranfied studies" are an example of
    (a) Case Studies (b) Survey Research
    (c) Experimental Research (d) Observation
68. "A Tentative Generalization" is also called
    (a) Hypothesis (b) Case Study
    (c) Research Design (d) Formulation of topic
69. Document are primary source of Information in
    (a) Historical Research (b) Scientific Research
    (c) Survey Research (d) All of the above
70. Modern age is concerned with which type of research
    (a) Pure Research (b) Applied Research
    (c) Both (a) & (b) (d) Relay Research
71. The "Delphi Technique" is mainly concerned with
    (a) Data collection (b) Data analysis
    (c) Data Interpretation (d) Data Recognisation
72. In which type of Research "Control Group" are used ?
    (a) Experimental Research (b) Survey Research
    (c) Observation (d) Historical Research
73. Scientific method of research can only be used in
    (a) Sciences (b) Human Sciences
    (c) Social Sciences (d) In All Discipline
74. Brandford and Zipf's Law are used for:
    (a) Quotation Analysis
    (b) Rank Frequency Analysis of data
    (c) Rank Analysis
    (d) None of the above

75. The term "Librametry was first coined by:
(a) Allen Kent
(b) S.R. Ranganathan
(c) Pritchard
(d) A. J. Lotka

76. The term Bibliometrics was first used by
(a) A Pritchard
(b) S.R. Ranganathan
(c) Allen Kent
(d) S.C. Brandford

77. Statistical Bibliography is written by
(a) Allen Kent
(b) A.J. Lotka
(c) A Pritchard
(d) S.C. Brandford

78. The highest point of spiral method is
(a) Nadir
(b) Zenith
(c) Accendant
(d) Descendant

79. Conversion of Response into a set of number is called
(a) Coding
(b) Classification
(c) Number building
(d) Setting of Number

80. The Preliminaries in the Research Report include
(a) Appendics
(b) Introduction
(c) List of books Referred
(d) Glossary

81. Citation Analysis help in
(a) Subject Indexing
(b) Selective Cataloguing
(c) Descriptive Cataloguing
(d) Indentification of core subject

82. Formulation of Fundamental law is
(a) Pure Research
(b) Applied Research
(c) Relay Research
(d) Research Design

83. In a research an "Information Need of Charted Accountant" a questionnaire is sent to every fifth member of official register of charted accountant would this be
(a) Stratified Sampling
(b) Random Sampling
(c) Purposive Sampling
(d) Quota Sampling

84. In a questionnaire Open-Ended question are
(a) The question are open to interpretation
(b) Those where long answers are required
(c) The answers may be incomplete
(d) The question are open completely

85. In a questionnaire close ended question are those where
(a) The question and answer are close to each other
(b) The answer are given as option
(c) Short answer are required
(d) The question are clear and distinct

86. The study aimed at finding out best method of charging of book is
(a) Basic Research (b) Applied Research
(c) Relay Research (d) No Research at all

87. Formulation Hypothesis is an important component in
(a) Research Design (b) Content Analysis
(c) Report Writing (d) Collection of data

88. In a Research Report, to refer to an earlier but not immediately preceding reference the following term is used :
(a) Op. cit (b) Loc. cit
(c) Ibid (d) Any of the above

89. A research on performance of sections of library science department, and if researchers take every fifth person from each category of staff (e.g. reference section, circulation section, technical section, periodical section) it would be
(a) Random Sampling
(b) Stratified Sampling
(c) The whole population
(d) Purposive sampling

90. A foot note is:
(a) A bibliographic reference
(b) A supplementary information to text
(c) Both (a) and (b)
(d) Neither (a) and (b)

91. Research Design Gives the:
(a) Blue print of research activity
(b) Correct Procedure of Research
(c) Method for collecting data
(d) Procedure of Research

92. In a research report to information undertake previous reference, the following term is used:
    (a) op. cit. (b) Ibid
    (c) loc. cit. (d) None of the above
93. In an empirical study of the effect of open access on borrowing patterns, open access is :
    (a) An independent variable
    (b) A dependent variable
    (c) Not a variable at all
    (d) An intermediate variable
94. Citation Analysis can be used to Identify:
    (a) Half life of Periodical
    (b) Less used journal
    (c) Journal with highest impact factor
    (d) All of the above
95. Hypothesis is a :
    (a) Rule (b) Postulate
    (c) Canon (d) Speculation
96. Mean, Median and modes are:
    (a) Measure of central tendency (b) Measure of deviation
    (c) Way of coding (d) Way of the sampling
97. A research design should not include:
    (a) Findings (b) Hypothesis
    (c) Methodology (d) Scope
98. A hypothesis that is tested for its rejection is :
    (a) Null Hypothesis (b) Alternative Hypothesis
    (c) Research Hypothesis (d) Statistical Hypothesis
99. In a Research Design, which is considered as the most important component ?
    (a) Formation of Hypothesis (b) Review of Literature
    (c) Case study (d) Defining Problem
100. Interview is a :
    (a) Tool of Research
    (b) Process of Research
    (c) Types of Research
    (d) Method of data presentation

Answers

1. b	2. d	3. c	4. b	5. a
6. b	7. d	8. b	9. c	10. c
11. d	12. a	13. c	14. a	15. b
16. a	17. a	18. c	19. b	20. c
21. d	22. c	23. a	24. d	25. a
26. b	27. c	28. c	29. d	30. b
31. b	32. b	33. c	34. d	35. d
36. c	37. c	38. b	39. c	40. b
41. d	42. d	43. b	44. b	45. a
46. d	47. b	48. b	49. a	50. a
51. b	52. a	53. d	54. c	55. a
56. b	57. a	58. a	59. d	60. b
61. b	62. a	63. d	64. a	65. b
66. a	67. c	68. a	69. a	70. b
71. b	72. b	73. d	74. b	75. b
76. a	77. c	78. b	79. a	80. b
81. d	82. a	83. b	84. b	85. b
86. b	87. a	88. a	89. b	90. c
91. a	92. b	93. a	94. d	95. d
96. a	97. a	98. a	99. b	100. a